THE CAMBRIDGE COMPA
"ROBINSON CRUSC

CW01022890

An instant success in its own time, Daniel Defoe's *Crusoe* has for three centuries drawn readers to its archetypal hero, the man surviving alone on an island. This Companion begins by studying the eighteenth-century literary, historical and cultural contexts of Defoe's novel, exploring the reasons for its immense popularity in Britain and in its colonies in America and in the wider European world. Chapters from leading scholars discuss the social, economic and political dimensions of Crusoe's island story before examining the 'after life' of Robinson Crusoe from the book's multitudinous translations to its cultural migrations and transformations into other media such as film and television. By considering Defoe's seminal work from a variety of critical perspectives this book provides a full understanding of the perennial fascination with, and the enduring legacy of, both the book and its iconic hero.

John Richetti is A. M. Rosenthal Professor (Emeritus) at the University of Pennsylvania. His published books include: *Popular Fiction Before Richardson: Narrative Patterns 1700–1739* (1969); *Defoe's Narratives: Situations and Structures* (1975); *The Life of Daniel Defoe: A Critical Biography* (2005); and *A History of British Eighteenth-Century Literature* (2017). He has also edited two *Cambridge Companions, The Eighteenth-Century English Novel* (Cambridge, 1996) and *Daniel Defoe* (Cambridge, 2009), as well as *The Cambridge History of English Literature, 1660–1780* (Cambridge, 2005).

A complete list of books in the series is at the back of this book.

THE CAMBRIDGE COMPANION TO

"ROBINSON CRUSOE"

EDITED BY
JOHN RICHETTI
University of Pennsylvania

CAMBRIDGE
UNIVERSITY PRESS

CAMBRIDGE
UNIVERSITY PRESS

University Printing House, Cambridge CB2 8BS, United Kingdom

One Liberty Plaza, 20th Floor, New York, NY 10006, USA

477 Williamstown Road, Port Melbourne, VIC 3207, Australia

314–321, 3rd Floor, Plot 3, Splendor Forum, Jasola District Centre, New Delhi – 110025, India

79 Anson Road, #06-04/06, Singapore 079906

Cambridge University Press is part of the University of Cambridge.

It furthers the University's mission by disseminating knowledge in the pursuit of education, learning, and research at the highest international levels of excellence.

www.cambridge.org
Information on this title: www.cambridge.org/9781107043497
DOI: 10.1017/9781107338586

First published 2018

Printed in the United Kingdom by TJ International Ltd. Padstow Cornwall

A catalogue record for this publication is available from the British Library.

Library of Congress Cataloging-in-Publication Data
Names: Richetti, John, editor.
Title: The Cambridge companion to "Robinson Crusoe" / edited by John Richetti.
Description: Cambridge; New York: Cambridge University Press, 2018. |
Series: Cambridge companions to literature |
Includes bibliographical references and index.
Identifiers: LCCN 2018000011 | ISBN 9781107043497 (hardback)
Subjects: LCSH: Defoe, Daniel, 1661?–1731. Robinson Crusoe. |
Crusoe, Robinson (Fictitious character) | Shipwreck survival in literature.
Classification: LCC PR3403.Z5 C36 2018 | DDC 823/.5–dc23
LC record available at https://lccn.loc.gov/2018000011

ISBN 978-1-107-04349-7 Hardback
ISBN 978-1-107-69680-8 Paperback

CONTENTS

CONTENTS

ILLUSTRATIONS

CONTRIBUTORS

EVE TAVOR BANNET is George Lynn Cross Emeritus Professor of English at the University of Oklahoma. Her recent books include *Transatlantic Stories and the History of Reading: Migrant Fictions, 1720–1810* (2011), *Empire of Letters: Letter Manuals and Transatlantic Correspondence 1688–1820* (2005), a critical edition of *Emma Corbett* (2011) and with the late Susan Manning (ed.), *Transatlantic Literary Studies, 1640–1830* (2012). She has just published a monograph, *Eighteenth-Century Manners of Reading: Print Culture and Popular Instruction in the Anglophone Atlantic World*.

DAVID BLEWETT (1940–2015) was Professor of English Literature at McMaster University, Senior Research Associate at Trinity College, University of Toronto, and Founding Editor (1988–2003) of *Eighteenth-Century Fiction*. His books included *Defoe's Art of Fiction* (1979) and *The Illustration of Robinson Crusoe 1719–1920* (1995). He edited *Passion and Virtue: Essays on the Novels of Samuel Richardson* (2001) and editions of Henry Fielding, *Amelia* (1987), Tobias Smollett, *Roderick Random* (1995), Daniel Defoe, *Roxana* (1982), *Moll Flanders* (1989), and Defoe's *The Conduct of Christians Made the Sport of Infidels* and *The Continuation of Letters Written by a Turkish Spy* (2005).

REBECCA BULLARD is Associate Professor of English Literature at the University of Reading. She is the author of *The Politics of Disclosure, 1674–1725: Secret History Narratives* (2009), editor of *The Ambitious Step-mother* and *The Fair Penitent* for *The Plays and Poems of Nicholas Rowe* (2016), and co-editor, with Rachel Carnell, of *The Secret History in Literature, 1660–1820* (2017).

JILL CAMPBELL is Professor of English at Yale University. She has recently completed a series of essays on adaptations of *Robinson Crusoe* for young people, including a study of Joachim Heinrich's Campe's *New Robinson Crusoe* in *Story Time! Essays on the Betsy Beinecke Shirley Collection of American Children's Literature* (2016), and an article on *Swiss Family Robinson*. Her essay on Maria Edgeworth's children's tales appeared in *Imagining Selves: Essays in Honor of Patricia Meyer Spacks* (2008). She is also the author of *Natural Masques: Gender and Identity in Fielding's*

Plays and Novels and essays on topics ranging from satire and eighteenth-century representations of female old age to newspaper advertising and the rise of the novel

ANN MARIE FALLON, Ph.D., is the Dean of the School of Arts and Sciences at St. John Fisher College in Rochester, New York. Her work includes *Global Crusoe: Comparative Literature, Postcolonial Theory and Transnational Aesthetics* and several books, chapters and articles on Comparative Literature, Public Humanities, American Studies and Feminist Theory.

CARL FISHER is Professor of Comparative Literature at California State University, Long Beach. He has co-edited two books on Defoe, *Approaches to Teaching World Literature: Defoe's* Robinson Crusoe (2005) and *Defoe's Footprints: Essays in Honour of Maximillian E. Novak* (2009). He has published numerous articles, including on Rabelais, Rousseau, Defoe, Fielding, Sterne, Godwin, and graphic satire in the eighteenth century.

J. PAUL HUNTER is Barbara E. and Richard J. Franke Professor Emeritus at the University of Chicago. Among his many books are *The Reluctant Pilgrim: Defoe's Emblematic Method and Quest for Form in Robinson Crusoe* (1966), *Occasional Form: Henry Fielding and the Chains of Circumstance* (1976), and *Before Novels: The Cultural Contexts of Eighteenth-Century English Fiction* (1990). He has recently edited, with Stephen Arata and Jennifer Wicke, *A Companion to the English Novel* (2015).

ROBERT MAYER is Emeritus Professor of English at Oklahoma State University. He is the author of *History and the Early English Novel: Matters of Fact from Bacon to Defoe* (1997) and *Walter Scott and Fame: Authors and Readers in the Romantic Age* (2017), and the editor of *Eighteenth-Century Fiction on Screen* (2002). He has published numerous articles on the history and theory of the novel, early modern historiography, and cinema and the eighteenth century, including "Three Cinematic Robinsonades," in *Eighteenth-Century Fiction on Screen*.

MAXIMILLIAN E. NOVAK is Distinguished Research Professor, Department of English, UCLA. He has published widely on the literature of the Restoration and eighteenth century, including a biography of Defoe, *Daniel Defoe: Master of Fictions: His Life and Ideas* (2001). The three-volume Stoke Newington *Robinson Crusoe*, which he edited with Irving Rothman and Manuel Schonhorn, is now at AMS Press.

JOHN RICHETTI is A. M. Rosenthal Professor (Emeritus) of English at the University of Pennsylvania. He has edited the *Cambridge Companion to the Eighteenth-Century Novel* (1996), the *Cambridge Companion to Daniel Defoe* (2008), and the *Cambridge History of English Literature 1660–1780* (2005). He has written several books on Defoe and his writings, the most recent *The*

Life of Daniel Defoe: A Critical Biography (2005). His latest book is *A History of Eighteenth-Century British Literature* (Oxford: Wiley-Blackwell, 2017), the eighteenth-century volume of the Blackwell History of English Literature.

PAT ROGERS is Distinguished University Professor (Emeritus) at the University of South Florida, having served as DeBartolo Chair in the Liberal Arts from 1986 to 2015, and having previously held posts at Cambridge, London, Wales, and Bristol. He has published chiefly on the eighteenth century, including several books on Alexander Pope, in addition to works on Swift, Defoe, Fielding, Johnson, Boswell, Austen, and others. Many publications on the bookseller Edmund Curll, including (with Paul Baines) a biography and a bibliography (nearing completion after forty-five years). Rogers has written on topics ranging from the rise of weight watching, the evolution of modernity, gout, and the breeches role, to the history of surveying, the Venus flytrap, the quest for the longitude, and gaolbreakers.

G. A. STARR has taught since 1962 in the University of California, Berkeley, English Department. While working on the *Serious Reflections … of Robinson Crusoe*, he came across *Christianity Not as Old as the Creation* (1731), which he edited with the subtitle, *The Last of Defoe's Performances* (2012). His current research calls in question some postcolonial readings of Defoe on slavery, piracy, and other adjuncts or threats to trade.

RIVKA SWENSON is Associate Professor of English at Virginia Commonwealth University. Her first book, *Essential Scots and the Idea of Unionism in Anglo-Scottish Literature, 1603–1832*, appeared in 2016. Recent publications include essays in *The Cambridge Companion to British Women's Writing, 1660–1789*, *Oxford Handbook of British Poetry, 1660–1800*, and a co-edited (with Manushag N. Powell) special issue of *The Eighteenth Century: Theory and Interpretation* ("Sensational Subjects"). She is co-editing with John Richetti an edition of Daniel Defoe's *The Farther Adventures of Robinson Crusoe*.

HELEN THOMPSON is Professor of English and faculty affiliate of Gender & Sexuality Studies at Northwestern University. Her first book was *Ingenuous Subjection: Compliance and Power in the Eighteenth-Century Domestic Novel* (2005). She has recently completed a book about chemistry, corpuscles, and the non-mimetic production of perceptible qualities, *Fictional Matter: Empiricism, Corpuscles, and the Novel* (2017).

DENNIS TODD is Professor of English at Georgetown University. He has authored *Imagining Monsters: Miscreations of the Self in Eighteenth-Century England* (1995) and *Defoe's America* (2010) and has co-edited, with Cynthia Wall, *Eighteenth-Century Genre and Culture: Serious Reflections on Occasional Forms. Essays in Honor of J. Paul Hunter* (2001). He has also written essays on Swift, Pope, Arbuthnot, and Hogarth.

PREFACE

Daniel Defoe's *The Life and Strange Surprizing Adventures of Robinson Crusoe, of York, Mariner: Who lived Eight and Twenty Years, all alone in an un-inhabited Island of the Coast of AMERICA, near the Mouth of the Great River of OROONOQUE; Having been cast on Shore by Shipwreck, wherein all the Men perished but himself. With An Account how he was at last as strangely deliver'd by PYRATES. Written by Himself* (1719), to give the full title of the original edition, occupies a crucial place in literary history's account of the emergence of the modern English novel and for that matter of the beginning of the modern European novel. A standard text in college and university courses on the "rise" of those long prose fictions that we now call the novel, *Robinson Crusoe* is a perennially interesting narrative fiction that has provoked scholarly and critical debate about its cultural and moral implications and its literary significance. Is it, the argument goes, a spiritual autobiography about a man who in his dramatic isolation on an uninhabited island seeks to understand the puzzling relationship between sinful man and an elusive Providence who has arranged this strange fate for him? Or is it essentially an adventure story, an exemplification in Crusoe himself of the European imperialistic drive from the sixteenth century onward to conquer and exploit the non-European world? Is the island a punishment and trial sent by God? Or is it an opportunity for colonization and conquest and a stage for Crusoe's triumphant survival and prosperity? There is, in my view, a great deal of truth in both of these explanations, and that ambiguity is a sign of the novel's richness and enduring fascination for readers over the centuries.

Whatever the answer one chooses, *Robinson Crusoe* was from its original publication immensely popular in Britain and in its colonies in North America and in the wider European world, with Defoe producing a sequel, *The Farther Adventures of Robinson Crusoe*, that same year, 1719, and in 1720 a third volume, *Serious Reflections during the Life and Surprising Adventures of Robinson Crusoe*, followed by seven reprints of the first two parts in the next seven years. The book (the first part) has been continually in print ever since. It is worth noting that like all his other works of fiction and many of his non-fictional works, the *Robinson Crusoe* books were published anonymously. The book's strong claim is, of course, that it is a true auto-biography of an actual person. His other fictional narratives make the same claim, but a few scholars have recently cast doubt on Defoe's authorship of some of the novels attributed to him, even two of his most popular, *Moll Flanders* (1722) and *Roxana* (1724). But in the case of *Robinson Crusoe*, we know from one contemporary attack on the book the same year it was published that Defoe was indeed the author. Shortly after *Robinson Crusoe* appeared, a rival and jealous author, Charles Gildon, published a satirical pamphlet entitled *The Life and Strange Surprizing Adventures of Mr. D— De F—, of London* and addressed contemptuously to Daniel Defoe "*hosier.*" (Defoe was for a time a wholesale dealer in hosiery!) In an amusing scene the pamphlet narrates how Defoe's characters appear to him in a dream and take him to task for making them look ridiculous. They take their revenge by making him eat a copy of the book (both volumes!) and then tossing him in a blanket. Gildon then ridicules the novel as implausible and attacks it as dangerously impious.

But Gildon was in the minority, as he himself complained when he had his Defoe respond to the angry character he has created, Robinson Crusoe, that "there is not an Old Woman that can go the price of it, but buys thy Life and Adventures." From 1719 onwards, Defoe's novel was immensely popular. Over three centuries *Robinson Crusoe* has had near-universal, world-wide appeal; it is much more than simply an academic text and node of literary-historical and critical controversy. Of Defoe's many works, fictional and non-fictional, the story of Crusoe's lonely survival on his island continues to be the only one familiar to large numbers of general readers, many of whom know only the title of the book and nothing about its author. As Ian Watt put it in his 1996 study, *Myths of Modern Individualism*, the Crusoe story is a "myth of modern individualism," and Crusoe himself is compar-able to Faust, Don Quixote, and Don Juan as a human and modern or at least European/Western archetype. In its hero's confusion and terror when he finds himself alone on the island as well as in his transition to resourceful management of his environment for survival and ultimate mastery of him-self, as well as of hostile visitors like cannibals and mutineers, *Robinson Crusoe* may be said to stage the tension in the early European eighteenth century between an emerging modern secular and activist individualism embodied and enacted in Crusoe, and what were in Defoe's day older and still powerfully persuasive religious modes of understanding personal identity and pondering one's destiny and fate in relation to the mysteries of providential ordering.

Moreover, like Cervantes' Don Quixote, Defoe's Robinson Crusoe may be in world literature a deeply familiar figure, indeed instantly recognizable, a truly iconic character (on his island, in his goat-skin clothing, carrying his umbrella and his musket, and accompanied by his faithful dog). Defoe's 1719 novel was within a year translated into French, German, and Dutch, and it has in those nearly three hundred years since its initial publication been translated into over a hundred languages, including Inuit and Coptic. Defoe's story has also since it appeared provoked scores of imitations, so called Robinsonades, and from the eighteenth to the twentieth century inspired a minor narrative sub-genre of island and adventure stories. More recently, novels have appeared imagining alternative versions of Defoe's story such as Michel Tournier's *Friday or the Other Island* (1977) and J. M. Coetzee's *Foe* (1986). There have also been children's versions, notably Johann David Wyss' German *Der Schweizerische Robinson* (1812), published in an English translation by the philosopher William Godwin as *The Swiss Family Robinson* in 1816. (As a child, I first encountered the Crusoe story in this book, the source later of a Disney movie.) *Robinson Crusoe* has also inspired a good number of film versions, including a fine one in 1954 by the great Spanish director Luis Buñuel, in both English and Spanish versions (*Las Aventuras de Robinson Crusoe*) as well as perhaps the laughably worst film version ever perpetrated starring the improbably handsome actor Pierce Brosnan in 1997, in which Crusoe is a Scotsman who kills his rival for the affections of a girl in a duel and has to escape by going to sea, eventually returning to marry Mary, the girl he left behind. There have also been various dramatizations for children, sometimes in cartoon form, and other often enough ludicrous modern adaptations (for one example, a Disney version in 1966 with Dick Van Dyke as Lieutenant Robinson Crusoe, a pilot who is stranded on an island), as well as television shows such as the immensely popular *Lost*, which rehearsed with many contemporary variations the archetypal plot of survival on a deserted island. More convincing as well as popular was the movie *Cast Away* (2000), in which Tom Hanks is a FedEx manager who, when his plane crashes, is the lone survivor stranded on a desert island, and the recent film, *The Martian* (2015), which is yet another iteration of the Crusoe story in which Matt Damon plays an astronaut, a scientist stranded on Mars who survives through Crusoe-like ingenuity and perseverance.

The chapters in this *Cambridge Companion to "Robinson Crusoe"* range from discussions of the book's literary, political, and cultural meanings in its own day (in England, in America, and in Europe) to its continuing resonances into our own times in popular as well as literary culture, including its migrations and transformations into other media over the last three centuries. The opening sections of our book are devoted to literary-historical and cultural explorations of *Robinson Crusoe* as one of the founding texts of the modern novel in England and indeed in Europe. Several chapters consider *Robinson Crusoe* in the context of Defoe's multifarious career as a political and moral writer and polemicist. Other chapters include in-depth discussions of Crusoe's story in its social, psychological, and political dimensions. One chapter traces the history of Defoe's novel as he expanded it to include two sequels; another considers selected eighteenth-century translations and imitations (Robinsonades), with attention paid to the eighteenth-century influences of Defoe's story on psychology and philosophy. For example in his novel of education, *Émile, or On Education* (1762), Jean-Jacques Rousseau stipulates that his young hero will read at first only one book – *Robinson Crusoe*. Several chapters consider the past and the future of Defoe's book: one looks back to precursors and sources for Defoe's island story, and another traces the fascinating numerous versions of the Crusoe story as adapted and transformed for children in the nineteenth and twentieth centuries. A key chapter surveys illustrations and images of what quickly became the iconic Crusoe from the eighteenth to the twentieth century. Two chapters remind readers of *Robinson Crusoe*'s popularity in colonial America, mostly in severely abridged versions, and of the book's influence in helping to form and to reinforce the ideology of European colonialism. And various chapters in Part III deal with latter-day revisions or extensions of the story in nineteenth-century desert island novels aimed at young audiences by Frederick Marryat, R. M. Ballyntyne, and Robert Louis Stevenson. And, finally, several chapters in the last section deal with the many popular revisions and contemporary literary adaptations, some serious and provocatively transformative, some to the point of travesty, of the Crusoe story in literature, in film, and on television.

We dedicate this book to the memory of our late colleague, David Blewett, who near the very end of his life wrote the chapter in this volume on the illustrations of *Robinson Crusoe. Frater, ave atque vale.*

CHRONOLOGY

1660 or 1661	Daniel Foe born in London (exact date unknown), son of James and Alice Foe
	Restoration of the Stuart monarchy as Charles II returns to England
1662	Act of Uniformity passed, mandating conformity in religious services to the Church of England Book of Common Prayer and requiring office holders to be members of the state church. The Foes followed the lead of their minister, Samuel Annesley, and left the Church of England to become dissenters
1663	Drury Lane Theatre in London reopens
1664	The Conventicle Act outlaws Nonconformist worship in gatherings of more than five people
	Second Anglo-Dutch War (to 1667). Dutch ships sail up the Thames and destroy much of the English fleet
1665–6	The Great Plague (kills over 70,000 people in London) and the Great Fire of London (consumes most of the old wooden city)
c.1671–9	Attends school of the Rev. James Fisher at Dorking, Surrey, and then the Dissenting Academy of Rev. Charles Morton, Newington Green, north of London
1675	Greenwich Observatory established by Charles II
1678	"Exclusion Crisis" as the Earl of Shaftesbury leads a movement to exclude James, Charles II's Roman Catholic brother, from the succession to the throne
c.1683	Established as a wholesale hosiery merchant, living in Cornhill, near the Royal Exchange
1684	Marries Mary Tuffley and receives a dowry of £3,700
1685	Death of Charles II – succeeded by his brother, the Catholic James II
	Louis XIV revokes the Edict of Nantes, ending religious toleration in France
1685	Participates in the unsuccessful rebellion against James II led by the Duke of Monmouth, one of Charles II's illegitimate sons

1685–92	Becomes a prosperous businessman dealing in hosiery, tobacco, wine, and other goods. Seems to have travelled extensively on business in England and in Europe
1688	"Glorious Revolution" (James II forced to vacate the throne) and Prince William of Orange in the Netherlands invited to reign as William III of England, with James' daughter, Mary, as his queen
1690	William III defeats James II at the Battle of the Boyne in Ireland
1692	Declares bankruptcy for £17,000 and imprisoned for debt
1694	Founding of the Bank of England
	Establishes a brick and tile factory at Tilbury, in Essex
1695	Daniel Foe begins to call himself Defoe
1697	Defoe's first published book, *An Essay on Projects*, a series of proposals for radical social and economic change
	Death of Queen Mary
1697–1701	Defoe acts as an agent for William III in England and Scotland
1701	James II dies in exile
	Act of Settlement establishes Hanoverian succession
	The True-Born Englishman, a poetic satire of English xenophobia and a defense of William III, who was Dutch by birth
1702	Death of William III, accession of Queen Anne, James II's daughter
	England declares war against France and Spain: War of the Spanish Succession
	John Churchill, Duke of Marlborough, named Captain-General of the English army
	The Shortest Way with the Dissenters, a satiric attack on High Church extremists
1703	Defoe arrested for writing *The Shortest Way with the Dissenters*, charged with sedition, committed to Newgate Prison and sentenced to stand in the pillory for three days. He published the poem *A Hymn to the Pillory* and an authorized collection of his writings, *A True Collection of the Writings of the Author of The True-born Englishman* (a second volume in 1705). Released through the influence of the powerful politician and Speaker of the House, Robert Harley, but his brick and tile factory fails while he is in prison. Bankrupt again
1704	English capture Gibraltar; Duke of Marlborough defeats the French at Blenheim on the Danube in southern Germany
	Defoe begins *The Review,* a pro-government newssheet appearing as often as three times a week (through 1713)
1704–13	Defoe acts as secret agent and political journalist for Harley and other ministers, traveling widely in England and Scotland promoting the union of the two countries.

1707	Union of England and Scotland
1710	Tories gain control of Parliament under leadership of Robert Harley (later Earl of Oxford) and Henry St. John (later Viscount Bolingbroke)
	Statute of Queen Anne passed by Parliament, limiting copyright to twenty-eight years and recognizing authors' rights
1711	Founding of the South Sea Company
1713	Treaty of Utrecht, ending War of the Spanish Succession
1713–14	Defoe arrested several times for debt and for his political writings but released through government influence
1714	Death of Queen Anne
	Accession of George I, the Elector of Hanover
	Fall of the Tory government
1715	*The Family Instructor*, the first of Defoe's conduct books
	Jacobite Rebellion in support of James II's son, "James III," the "Old Pretender"
	Death of Louis XIV of France
	Robert Harley (Earl of Oxford) and Henry St. John (Viscount Bolingbroke) are impeached for high treason. Bolingbroke flees to France
1719	*Robinson Crusoe*, *The Farther Adventures of Robinson Crusoe*
1720	*Captain Singleton*, *Serious Reflections of ... Robinson Crusoe*
	War with Spain declared
	South Sea Company fails ("South Sea Bubble")
1721	Robert Walpole appointed First Lord of the Treasury and Chancellor of the Exchequer
1722	*A Journal of the Plague Year*, *Moll Flanders*, and *Colonel Jack*
1724	*Roxana*, *A General History of the Pyrates*, *A Tour Thro' the Whole Island of Great Britain* (3 volumes, 1724–6)
1725	*The Complete English Tradesman* (volume I)
1726	*The Political History of the Devil*
1727	*Conjugal Lewdness*, *An Essay on the History and Reality of Apparitions*, *A New Family Instructor*, *The Complete English Tradesman* (volume II)
	Death of George I
1728	*Augusta Triumphans*, *A Plan of the English Commerce*
1729	*The Compleat English Gentleman* (not published until 1890)
1731	Defoe dies April 24 in Ropemaker's Alley, London, in debt, hiding from creditors

PART I

Robinson Crusoe and Daniel Defoe: The Eighteenth Century

I

J. PAUL HUNTER

Genre, Nature, *Robinson Crusoe*

In *The Dunciad* of 1728, Alexander Pope ironically celebrates the victory of popular over polite literature:

> Books and the Man I sing, the first who brings,
> The Smithfield Muses to the Ear of Kings.

And one of his satiric targets is of course Daniel Defoe, memorialized as "restless Daniel," the sometime poet and prose pamphleteer who had been pilloried a quarter century before and who now got repilloried in print in a kind of silver anniversary moment.

> Earless on high stood unabash'd Defoe.

> (*The Dunciad*, II, 139)

The Dunciad argues powerfully for a firm divide between popular, everyday, and ephemeral journalism on the one hand and a tradition of responsible, witty, ambitious, dignified, and venerable "literary" texts (mostly poetry) on the other. Pope was far from alone in his efficient attempt to divide the textual universe in Manichean terms, dismissing Smithfield and Grub Street productions as unworthy of attention or even existence. Observers from many backgrounds and perspectives – Dryden, Addison, Swift, Fielding, Sir Richard Blackmore, Joseph Trapp, and indeed Defoe himself in his poem, *The Pacificator* – all produced what we might call "sorting texts" which effectively divided the print world into the acceptable and unacceptable with little grayness in between. The dominance and proliferation of such binaries suggest that the larger cultural climate accepted and enforced the contrasts between the lower and the higher and the fit and the unfit, even though there was wide disagreement about the grounds or criteria for placing who where and for what reasons.

Now we know from Joseph Spence's conversations that Pope himself was capable of more nuanced analysis and appreciation. As recorded by Spence,

Pope said that Defoe wrote "a vast many things; and none bad, though none excellent except ... the first part of *Robinson Crusoe*." Still, in his public persona as literary guardian and gatekeeper of the noble tradition there was no compromise, little sympathy for popular taste, and scant tolerance for any kind of literary leveling. Now it is of course true that there were profound social, political, philosophical, and cultural differences that sharply divided habits and values as well as loyalties in early eighteenth-century England, and these distinctions are not arbitrary or trivial. I have no intention of obscuring very real divisions in authorial loyalties and socio-cultural aims. But I do wish to use Defoe to point to some textual practices that cross habitual lines and think across received historical categories, allowing the aspiring literary traditions of high culture to interact with less ambitious and less self-conscious workaday texts that could readily circulate across class and educational lines. These are utilitarian, often ephemeral, texts of everyday life and popular culture – what used to be disparagingly called paraliterature, subliterature, or popular literature – texts that seemed to have little likelihood of achieving posterity but that provided practical information, urgent rhetorical sallies, or entertainment for varieties of readers; they are – whether stories, guidebooks, or reflections – the unvarnished and unambitious texts of ordinary life.

What I want to consider here is how one major critical category of delineation (of genre or literary kind) works in practice when activated across the high/low cultural divide. I worry about two things. The first involves the discomfort inherent in using the troubled word "genre" itself, which tends to bring forward the habits of a tradition of usage that is at once too loose and baggy on the one hand, and (on the other) too narrowly applied to a limited and artificial set of familiar literary categories. At the heart of this issue, there is a basic philosophical question about whether it is right to appropriate a term from the life sciences in the service of artificial, invented, human-made categories as if they were a product of Nature or the eternal fitness of things. I would like to sideline that worry by putting aside the word "genre" and substituting here the term "textual traditions" in its place. This term, however inelegant and unmusical, has the virtue of being neutral across the privilege/popular divide. It more easily applies to new or newly identified categories of writing and is friendly to expansion. And the old, big, enduring genre categories like tragedy or elegy or pastoral or epic or georgic can function equally well under the term "textual traditions." It is just that under this rubric they can bear a wider, more flexible, and more comprehensive reach, and be applied more directly to readers' expectations than to writerly intent. So I mean my term "textual traditions" to comprehend both classic formal categories (like genre, species, kind, mode, etc.)

4

and less rigid groupings such as travel books, adventure stories, captivity and isolation narratives, and didactic treatises of several sorts, offering a less narrowly precise but more representatively comprehensive system to encompass distinct and definable but less talked about categories of reading materials. I am more concerned here with the way readers' expectations work than what authors intend or critics measure.

The second worry has to do with the teleology issue in literary history, that is, the tendency to find definitions in the way history turns out rather than in the way it developed. There is no doubt in my mind that Defoe studies are healthier and sounder now than they have ever been, and that literary history has come a long way in positioning Defoe securely among the eighteenth-century writers who most matter. But the enhanced standing has come at some price. Defoe comparisons are now more likely to be with his novelist successors and heirs rather than with his contemporaries and their texts, and the critical sense of where his writings come from seems now to have diminished (except among biographers) rather than enlarged. We are critically more apt to see a modern Defoe as novelist rather than the explorer of narrative forms and methods that he was. I suggest we do more probing into his historical roots and the textual traditions available to him and his readers. There is nothing wrong (and many things right) in thinking about Defoe in relationship to Scott or Dickens or Eliot or Conrad, but we need as well to keep track of what his readers knew and expected when they first picked up his strange and surprising books, if we are to have a full and rich sense of where he belongs in literary history.

There was a time in Defoe criticism – nearly a century ago now – when sources and analogues were all the rage in literary study, and they were not very good times. The scope was wide, but the results were rather thin, especially on the "sources" side, and a lot of energy was expended looking for factual dependence and transmissions of information rather than common strategies or habits of writing and reading. But even though criticism of this kind became something of a dry well, at least the emphasis was on origins, history, development, and process rather than future trajectories and events, so that issues devolved in terms of accumulations and choices and not teleology. Even though the questions being asked then were not very sophisticated, Defoe got critical attention within some relevant contexts and traditions. But, ironically, as Defoe's formal reputation as a novelist grew and he became more solidly ensconced in the ever-higher-flying novel tradition, rather than being called "novelistic" or a proto-novelist, as was once the habit, his new, more elevated and secure place in the literary hierarchy has meant that he became more unmoored from his humbler beginnings and detached, in critical discourse, from the popular textual traditions that his contemporary readers were familiar with and that constituted some of his own early reading materials. I believe there is still value in reading the traditions that Defoe's contemporaries read and that he himself to some extent followed, altered, and developed.

Compared to works like *The Dunciad*, or *Trivia*, or *A Tale of a Tub*, or even *Clarissa* and *Tom Jones*, *Robinson Crusoe* is not a very bookish book; that is, previous texts don't make much of an appearance there, and the text makes little direct reference or allusion to other books, although Crusoe's account of his time as a slave in North Africa (Sallee) and his escape from his master there links his story to other popular captivity narratives. Crusoe himself puts together on his Island of Despair a small library of volumes he rescues from his own shipwreck: "books of navigation ... three very good Bibles ... some *Portugueze* books also, and among them two or three Popish prayer-books"; and then he adds: "and several other books" – all unspecified.[1] These volumes, along with paper and ink, are the last things he mentions having rescued from the ship, almost as if books were some kind of leisurely afterthought, not so pressing in the contexts of physical survival. He makes good use of the paper and ink (the grounds of his own art), but never tells us whether he consults the resources of his library, with the exception of the Bibles which he says he reads daily and which he quotes liberally and echoes often, especially early on when he narrates in detail his repentance and conversion.

Otherwise, Crusoe seems to lead pretty much an unprecedented life, unconnected to earlier figures or situations; he is content to be only in the lineage of Jonah, Job, and the prodigal son, without reference to modern or other classic wayfarers or colonists or solitaries who preceded him and shared their experiences in print. There are no invocations of Alexander Selkirk or any of the other castaways and island solitaries of his time, and he seems to think of himself in vaguely mythic terms rather than allusive ones: he is a maker of things and a doer of deeds. He thinks of his story as telling itself without invoking precedents or citing models. But this total-originality, *tabula-rasa* pose is something of a ruse. There is frequent awareness that even in his newness he is participating consciously in traditions, themes, expectations, and methods, following the habits and patterns of whole clusters of readily accessible texts – books, pamphlets, *vade mecums*, ballads, guides – that dealt with travels and exploration and trade and cultural overlap. Sometimes these contemporary materials were organized along a narrative line, and sometimes involved just piled-up information, maps, tables, illustrations, charts, and preachy advice as well as running commentary. Defoe may well have cherrypicked here and there hints or ideas for activities or episodes or tools or geographical facts, as the old source hunters believed, but the real dependence on traditions here involves what he leads the reader to expect by his very presence within some of the textual traditions of their informal reading. I see no reason to believe that Defoe needed specific written "sources" for his accounts of Crusoe making or discovering things – clothing, earthenware pots, umbrellas, walls, ladders, canoes, creeks, currents – but he certainly knew that his readers expected such details. These expectations were created by what was already there in the textual traditions and their contexts rather than by any particular book or model or critical directive. The many varieties of travel books in his time, for example, carried suppositions and expectations that he virtually *had* to satisfy – about the facts of climate and weather, flora and fauna, geography, physical features of the natives, skin color, diet, language, rituals, tools and building projects, etc. Defoe's text dutifully fulfills such expectations quietly, smoothly, and realistically without any fanfare or direct acknowledgment that even in his distinctiveness and originality he was participating in established textual traditions. Here are storms at sea, shipwrecks, seamen's language, details of location and sailing conditions, pirates, mutinies, diverted plans and voyages, cargo arrangements, opportunities for trade, money exchange values, and both realized and lost commercial opportunities. Some of these expectations – adventures, pirates, strangeness, America, uninhabited islands – are highlighted on the title page; others show up later in the unfolding of the narrative. In the *Farther Adventures* (the sequel published the same year as *Robinson Crusoe* and included with subsequent editions of the novel) Defoe very self-consciously claims that he is avoiding all these conventions and he gives a list of them: "I shall not pester my Account, or the Reader, with Descriptions of Places, Journals of our Voyages, Variations of the Compass, Latitudes, Meridian-Distances, Trade-Winds, Situation of Ports, and the like; such as almost all the Histories of long Navigation are full of, and makes the reading tiresome enough, and are perfectly unprofitable to all that read it."[2] But on second look (as with the money he finds in the shipwreck) he includes the very kinds of information he pretends to rail against.

These expected "facts" and details are not necessarily trustworthy or accurate of course; Percy Adams' classic account in *Travelers and Travel Liars 1660–1800* (1962) remains a lively read for its detailing of falsified "facts" and information mistakenly copied from one inaccurate book to another but often cobbled together in London by hacks whose sea experience was all in their garrets. The point is that the conventions were set not by design or necessity but by habit and repetition, and often accurate cultural facts about one location were relocated on another batch of natives on another continent. What is common in travel books is a thirst for cultural information about far-off places, especially Africa and the Americas – often because such "facts" are strange and surprising in themselves and minister to a taste for the exotic, but sometimes because (more practically) they hinted at potential future markets, possibilities for expanding trade, or religious, cultural, and commercial evangelism. It was an acquisitive age, and the acquisitiveness included customs and behaviors and languages and habits of mind as well as goods, and products, and slaves. And the same kind of habits obtained in many different kinds of textual traditions, some of them discursive and didactic, as well as narrative and reflective.

A couple of years ago, when I was preparing a talk for a narrative conference in Finland, I decided to make a list of as many definable textual traditions as I could think of that were, one way or another, embodied or drawn upon in the pages of *Robinson Crusoe*. I quickly came up with a list of thirty-some of them. And when I delivered that paper a few weeks later, one listener jumped up straightaway at the end to add five more he had thought of during the talk. Ultimately, others suggested several more: each of these embodied distinct habits and conventions, and it is something of a feat to meet those expectations and fit them smoothly into something definite, distinctive, and new. I won't repeat the entire list here, but let me mention in passing just a few examples of these textual traditions and then briefly discuss two of them.

1. Personal journals (or diaries), usually Puritan in background, tone, and spirit and often Calvinistically motivated, that detail daily events and behaviors, with rich details about spiritual triumphs and failures.
2. Spiritual autobiographies that trace patterns in personal journals and summarize, from a later perspective, spiritual progress and regress.
3. Missionary accounts of conversions and tutorial successes in the New World.
4. Accounts of observations of natural phenomena, some from a scientific perspective (such as Royal Society reports and transactions), some from a meditational interest (such as Sir Robert Boyle's "meletetic lucubrations," Protestant meditations on everyday events that help to reveal truths about God and man).
5. Captivity or fear-of-captivity narratives.
6. Guides for conduct in specific callings, occupations, and circumstances, ranging from *The Young Man's Guide*, *The Young Man's Calling*, *A Christian Directory*, and Defoe's own *Family Instructors* to *The Tradesman's Calling*, *The Husbandman's Calling*, *The Seaman's Monitor*, and *Navigation Spiritualized; or a New Compass for Seamen*.
7. Stories of sinners, backsliders, reprobates, and rebels whose lives were cautionary or evitational.

8. The sequel tradition in which an original text is elaborated or extended into a new and quasi-independent narrative.
9. Wonder books that describe persons, circumstances, and events that seem to violate normal behaviors and natural laws, matters often going beyond the strange and surprising and sometimes crossing into the miraculous, eerie, bizarre, or supernatural.
10. Providence books relating special divine interventions in the natural processes of things and events.

Let us look in a little more detail at the first and last of these traditions – daily journals and Providence books, for both of these textual traditions bear a special relationship to a larger sense of order and the nature of things. Providence books first. In Defoe's time, there was nothing new in the idea that God actively watched over human events and monitored individual human lives through the orderly processes of Nature (General Providences) and that he sometimes intervened in specific moments and cases to punish or reward specific peoples or individuals (this involved Special Providences and occasionally Miracles). The theological debate about where to draw lines without lapsing into total solipsism was an old one, but what was new in emphasis in the late seventeenth century involved the increased pressures from science to discover and extend the orderly processes of Nature. Exceptions were a conceptual problem. Theology fought back largely through stories of special interventions that challenged the inviolability of natural laws. And the stories poured from the presses. One Matthew Poole in the 1670s was reported to be attempting to assemble an exhaustive collection of stories of providential interventions, and in 1697 William Turner published *A Compleat History Of the Most Remarkable Providences, both of Judgment and Mercy, which have Hapned in this PRESENT AGE*, a collection of about five thousand stories and anecdotes scattered over almost 600 folio pages. Similar collections were assembled in America, engineered by Cotton and Increase Mather, and (besides such massive anthologies) there were (on both sides of the Atlantic) scores of pamphlet-size volumes of judgments and punishments as well as rescues and deliverances. Providence books often involved doctrinal discussions and ambitious (or at least long) defenses of theory, but the emphasis was on examples, anecdotes, and narratives that illustrated or suggested providential intervention or special care in particular circumstances. It was a highly polemical (and repetitious) tradition, and it is probably safe to say that it had little impact on serious philosophical discourse or the rising Deistic challenges more generally. But it was appealing comfort reading for believers and had the cumulative effect of providing comparative test cases of credibility, for the examples were

argued vigorously, but varied widely in their rhetorical success. Readers of
the Providence tradition were not necessarily skilled critical readers, and
religious bias or gullibility were obviously friendly to Providential accounts.
But readers of Providence books were trained by reading experience to
assess gradations in credibility, and Defoe has the early pre-conversion
Crusoe work his way carefully through basic questions of agency. When
Crusoe discovers a few stalks of barley growing (apparently miraculously)
just outside his fortification, he reports "the astonishment and confusion of
my thoughts on this occasion" and begins "to suggest, that God had miraculously caus'd this grain to grow without any help of seed sown." But with
the help of his memory, he works out a rational explanation involving his
dumping out the dregs of a bag of seed, but then he loses his sense of being
singled out for special intervention. "And then," he reports, "the wonder
began to cease; and I must confess, my religious thankfulness to God's
Providence began to abate too upon the discovery that all this was nothing
but what was common; tho' I ought to have been as thankful for so strange
and unforeseen Providence, as if it had been miraculous; for it was really the
work of Providence as to me." Here Defoe draws directly on the insistent
distinction in Providence books between miracles and special providences,
the former involving direct interventions in the processes of Nature, and
the latter unusual favorable outcomes that happen within normal cause-
and-effect sequences. Defoe knows the vocabulary and the rhetoric of the
tradition and counts on readers to be able to navigate the turbulent waters
of theological controversy. In *The Farther Adventures*, Crusoe's mention of
providential doings trails off noticeably: he doesn't forget about it, but like
Moll Flanders, he is perhaps "not so extraordinary a Penitent as [he] was
at first."

If reader experience with the textual tradition of Providence books was
useful preparation for reading some parts of *Robinson Crusoe* where religious interpretation and critical rationality disagree, the whole life experience of keeping and re-reading a journal resonates throughout the novel,
even though strictly speaking the journal itself takes up only a dozen or so
pages and is much more often summarized than quoted directly.[3] Still, the
very idea of recording events daily, reviewing their patterns periodically, and
reflecting on them long-term sets up a complex method of interpreting and
evaluating events and reactions. It also enables Crusoe to keep a time line
that orders events and feeds his rage for order in his unfamiliar and puzzling
new world. He is obsessed by the idea of order during his entire stay on the
Island of Despair and is especially anxious in his first nine months when
keeping his journal is both a reminder of his discomfort and a steadying
force in facing it.

It well may be that the whole idea of Crusoe's journal came to Defoe late and gradually; the delayed mention of his finding ink in the shipwreck suggests that he hadn't initially planned to interleave retrospection with on-the-spot observation; the first fifth of the book is cast as a typical I-was-born Life narrative in retrospect. And the title page contributes here by featuring "Life" as the largest and most prominent word, a sometime guide/hint to emphasis even when authored by an editor or typesetter. But in any case the idea of the journal (once introduced) quickly becomes crucial to the sense of time and order that sets up the coherence of Crusoe's writing and perspective. First of all, the journal triggers the tripartite observation/digestion/reflection tension that animates the second fifth of the novel (and the whole first year on the Island of Despair). Defoe's use of the journal is somewhat irregular and seemingly casual – Crusoe often paraphrases or summarizes in blocks of several days – but his strategy sets up a pattern of observing events and writing-to-the-day, then reviewing, and then interpreting again from a lifelong retrospective. In effect, Defoe traces the narrative move from daily journal to reflective spiritual autobiography but inserts a middle-distance that mediates the observation/reflection. The journal's effectiveness in recording change of perspective underscores the way Crusoe comes to understand not only himself but the universe in its unexpected and (at first) unwelcome variety. And beyond the layered time perspectives, the journal provides an anchor and authority for time and for order itself.

Crusoe is understandably overwrought and confused when he is first cast up on dry land, and everything seems disordered or unknown; he is an alien in a place so unnerving that he sleeps in a tree during his first night on the island. Once he gets his minimal bearings he remarks on his disorder and spends his early weeks and months trying to make sense of his environment, only to discover that the island is in fact stable and ordered in its own way, and that it is he who must adjust once he finds out the order of nature in this particular place. For there are here different kinds of growths and wildlife, different terrains, different seasons (in fact different kinds of seasons – rainy and dry rather than summer and winter), and ultimately (though it takes him years to document it) different human traits and habits and customs, including of course much later its use by cannibals for killing and consuming their prisoners of war.

His first thoughts on the island, naturally enough, are about physical security, but he soon discovers that what he really lacks in his new world is any sense of Order, both in his environment and in his life. And only when he begins to keep his journal – some weeks into his island residence and when he has recovered as much of his past as he can from the shipwreck – does he begin to gain some coherent perspective: writing and keeping a record of himself enables him to sort out climate, growth cycles, and seasonal patterns. At first he sees his carefully harvested legacy from the shipwreck as "a confus'd heap of goods which ... lay in no order" (55), but with paper and pen in hand he can sort things out in a vertical written ledger of the Good and Evil in his condition and situation. "[I]t was a great Pleasure to me to see all my Goods in such Order," he later reports, and his journal soon records his satisfaction with being in control of his time: "This morning," he writes in his journal on November 4, "I began to order my times of work, of going out with my gun, time of sleep and time of diversion, *viz*. Every Morning I walk'd out with my gun for two or three hours if it did not rain, then employ'd my self to work till till about eleven a-clock, then eat what I had to live on, and from twelve to two I lay down to sleep, the weather being excessive hot" (58). What is remarkable about Defoe's adaptation of the journal tradition here is the way Crusoe learns that he needs a larger sense of order, and at the same time discovers the relativity of regional and cultural norms. Travel is discovery, and what is Nature in one place is not necessarily Nature in another.

Crusoe as a land owner, trader, and accumulator was probably temperamentally and intellectually more interesting and important to Defoe than Crusoe as builder, gardener, and grower: his other novels are preoccupied with exchange and accumulation much more than production. But readers of *Crusoe* over the years have usually seen it another way, being more fascinated by the island section of the novel, with Crusoe's need to create, with his human challenges in isolation rather than with his global business decisions and accumulated wealth. In other words, readers have been more intrigued by the potential of a book Defoe never wrote, *The Compleat English Husbandman*, rather than *The Compleat English Tradesman* that Defoe published in 1725–7. The association of reading with survival may account for part of the success of narration in the early part of the island years, but some of the narrative power results from the sheer force of "how" answers that are particular to the discrete island isolation: how can Crusoe come to understand Nature halfway across the world when his native experience is otherwise? How can he use the leftovers from the shipwreck to build a new life in a new and contrary setting? How can solitude and survival be framed as creative if not satisfying? How do things learned in one location translate to a different part of the world? How do people create or grow things as distinguished from selling or exchanging them? Among other things, the first year of the island section reconciles, largely through the conversion episode that animates Crusoe's perception and understanding and leads to his mastery of the physical through the spiritual. That is to say, Crusoe's needs and assets come into a do-it-yourself kind of balance.

Rousseau was essentially right in his novel, *Émile or On Education* (1762), about the educational dimensions of *Robinson Crusoe*: exploring here is instruction, and what has to be mastered once the self is ordered is Nature itself in all its particulars and variety and fundamental order. Crusoe's monocultural teaching of Friday about language and religion and diet takes over and tests the instructional function later in the novel, and in a sense *Robinson Crusoe* becomes for a while a kind of *Rough Guide* to the New World.

Pat Rogers has suggested that *Robinson Crusoe* has a good deal in common with the georgic mode, a type of verse imitating the Roman poet Virgil's poems, *The Georgics*, dealing with rural and agricultural life. Rogers makes the connection via Defoe's *A Tour thro' the Whole Island of Great Britain* (1724–6), where it applies very nicely, but he could just as well have made his point with *A Tour through the Whole "Island of Despair,"* Crusoe's name at times for his island.[4] More recently Stephen Gregg has very suggestively sorted out affinities in *Robinson Crusoe* for the languages of both georgic and pastoral.[5] It is provocative to contemplate some of the concerns of *Robinson Crusoe* with Virgil as our guide. We might ponder for a moment parallel functions that Defoe here performs, much in the spirit of recalling some of the popular textual traditions that he drew upon for reader guidance. Defoe explores many of the same issues and functions that the georgic articulates for eighteenth-century poetry. In the central island portion of the novel, he sorts out the processes of Nature, climate, discovery, cultivation, labor, husbandry, and productivity, in concrete, particular, and narrative working terms. In fact, for the central three-fifths of the novel (that is, all of the "transformed island" narrative), Crusoe's busyness in creating an isolated economy of his own is front and center both in conception and in particular details. It is the intricate managing of these themes and concerns (especially the devotion to everyday labor within the framework of the deciphered processes of Nature) that constitutes the striking and insistent coherence of that section of the narrative. If *Robinson Crusoe* has observable affinities with the georgic they would seem to be broadly cultural and pragmatic rather than traditional or formal, but they are visible to readers across the cultural divide.

A strict interpretation of the georgic as a textual tradition would need to start with Virgil and virtually end there as well. There are a modest number of formal georgics in the eighteenth century, but there are hundreds of georgic derivations, spinoffs, and allusions. Literary historians are pretty well agreed that signs of the georgic pop up everywhere in the English-speaking world after Dryden's translation of Virgil's poem and Addison's influential essay of 1697, "An Essay on Virgil's *Georgics*," accompanying that translation. And the proliferation and amalgamation of other closely related textual traditions is abundantly manifested in texts throughout the eighteenth century: in house and estate poems, prospect poems, garden and landscape poems, poetry of description, occupational and work poems, rural community poems, mock georgics, urban georgics – lots of familial variants that recall similar themes and emphases. And beyond this (mostly in prose) there is a broad spectrum of agricultural and rural improvement texts (such as Jethroe Tull's 1731 *Horse-Hoeing Husbandry*) that rise up in a kind of quiet rebellion against urbanization and its discontents and that reassert and celebrate the cultural heritage of labor, instruction, and orderly rural creativity. This kind of observation is part of the context that many readers, both early and late, brought to their reading of *Robinson Crusoe*, hardly a source or allusion in the usual sense but a frame of reference that quietly (as in other textual traditions) becomes part of the reach of the novel; textual traditions – learned or popular, in poetry or prose – assert and insert themselves into reader practices and habits. This constitutes one set of reasons for thinking about traditional formal distinctions and broader textual traditions at one and the same time on more or less an equal basis.

I have been trying to think about textual traditions in a comprehensive way that includes how readers are trained and habituated by them, as well as for their thematic and formal features. But I have also been trying to complicate two broad distinctions that we seldom question hard enough: between traditional and popular literature, for one, and (second) for poetry and prose. I began with Pope's sharp division of writing into the worthy and lasting, on the one hand, and, on the other, the transitory and the inferior, a would-be distinction that once had its day in literary studies but has proved to be illusory as the novel claimed a larger and larger share of both readership and reputation. In practical terms, not many eighteenth-century scholars and critics have actual difficulty with multiple citizenship in traditional categories. Pope's *The Rape of the Lock* (1714), for example, can readily be conceived as many different things at the same time, fed by multiple forms and textual traditions: rhymed poem, mock epic, couplet lyric, neoclassical poem, social comedy, five-act comedy honoring the unities of space and time, social satire, occasional poem, etc., and there is some profit in tracing its relationship to any of these traditions. But no category cancels the rights of any other one: there is no reason for any either/or rather than both/and. Perhaps Pope in his own private taste and conversations was less consistent and more generous than he was as a would-be canon maker, but in any case Defoe's catch-all lifetime habit of gleaning and gathering multiple textual traditions and transforming them into new configurations continues to have a pretty good run. What I have tried to do here is to provide some reasons for thinking more broadly about textual traditions in both prose and poetry, and for seeing affinities by complicating some of the usual polar distinctions – traditional versus experimental or improvisational, poetry versus prose, literary establishment versus outside innovators, formal loyalties versus instinctive absorption and intermixing of multiple textual traditions into something new. These are strange and surprising adventures indeed.

NOTES

1 All references in the text to *Robinson Crusoe* are to *Robinson Crusoe,* ed. John Richetti (London: Penguin Books, 2001), 52–3.
2 *Farther Adventures*, ed. W. R. Owens, *The Novels of Daniel Defoe*, vol. 2 (London: Pickering & Chatto, 2008), 127.
3 *The Fortunes and Misfortunes of the Famous Moll Flanders*, ed. G. A. Starr (London: Oxford University Press, 1971), p. 5.
4 Pat Rogers, *The Text of Great Britain: Theme and Design in Defoe's Tour* (Newark, DE: University of Delaware Press, 1998), 135–46.
5 Stephen H. Gregg, *Defoe's Writings and Manliness: Contrary Men* (London: Ashgate, 2009), 64–70.

2

RIVKA SWENSON

Robinson Crusoe and the Form of the New Novel

Defoe's first novel (and its sequel, *Farther Adventures* [1719])[1] gave rise to the Robinsonade, a microgenre still inspired today by Crusoe's lessons about surviving on a desert island. But what is *Robinson Crusoe*? Where does it fit within the larger history of realism and of novelistic form? Answering these questions requires readers to consider Defoe's approach to visual description, his inclusion of what seem to be (on the surface) numerous errors and internal contradictions, and his claim – in *Serious Reflections* (1720), the meditative addendum to *Crusoe* and *Farther Adventures* – that the *Crusoe* story was an "allusive allegorical history" and an "allegorical" and "historical" rendition of the life-story of a "man alive, and well known too."[2] In the first case, *Crusoe* contains copious details but the descriptions famously lack fullness; modern readers have trouble visualizing Crusoe's world. But what descriptive treasures appear if readers momentarily disregard the wisdom that *Crusoe* is simply the unadorned equivalent of (as Virginia Woolf wonderfully suggested) a "plain earthenware pot"?[3] Second, what kind of formal unity emerges if readers recognize that *Crusoe*'s apparent errors and inconsistencies are actually the means by which Defoe dramatizes the difficult process not simply of building a world but of building a narrative and of building a world through narrative? Third, what helpful connection is revealed at the juncture of genre, history, and novelistic form, if readers see how Defoe's oft-overlooked claim that *Crusoe* was an allusive allegorical history actually points to *Crusoe*'s allusive engagement with the forming of Great Britain in which Defoe himself had recently had such a prominent authorial hand as a paid propagandist?

What is *Robinson Crusoe*'s place in the history of the novel? Within the critical history, *Crusoe* has traditionally been taken as a hesitant but rough step toward the novel: Ian Watt saw "episodes" rather than fully fleshed formal realism; Dorothy Van Ghent saw "anecdotes" and "naively patched" scenes, not a "world," not a "novel, coherent in structure, unified and given its shape and significance by a complex system"; Ralph Rader saw something "genuinely but ambiguously and incoherently literary"; while, on the other hand, Cynthia Sundberg Wall wisely cautions modern readers to be wary of our "expectations" about early prose fictions, even as Maximillian E. Novak calls Defoe a master of fictions, Patricia Meyer Spacks sees *Crusoe*'s psychological depth, and Stuart Sherman, David Marshall, and Michael Seidel perceive *Crusoe*'s metafictional richness.[4] The novel genre does not simply develop in linear fashion from allegory, abstraction, and emblem, through a period of proto-novelistic fumbling, toward modern realism. Quick to deem early fictions the primitive, failed forebears of realism, modern readers risk missing out on *Crusoe*'s richness; postmodern writing does not hold exclusive title to meaningfully implausible claims, internal contradictions, troubled syntax, self-referential inquiry, or narrative discontinuity.

Familiar as it is, *Crusoe* still holds surprises. First, is *Crusoe* really the unswerving equivalent of the unadorned pot we have come to take it as? No. Readers should press hard upon the oddly under-examined but climactic episode within the cave of "a hundred thousand lights" wherein the protagonist catalogues the attributes of a "stark naked" Carib who slumbers in full color and texture (141, 163). Friday's colorful, texturized, particularized body, shimmering anomalously in the cave's crucible like a time-traveling slice of description from a modern novel, compels a closer look. Second, the presence of errors in a "naïve" pre-novelistic text would hardly be surprising, but is *Crusoe* naïve? No. Even fans of the book sometimes feel that *Crusoe* is clumsily rendered (if innovative), but, rather than seeing the book as realism's loved but lumpy ancestor, readers should take *Crusoe* on its own un-simple terms: this is a carefully crafted, formally self-aware narrative that the protagonist explicitly labors to fashion from life's messy incidents and accidents. *Crusoe* is not a character's life-story but a story about a writer who overtly composes and revises his life's fiction; readers watch him visibly manipulate details so that they seem to tend toward an "end" and parts seem to serve an emergent whole, since, as Crusoe asserts at the beginning of *Serious Reflections*, "the Design of every Thing is ... in the Intention" and is made manifest "last in the Execution."[5] Readers should neither apologize for nor gloss over *Crusoe*'s obvious internal irregularities. Instead, readers should recognize how such contrivances dramatize Crusoe's consciousness-in-action as would-be-master-of-reality. Like any storyteller, he needs an audience, and he marvels at how his life's chaotic "collection of wonders" is transformed by the telling into a "chain of wonders" (203, 215); he revises in the foreground, as readers can see, "in miniature, or by abridgement" (155), while bringing others (and us) into an assimilating circle of influence that is the narrative equivalent of Crusoe's fence or "pale" (Crusoe uses the older term). By taking seriously how *Robinson Crusoe* performs its own progress from collection to chain (words with strong narrative and national–colonial–global associations), readers will see how content and form generate a self-avowed selective accounting that seeks to master the chaos of misshapen pots, misremembered days, mismatched shoes into a unified world. Readers will also see that if *Crusoe* offers a metafictional allegory-of-its-own-becoming, it resonantly conjures Defoe's own personal obsession with the idea of England and Scotland coming together to form the personified nation-as-man, an image that *Crusoe's* "allusive allegorick history" encodes within the spectacle of Friday's own body in the cave of many lights.

Describing Friday 1: A Plain Earthenware Pot?

It is a truism that *Crusoe* (among other early novels including Defoe's) lacks particular, tactile, colorful, sensational description. Samuel Taylor Coleridge lauds Crusoe as "a representative of humanity in general," "the universal representative, the person, for whom every reader could substitute himself," with a story that can "make me forget my specific class, character, and circumstances, and ... raise me while I read him, into the universal man"; similarly, Woolf, seeing the narrative as the equivalent of a "plain earthenware pot," indeed "nothing but a large earthenware pot," applauds how *Crusoe* makes us ponder, abstractly, the vast "solitudes of the human soul."[6] It is true that *Crusoe* has plenty of *things* that cannot be pictured by a reader; Jenny Davidson's apt phrase is "bare novelistic minute particulars."[7] But such details are not insignificant; bald or flavorless, they still reveal the psychology. When shipwrecked-Crusoe melancholically muses that the sea has coughed up "two shoes that were not fellows" (38–9), the flotsam reifies Crusoe's (and *Robinson Crusoe's*) condition of fragmented self-difference. Moreover, not all *Crusoe's* details are as baldly figured as those shoes. Indeed, in a passage somewhat neglected by critics for all its intimacy, the vibrant inscription of Friday's body upon the formerly dark cave of Crusoe's consciousness stands in stark contrast to the narrative's otherwise typical colorlessness.

The general plainness of *Crusoe's* things and spaces is undeniable, which is what makes a rare vivid palette so remarkable. As Van Ghent says, Defoe's things are usually "not at all vivid in texture."[8] Where are the tropical colors? What color is Poll, or the hair and eyes of the woman Crusoe later marries and has children with? Readers do not know, but we see Friday's hair, eyes, and more. As Friday slumbers stark-naked (a detail often missed) "upon rice straw, and a blanket," Crusoe queerly observes:

> He was a comely handsome fellow, perfectly well made ... He had ... something very manly in his face, and yet he had all the sweetness and softness of an *European* in his countenance too, especially when he smil'd. His hair was

long and black, no[t] curl'd like wool; his forehead very high, and large, and a great vivacity and sparkling sharpness in his eyes. The colour of his skin was not quite black, but very tawny; and yet not of an ugly nauseous tawny, as the *Brasilians*, and *Virginians*, and other natives of *America* are; but of a bright kind of a dun olive colour … very agreeable … His face was round and plump; his nose small, not flat like the Negroes, a very good mouth, thin lips, and his fine teeth well set, and white as ivory. (162)

With this spectacle – though it be "not very easy to describe" – the reader is treated to a kind of racist buffet consisting of black hair, tawny skin, white teeth (162). Coleridge was right that Crusoe himself is drawn abstractly, such that anyone (provided they be English, Protestant, white, male, able-bodied, literate) can see themselves in his Platonic form: here is "the universal representative, the person, for whom every reader could substitute himself."[9] Yet Friday, in the cave's cabinet of wonder, is particularized ("thin lips"), texturized ("curl'd like wool"), colorized ("a bright kind of dun olive colour"): his "very agreeable" body, objectified as surely as a beloved lady in any Renaissance sonnet, glows like emblazoned booty in the cave of Crusoe's mind and narrative, amid the novel's hoard of otherwise-loosely-drawn things (162).

The anomalously vivid portrait is practically edible; we could eat Friday up. A disturbingly tasty object whose "softness" melds with "manly" mien, he is conflated with consumable desiderata: "olive," "ivory," "wool" (162). Alarmingly, in his caramel "tawny" "sweetness" he resembles sugar, a product Crusoe knows well. Pre-shipwreck, Crusoe "was recommended," he says, "to the house of a good honest man like himself, who had an *Ingenio*," and "I lived with him … and acquainted myself … with the manner of planting and making of sugar; and … I resolved … I would turn planter" (29); he "planted some tobacco" and got "a large piece of ground ready for planting canes in the year to come, but" he "want[s] help" and regrets having sold "my boy Xury," and so he has to wait until he is rescued from his desert island to enjoy the financial fruits of the cane-plot his partner built for him and cultivated (28, 29).

But what is this passage – one of the most descriptively modern moments in eighteenth-century novels – doing here, inside a formerly dark cave that glitters, once illuminated, with "a hundred thousand lights, whether from diamonds, or any other precious stones, or gold" (141)? Looking back from the vantage-point of modern novels, the passage looks like a missing link that anticipates, even engenders, realism's rise. At the same time, the description of the sleeper explodes realism, disrupting the time–space continuum with information about Friday's smile, teeth, eyes. The passage is dually important, then, both for the unexpected appearance of descriptive realism and for the way Crusoe's acts of narrative compression and transposition unexpectedly explode that realism.

Two Shoes Without Fellows, and the Grammar of Becoming

Every reader butts up against the novel's retinue of seeming-errors, including the awkward implication that the sleeping man grins, open-eyed, in slumber. Are these marks of hasty indifference, or sophisticated craft? Arguably, Crusoe's errors and self-contradictions are the signal evidence of his own foregrounded composition-and-revision methodology (omitting, expanding, transposing, consolidating, making-things-up). *Robinson Crusoe* instantiates the writer-protagonist's process of making "Crusoe" and the novel he's a part of. Latter-day Crusoe reads the desired-present into the past, displaying a history of his development as a writer-storyteller who learns – with help from his parrot – to build and shape his narrative toward a desired reality. A splendid metafiction (a fiction about fiction, in this case a fiction about making and conveying fiction), *Crusoe* emphasizes the work it takes.

Crusoe's journal, from his early island years, exemplifies the book's foregrounding of writerly manipulation, of revisionary-craft-in-process. Preceding the journal is Crusoe's detailed, and very different, decades-later summary of coming to the island, and a revealing comment about the clarifying benefits of hindsight, wherein he attests that if he had started writing right away, "my journal would have been full of many dull things" such as "vomiting" and beating his "head and face" (56). The journal is then introduced with two self-reflexive claims: first, that this is a "copy" rather than the original; second, that the journal will merely repeat "all these particulars over again" (56). But these claims cannot be taken at face value any more than the novel's prefatory claim (from the faux-editor) that "the thing" – *Robinson Crusoe* – is "a just history of fact" without "any appearance of fiction in it" (3). The claim is farcical on the face of it: sometimes Crusoe says all is exactly rendered, sometimes he says he lost a day in his reckoning, and sometimes he says he lost more than a day. But the problems are more pervasive than that; the journal, a particularly concentrated example of fictionalizing-at-work, quickly exposes itself as anything but a copy of the original (latter-day Crusoe interrupts often), and the journal consistently contradicts (in chronology and substance both) the earlier hindsight-telling. In the hindsight version with which the novel begins, Crusoe spares a wildcat and feeds it; in the journal, he kills and skins a wildcat. In the hindsight-version, Crusoe successfully kills a she-goat, trapping its kid in an enclosure; in the journal, enclosure is impossible because he has merely marked a semi-circle for future enclosure. Dozens of disjunctions have been documented since Charles Gildon's ungenerous (if hilarious) attack on Defoe's supposed accidental errors in *The Life and Strange Surprizing Adventures of Mr. D— De F—, of London, Hosier* (1719).[10] But Gildon's piece was satire, and, like some others after him who misunderstand Defoe as a careless writer for-money, Gildon does not account for the fact that *Robinson Crusoe* is a highly self-aware story about a storyteller/writer.

The malformed grammar within the journal, produced when latter-day-Crusoe interrupts and contradicts himself, is an allegorical formalism that both reflects and produces the hero's disordered psychology in which one thought is not the fellow of another. The internal competition between storytellers/versions (young-Crusoe; hindsight-Crusoe) manifests as an aggressive dissonance between the *deictic* referents – the pronouns, temporal-spatial adverbs, and verb tenses that signal the sources of utterance.[11] Not only do details contradict, the shifting "time deictics" (e.g., "now," "then") wrench the relationship between past and present into strange shapes. In the journal, two voices overlap awkwardly, two Crusoes, constituting a formal-psychological corollary to the problem of unmatched shoes. Consider the journal's entries for January 2 and 3: "*Jan.* 2. Very hot still, but I went abroad early and late with my gun, and … I found there was plenty of goats, tho' exceeding shy and hard to come at, however I resolv'd to try if I could not bring my dog to hunt them down. *Jan. 3.* Accordingly, the next day, I went out with my dog" (61). The hindsight-voice encroaches, making meaning after-the-fact by skewing facts, making what should be "today, I went" into "the next day, I went" (61). Narrative versions and grammars compete; Crusoe makes many misshapen pots before he gets one right, and the task of *making* history, of comfortably designating the past and its truths "a place I had lived in, but was come out of," is overtly arduous (102).

Finally, however, Crusoe's encroaching hindsight-voice begins to pre-vail, to inhabit more space, from sentences to pages, as he makes order. The eat-or-be-eaten voice of latter-day Crusoe submits the Otherness of his old self to acts of grammatical enclosure and incorporation, subsuming the journal, pursuing a tidier progress toward who he says he is now. Crusoe, always losing himself or giving himself over for lost, always frightened of being devoured, swallowed up, eaten by external forces (ocean, earth-quake, cannibal, cat), syntactically consumes his internal Otherness. The present overwrites the past as Crusoe's nonmatching shoes (so to speak) are synthesized toward an end.

But rather than simply dismiss the journal, Crusoe gives a reason for its disappearance that tests the bounds of the realistic, if not realism itself. Namely, before the journal even begins, Crusoe constructs a path toward its disappearance that is as implausible as it is convenient, asserting, "while my ink lasted, I kept things very exact" (this in defiance of confessions elsewhere about losing days), "but after that was gone, I could not, for I could not make *any* ink by *any* means that I could devise" (53, italics mine), and, so, "having no more ink, I was forc'd to leave it off" (56). The repetition ("I could not, for I could not") underscores the unlikeliness (53). How hard did he try to make ersatz ink? Why is there nary a numbingly detailed account of missteps with charcoal or plant-tinctures? The claim is as silly as the claim that Crusoe accidentally built a canoe that was big enough for twenty-six men. Hindsight-Crusoe makes the abandoning of the journal into something significant, as it coincides, in his retelling, with the anniversary of his birth and of his coming to the island (106). Later, upon leaving the island, the hero keeps journals assiduously, but the streamlined narrative, which picks up pace as it goes, "omit[s]" many "adventures" as he explicitly declines to "trouble" us with either his "sea-journals" or new "land-journal" (227).

Upon abandoning the journal, Crusoe has a sort of conversation with Poll, the parrot, that expresses the hero's development into a writer committed to streamlining his story toward an end. Poll parrots questions that the hero has, clearly, asked aloud ad infinitum: "*Robin, Robin*, poor *Robin Crusoe*, where are you *Robin Crusoe*? Where are you? Where have you been? ... *How come you here?*" (113). If these questions are strange, the use of second-person pronoun is stranger still, marking an Otherness-within. The voice is Crusoe's own; Poll queries him "in such bemoaning language I had used to talk to him; and he learn'd it so perfectly," just as "I had taught him" (113). In line with Paula Backscheider's observation that Defoe uses "dialogue ... to externalize inner conflict," the parrot's mock-invitation-to-dialogue is an exposure.[12] Crusoe's deictic dissonance suggests *internal* ambivalence, a crisis not fully solved until he conveys to an audience (Friday, the Spaniard, us) the crafted answers to Poll's question.

Describing Friday 2: Crusoe's Gift

Having already subsumed the journal, Crusoe rises to Poll's challenge and the narrative proceeds, but just when it seems young Crusoe's breakdowns have ended and he has become a skilled assimilator of Otherness both within and without himself, he stumbles on the mark of a competing author-owner-master upon the beach's sandy text: the footprint. The fellow-less print swallows Crusoe's; his fear of being devoured returns; eaten up by terror, he considers destroying all he has built. But instead, he steels himself to enter a dark, groan-filled cave: there, he is dazzled to find that the walls bear "reflections" of "a hundred thousand lights" from his two candles (141); and, burying the groaning-monster-turned-dying-goat in the cave's "mouth" after the old he-goat expires, Crusoe subsequently encloses a delicious sleeping man – Friday – within the renovated space (142). The gift to us of Friday's gemlike body in the illuminated interior of the new novel is an emblem of Crusoe's larger "great favor" to us (as the preface says), i.e., the story he bequeaths to those within his purview (3). Such gifts are self-serving; Crusoe becomes himself by giving others (Friday, the Spaniard, us) the (partial) story of his life, the story of how to be English, the story of how to make cheese, and bringing them within its scope. With this inheritance, the pale widens, and Crusoe at last finds that his disorderly "collection of wonders," as he calls it, has been transformed, by conveyance, into the "chain of wonders" that he subsequently deems it (203, 215).

When Crusoe first discovers this new cave, he is terrified, but facing this challenge transforms him. First, clearing the "mouth," he hears "a broken noise, *as if* of words half-express'd," and he sees "two broad shining eyes of some creature, whether Devil or man I knew not, which twinkled like two stars" (140). He steels himself: surely, "there was nothing in this cave that was more frightful than my self" (140). Rushing in with a firebrand, he finds the "monster" is but a dying he-goat, and, moreover, "never was such a glorious sight seen in the island, I dare say, as … the walls reflected a hundred thousand lights … whether [of] diamonds, or any other precious stones, or gold" (141). Now the space is "a most delightful cavity, or grotto," a place to bury the now-dead goat along with his fears, a storehouse for guns and powder (141). Now the time of "broken noise" ends; never again will Crusoe be lost and need to utter the phrase, as he does now for the last time, "I recover'd myself" (140). And although his parrots "all call Robin Crusoe," he no longer needs to "take the pains with them that [he] had done with [Poll]" (143).

Instead, Crusoe readies himself for a human parrot as he pores over the material of his life and guides that history toward the desired end. Steadying the "crowd of thoughts that whirl'd through that great thorow-fare of the brain, the memory, in this night's time," Crusoe coolly reviews "the whole history of my life in miniature, or by abridgement, *as I may call it*" (155). He sleeps, dreams of treasure: specifically, he imagines finding a "savage" who is pursued by others of his own kind and is ripe for the saving, and he dreams of "carry[ing] him into my cave," such that the man "became my servant" (157). Thus determined "to get a savage" or two "into my possession" and "make them entirely slaves to me" (157, 158), Crusoe keeps his eye on the telos, the prize, even while hindsight-Crusoe credits Providence with setting "such narrow bounds to his sight and knowledge of things" that although he "walks in the midst of so many thousand dangers" he "is kept serene, and calm" (155). "[A]dvanc[ing] towards" two cannibals and then "rushing at once" upon them, he carries another cannibal, their intended victim, "quite away" (162). There is one way, however, in which Crusoe modifies his dream's supposed providential mandate and "did not let my dream come to pass": namely, he does not take Friday first "to my castle" nor "into my grove for shelter"; instead, he immediately takes him "to my cave on the farther part of the island," i.e., into the formerly dark cave of lights (162). Thus follows, as discussed above, the stunning depiction of the nude sleeper.

As for the sleeper (now Friday), upon waking he serves a crucial role: he helps Crusoe become a confident Englishman who shores up his identity/ story by telling it to others. Simultaneously, Crusoe's island, full of non-native trees and plants, hardly untouched by humans (just as the novel genre was not untouched before Defoe came to it), becomes his through the telling. Before Friday came, Crusoe declared of this "delicious vale" that "this was all my own ... and [I] had a right of possession; *and if I could convey it, I might have it in inheritance*, as compleatly as any lord of a manor in England" (80, italics mine). Paradoxically, it is precisely by "convey[ing]" an inheritance – not just of real property but of language, thanks to the double connotations of "convey" – that Crusoe becomes the master of all he surveys. "I taught him," he says of ventriloquized-Poll, and now he teaches Friday; indeed, Crusoe fully becomes his own latter-day self as he teaches Friday about gunpowder, God, shoes. By conveying, Crusoe moves "past the operation of fear" into mastery (205). At the same time, it is a given that Friday loses himself in the process; Crusoe is Prospero to Friday's Caliban; Friday, losing his own name, is "taught to say *Master*" and informed "that was to be [Crusoe's] name" but is taught not the meaning (163).

By opening up the narrative pale to let Friday and others (including us) inside, colonist-Crusoe resists colonization himself, instead making everyone part of his story, incorporating them into his world. As he says of the mariners who alight on his shore:

> I gave them the whole history of the place, and of my coming to it; shew'd them my fortifications, the way I made my bread, planted my corn, cured my grapes ... I gave them a description of the way I manag'd the goats, and directions to milk and fatten them, and to make both butter and cheese. In a word, I gave them every part of my own story. (222)

The telling is everything, and readers are part of the chain; what is the above but a portrayal of *Crusoe* itself – not history but Crusoe's story? Crusoe emphasizes his generosity ("I gave them," "I gave them," "I gave them," he says thrice), but the telling and gifting discloses a complicated dynamic (222). The preface describes *Crusoe* as a generous "favor" to readers, but Crusoe's stories serve Crusoe first (1).

At the end of the day, *Crusoe* is perhaps best thought of as a novel about a writer who overtly manipulates his story and audience, shaping by hindsight, reading the present into the past, omitting and compressing toward an end, forging a chain of narrative reciprocity. *Crusoe*/Crusoe meditates self-reflexively on the story's erection as a narrative of personal development; *Crusoe* describes the labor of building a narrative architecture and conveys its inheritance – any author's final task, as Defoe knew from his early career as a pro-Union propagandist. No wonder Crusoe praises fellow Englishman Will Atkins for fabricating well to the sailors who had attempted to mutiny, as the ends justify the means: "[t]hough this was all a fiction of his own, yet it had its desired effect" (211). Readers might say the same about Crusoe's own proprietary projections, wherein the world reproduces Crusoe; he imagines that after he leaves, the islanders will parrot him into eternity and the birds will "all call *Poor Robin Crusoe* to this day" (141). The world around Crusoe is so transformed that it might well say as Crusoe himself does that "by the usual corruption of words in *England*, we are now call'd, nay we call our selves, and write our name *Crusoe*" (5). Thus, conveying his story to the captain who will deliver him from the island, Crusoe transforms his "collection of wonders" into a "chain of wonders" (215). This brilliant conceit encodes the element of control implicit in all Crusoe's language, even as it allegorizes the how he fashions a progressive-linear form. "Providence" is an alibi; Crusoe himself "order'd everything for the best" (87).

Whither Allegory? Crusoean Formalism and the "allusive allegorick history" of Nation

"[T]he Fable is always made for the Moral," Crusoe says, suggesting that his story's content and structure proceeds according to an "Intention" that produces "Design."[13] He insists moreover that *Crusoe*, "though allegorical, is also historical," that its every "Circumstance" makes "Allusion to a real story," to "the actions" of an actual "man alive, and well known too."[14] What did he mean by allegory, apart from the notion that *Crusoe* is a metafiction that performs its construction? What did he mean by man alive? Considering that Crusoe claims that his life consists of "a strange concurrence of days" (106), readers should observe that the marriage of English Will Atkins to the reformed and renamed savage Mary, in *Farther Adventures*, happens on May 1, the date of the British Act of Union; on April 10, 1695, Crusoe returned to the island, he stayed "five and twenty days," and he left "not above four days after" the emblematic weddings of Will Atkins et al. to newly baptized, renamed Indian women.[15] Having praised Atkins in *Crusoe* for manipulating others deftly through "fiction" in order to achieve a "desired effect" (211), Crusoe declaims in *Serious Reflections* against "People, who go about telling ... Stories forg'd in their own Brain" instead of offering "Facts that are form'd to touch the Mind"; in other words, he lauds fictions that inflect reality and that do so in order to affect it; such fictions belong to the genre of "allusive allegorick history," i.e., to the genre of *Crusoe* itself.[16]

In the propagandistic writing that Defoe produced for pay about the 1707 Act of Union of England and Scotland that formed Great Britain, he developed a scheme of metaphors, images, and formal designs that found fictionalized resonance in *Robinson Crusoe*. In Defoe's novel, readers can see an "allegorick" rendering of the narrative processes that informed the extra-legal construction of the nation as Defoe depicted those processes in *The History of the Union of Great Britain* (1709) – not surprisingly, his "history" was overtly presented as a progressively linear *interpretation*, a subjectively-known truth-told-slant that he explicitly hoped would help to complete the unification within the minds of still-hostile readers.[17] *Crusoe*'s Union resonances are complexly allusive. The hero's recovery from fragmentation, his coming-to-self-via-narrative, resonates with Defoe's dream for Anglo-Britain in which the nation unifies as a "Man" by imagining its *future self looking back* from the "high rock" of desired-hindsight and surveying the narrative path of the state's ship through history's "waves."[18] *Crusoe*'s self-contradictions illuminate the difficulty of crafting a smooth thread from competing versions and mismatched shoes. Naturally, where Defoe complained about the "Pen and Ink War" over Union taking place within contemporary journals (wherein his own salvos depicted the nation as a human body divided against itself, wracked in pain), Crusoe's own journal, as discussed above, manifests a pen-and-ink war between selves.[19]

Author and hero alike thus foreground instead of mask the revisionary processes they bring to their material. Crusoe triumphs by visibly remaking fragments into what Defoe's *History* called a "Thre[a]d of History."[20] Crusoe survives shipwreck and the practical and aesthetic disasters of enormous unabridged canoes (corollary to real history) and ugly pots (recalling Defoe's complaints about the "Abortions and disappointments" of early attempts at Union), fashioning what the *History* called a "true string"[21] – but, as in the *History*, the "true string" is overtly not the literal truth. Indeed, the *History*, in making for Britons a path-through-history, is adamant that the "true" string is the one that cuts through rocky contradictions to generate a desired reality. For Defoe and Crusoe, the promotion of some elements (e.g., Englishness, Protestantism) over others is part of a devouring narrative process and its correlational reality. Defoe admits he strategically "misplaces some things" in his "Account Current" while showing how the "thought of Union" thus makes "every thing retir[e] to its proper place" – as does Crusoe, in a manner of speaking.²² Through the force of contrived hindsight, latter-day Crusoe excels at Defoevian historiography, putting all of young-Crusoe's "goods in such order" (56).

Francis Bacon, Defoe's predecessor in pro-Unionist writing and thought, imagined future-Britain as a coalescence of lights, an image that finds legacy in Crusoe's cave. Where Bacon imagined "lights" that "meet in conjunction" to produce "admirable effects," Defoe, Bacon's inheritor, fantasizes in *Crusoe* about a cave wherein a "hundred thousand lights" "reflect" his light (141).²³ Providence (really Crusoe) sets "narrow bounds to [his] sight and knowledge of things" so that he can calmly face "dangers" both real and imagined (cannibal melee, dark cave of groans), the better to achieve the shared vision (of Friday's hybrid beauty) toward which his narrative leads and from which it proceeds (155). Resonantly, Defoe's *History* employs just such a "Thre[a]d"; he leads readers through a labyrinth toward the birth of no goat-y "chimera of the English Ministry," no "Monster," but instead a "Beautiful Creature"; from there, he hopes readers will do what he called for in a pre-Union essay: imagine their future selves "*look[ing] back*" as one unified man at their path through "the Dangers."²⁴ Like Crusoe, Defoe miniaturizes, abridges. In a manner of allusive speaking, Crusoe achieves the dream Defoe wanted for Great Britain.

What this means is that Gildon, while dismissive, was not wrong about everything. He was not wrong to conflate Crusoe with Defoe. Nor was he wrong to see the specter of nation in *Crusoe* when he altered *Crusoe*'s title-page to observe that Defoe had "liv'd above fifty Years in the Kingdoms of *North and South Britain*."²⁵ To boot, Gildon's satire is suitably metafictional: in fantastical "Dialogue" between Defoe, Crusoe, and Friday (a drunken Defoe is beaten as he stumbles home from a pub), Gildon's Defoe croons to his erstwhile protagonist, "You are the true Allegorick Image of thy tender father."²⁶

In Lieu of Conclusion: Crusoe's (Other) Things

If *things* are important in *Crusoe*, it is appropriate that *Crusoe* has spawned so many of them (in addition to Robinsonades) over the centuries. One such thing, an elaborate 7.5-inch "Robinson Crusoe" character mug (or Toby Jug), produced over the decades of the twentieth century's latter half by venerable ceramics company Royal Doulton, London, is arguably the perfect material homage to Crusoean formalism. The mugs, large as actual human heads, varied little over the years in their conflated depiction of Crusoe (head, shoulders), his world, and his narrative. In all cases, the handle, a palm tree, connects Crusoe's head to shoulders that double as a sandy beach. In front of the tree, on the sand/shoulder, is a single large footprint (absent in some of the smaller versions of the mug), and on the back are the carved-in-sand words "Robinson Crusoe" (see Figures 2.1 and 2.2). Friday, in English clothes and hat, hides behind the tree, to which he clings closely; poised as if whispering in Crusoe's cavernous ear, he gazes in apparent horror at the footprint, or at the gigantic Crusoe-head (whose alert eye skews toward Friday and footprint), or at us as we put our lips to the top of the skull.

Mugs, like novels, are readable texts, and the Royal Doulton mug offers a significant artifactual interpretation that appropriately wrenches the time–space continuum, engages key symbols, and conflates hero, story, world. First, the mug presents an abridgment: Crusoe's giant empty head, with snow-white beard, bears the face of aged hindsight-Crusoe but improbably wears island-Crusoe's goat-skin cap; similarly, Friday gapes at the footprint, but in the novel the footprint happens before Friday has appeared, much less gained clothes or indeed English clothes (not until the morning after

Figure 2.1 *Robinson Crusoe* (front). Colored ceramic Toby Jug, combining the head and shoulders of the protagonist with other elements of the novel. Height: 7.5 in. Made in London (1959) by Doulton & Co. Limited. Object and image are author's own.

Figure 2.2 *Robinson Crusoe* (back). Colored ceramic Toby Jug, combining the head and shoulders of the protagonist with other elements of the novel. Height: 7.5 in. Made in London (1959) by Doulton & Co. Limited. Object and image are author's own.

that first colorful night does Crusoe "let" the "stark naked" man "know I would give him some clothes" [163]). The mug performs appropriate slippage between *Crusoe*, Crusoe, and the island, even as the mug reifies the novel's form by compressing dichotomies, reproducing temporal dissonance, and otherwise violating its own realism. The clever vessel brings head-space, page-space, and island-space together. The mug's chorography of mind – specifically the footprint on the front versus the sand-writing ("Robinson Crusoe") on the back – pithily encompasses Crusoe's writerly, psychological, and social dramas. As we drink from this capacious cup (tea from China? rum from the Brasils?), our palm closes on the palm-tree and on the already-obscured figure that holds it all together; with just a whiff of cannibal-irony, we lift our mouth to the uneven mouth of the head's cave, we consume the prize.

NOTES

1 Thank you to John Richetti, Linda Bree, and Winnie Chan for their improving comments on a draft of this chapter. Daniel Defoe, *Robinson Crusoe (1719)*, ed. John Richetti (London: Penguin Books, 2001). All further page references

in the text are to this edition. The sequel followed immediately, and then a meditative coda: *The Farther Adventures of Robinson Crusoe (1719)*, ed. W. R. Owens (London: Pickering & Chatto, 2008); *The Serious Reflections during the Life and Surprising Adventures of Robinson Crusoe (1720)*, ed. G. A. Starr (London: Pickering & Chatto, 2008).

2 Defoe, *Serious Reflections*, 51.

3 Virginia Woolf, "*Robinson Crusoe*," in *The Second Common Reader*, ed. Andrew McNeillie (New York, NY: Harcourt Brace, 1932, 1986), 51–9, 54. *Crusoe*-as-plain-earthenware-pot is now a critical commonplace. See, e.g., Lydia H. Liu, "Robinson Crusoe's Earthenware Pot," *Critical Inquiry* 25.4 (Summer 1999): 728–57.

4 Dorothy Van Ghent, *The English Novel: Form and Function* (1953; rpt, New York, NY: Harper & Row, 1961), 131. Ian P. Watt, *The Rise of the Novel: Studies in Defoe, Richardson, and Fielding* (1957; Berkeley, CA: University of California Press, 2000), 42. Ralph Rader, "The Concept of Genre and Eighteenth-Century Studies" (1973), in *Fact, Fiction, and Form: Selected Essays*, ed. James Phelan and David H. Richter (Columbus, OH: The Ohio State University Press, 2011), 58–81, 64. Cynthia Sundberg Wall, *The Prose of Things: Transformations of Description in the Eighteenth Century* (Chicago, IL and London: University of Chicago Press, 2006), 108–14, 110. Maximillian E. Novak, *Daniel Defoe: Master of Fictions* (Oxford: Oxford University Press, 2003). Patricia Meyer Spacks, "The Soul's Imaginings: Daniel Defoe, William Cowper," *PMLA* 91.3 (1976): 420–35. Stuart Sherman, *Telling Time: Clocks, Diaries, and English Diurnal Form* (Chicago, IL and London: University of Chicago Press, 1996), 235; David Marshall, "Autobiographical Acts in *Robinson Crusoe*," *ELH* 71.4 (2004): 899–920, 899; Michael Seidel, "*Robinson Crusoe*: Varieties of Fictional Experience," in *The Cambridge Companion to Daniel Defoe*, ed. John Richetti (Cambridge: Cambridge University Press, 2009), 182–99, 185.

5 Defoe, *Serious Reflections*, 51.

6 Samuel Taylor Coleridge, "Lecture XI," in *The Complete Works of Samuel Taylor Coleridge*, ed. W. G. T. Shedd (New York, NY: Harper and Brothers, Publishers, 1853), 309–19, 311, 316, 312. Woolf, "*Robinson Crusoe*," 54, 58.

7 Jenny Davidson, "The 'Minute Particular' in Life-Writing and the Novel," *Eighteenth-Century Studies* 48.3 (2015): 263–81, 264.

8 Van Ghent, *English Novel*, 34.

9 Coleridge, "Lecture IX," 316.

10 Charles Gildon, *The Life and Strange Surprising Adventures of Mr. D— De F—, of London, Hosier, who has liv'd above fifty years by himself, in the Kingdoms of North and South Britain. The various Shapes he has appear'd in, and the Discoveries he has made for the Benefit of his Country* (London, 1719). William T. Hastings made a stab at enumerating basic errors in "Errors and Inconsistencies in *Robinson Crusoe*," *Modern Language Notes* 27.6 (1912): 161–6.

11 Stephen C. Levinson succinctly defines deictic types in *Pragmatics* (Cambridge: Cambridge University Press, 1983), 54–62.

12 Paula Backscheider, *A Being More Intense: A Study of the Prose Works of Bunyan, Swift, and Defoe* (New York, NY: AMS Press, 1984), xviii.

13 Defoe, *Serious Reflections*, 51, iii.

14 Ibid., 51. On *spiritual* allegory, see J. Paul Hunter and G. A. Starr. Hunter, *The Reluctant Pilgrim: Defoe's Emblematic Method and Quest for Form in Robinson Crusoe* (Baltimore, MD: Johns Hopkins University Press, 1966). Starr, *Defoe and Spiritual Autobiography* (Princeton, NJ: Princeton University Press, 1965).

15 Defoe, *Farther Adventures*, 119. See Rivka Swenson, *Essential Scots and the Idea of Unionism in Anglo-Scottish Literature, 1603–1832* (Lewisburg, PA: Bucknell University Press, 2016), 56–7.

16 Defoe, *Serious Reflections*, 115, 116, 115.

17 Defoe, *The History of the Union of Great Britain* (1709), ed. David William Hayton, in *Writings on Travel, Discovery and History by Daniel Defoe*, gen. eds. W. R. Owens and P. N. Furbank, vol. 7, *The Pickering Masters*, vol. 8, *The Works of Daniel Defoe* (London: Pickering & Chatto, 2002). See Swenson, *Essential Scots*, 25–66.

18 Defoe, *Essay at Removing National Prejudices against a Union with Scotland* (1706), 19.

19 Defoe, *History*, 7:124.

20 Ibid., 7:126.

21 Ibid., 7:152, 150.

22 Ibid., 7:167.

23 Francis Bacon, *The Letters and the Life*, vol. 3, *The Works of Francis Bacon*, vol. 10, eds. James Spedding, Robert Leslie Ellis, and Douglas Denon Heath (London: Longman, 1868), 102.

24 Defoe, *History*, 7:126, 7:167, 7:151, 7:37. *Essay at Removing National Prejudices*, 25.

25 Gildon, *Life*, title page.

26 Ibid., x.

3

MAXIMILLIAN E. NOVAK

Robinson Crusoe and Defoe's Career as a Writer

In 1879, in the process of attacking Daniel Defoe as a writer of immoral works of fiction, the novelist Anthony Trollope set aside *Robinson Crusoe* as a work that everyone agreed was an "accident." He did not elaborate on this comment, but it may be argued, to the contrary, that so far from being an "accident," Defoe seemed destined to write the work that brought him a degree of fame in his lifetime and continued fame over the centuries following his death in 1731.[1] Although he achieved some notoriety in the first decade of the eighteenth century as the writer of controversial political poetry, pamphlets, and journals, he sprinkled these works liberally with short fictions; so much so that one critic complained that this was his only real talent. It was not. From the very beginning, those critics who were not biased against him because of his Whiggish politics, his status as a religious Dissenter, and his pugnacious defense of his ideas recognized the vividness of his style and his ability to write powerful narratives, whether of battles, scenes of riots, or accounts of infamous Jacobite gatherings, forceful in a manner to be discovered in few of his contemporaries.

The publication date of *The Life and Strange Surprizing Adventures of Robinson Crusoe*, April 25, 1719, was significant as well. It reflected a time when publishers had begun to recognize a growing audience demand for book-length fiction. It would be a mistake to speak of an imaginary audience eagerly awaiting the publication of Defoe's work, as Richard Altick absurdly imagined the audience for the novels of Samuel Richardson and Henry Fielding,[2] but, aside from an amazing ability to involve readers in a work in which, once Crusoe lands on his island, almost "nothing" adventurous happens for almost fifteen years, until the discovery of the cannibal's footprint, there was much in Defoe's masterpiece that played to developing attitudes and interests of the time – ideas of isolation, concepts of the importance of the private life, a sense of exploring a new world, notions of the nobility of labor, and a fascination with the primitive. Along with these, the concept of what may be called anachronistically the Robinsonade, though hardly original with Defoe, seemed to strike a chord with Defoe's and with future audiences. Island fictions became popular in Britain and the rage in Germany, where that term was invented.

Before entering into an account of Defoe's writings before *Robinson Crusoe*, I want to address the notion argued by Defoe in his *Serious Reflections during the Life and Surprising Adventures of Robinson Crusoe*, the third and last of the *Crusoe* series, to the effect that the first two volumes were an allegorical account of his (Crusoe's and/or Defoe's) life and hence an allegory of his career as a writer. Having been exposed as the author of what purported to be an autobiography of a Robinson Crusoe,[3] Defoe, still writing as Crusoe, argued in his preface that his work was to be regarded as "Allegorick History."[4] He maintained that all of his reflections were a "just History of a State of forc'd Confinement, which in my real History is represented by a confin'd Retreat in an Island; and it is as reasonable to represent one kind of imprisonment by another, as it is to represent any Thing that really exists by that which exists not."[5] He then proceeded to enumerate all the incidents of his story: there really was a parrot, the footprint in the sand, and a Friday. For all his swearing to the truth of his statements, as if he were signing a legal document, all that we can actually rely upon from this seeming statement of fact, aside from its being a brilliant general defense of fiction, is that Defoe's writings on contemporary politics, both secular and religious, were so often controversial that he was indeed put into prison on a number of occasions. In so far, then, as Crusoe's island experience, which Crusoe at one point describes as being "a prisoner lock'd up with the eternal bars and bolts of the ocean,"[6] might bear some relationship to Defoe's imprisonment for using his talents to express his viewpoints in print, there is a degree of truth to Defoe's claim. And it may be allowed that Defoe felt deeply enough the anguish of these times in prison to have felt some imaginative empathy with Crusoe's island experience.

Defoe's earliest manuscripts, dating from around 1682 to 1684, have certain fictional interests and hence some relationship with *Robinson Crusoe*. The first involved a series of poetic meditations recounting his personal religious struggles. These certainly have importance in relation to Crusoe's discovery of his need for the comforts of religious belief, but while these were far more than exercises, the meditation, as a poetic form, was well established during the seventeenth century. More interesting are the "Historical Collections," a series of brief prose narratives with particular, pointed morals. These fell under the genre known as the apothegm, or brief fictions, which were popular at the end of the seventeenth century. Defoe's collection was dedicated to his future wife, Mary Tuffley (given the romance name Clarinda), and was almost certainly intended to give her an idea of his personality. They were fictions with a purpose, but it is surprising how many concerned events involving the emerging of powerful character to meet some difficult challenge. One, of particular interest to students of Defoe as the future creator of realist fiction, involved the ancient Greek painter, Zeuxis, who destroyed a painting for its failure to be real enough.[7]

What contemporary fiction did he read? He occasionally spoke of Miguel de Cervantes' *Don Quixote*. He certainly knew popular picaresque fictions, mentioning *The Spanish Rogue* and *The English Rogue* and seemingly drawing on *The French Rogue* for Crusoe's interview with his father. *The English Rogue*, from which he drew material for his novel, *Roxana*, was essentially a piece of libertine fiction, but as with his admiration for the libertine poet, John Wilmot, Earl of Rochester, this did not seem a barrier to his enjoyment.[8] It is hard to tell how many "novels," the successors to the long historical French romances, he might have read. The magnificent *Princess de Cleves*, by Madame de Lafayette, might have seemed to be too much about love to interest him. But he certainly knew the popular first-person fictional memoirs, which were the specialty of Courtilz de Sandras (1644–1712).[9] Of course he knew John Bunyan's *Pilgrim's Progress*, but although he often used brief allegories to illustrate economic or political arguments in his journal, the *Review*, begun in 1704, he never attempted a lengthy allegory of the kind written by Bunyan. His attraction to picaresque fiction, with its realist depiction of the lowest ends of society, was certainly a more important influence upon his writing.

After working as an effective propagandist for William III, especially in his role as a writer and political activist in moving the country toward war with France and publishing his first book, *An Essay upon Projects* (1697), dealing with the social and economic possibilities of contemporary England,[10] Defoe emerged from relative anonymity in 1700 as the author of a poetic satire, *The True-Born Englishman*, a clever attack upon English xenophobia through a rehearsal of the numerous peoples who had populated England over the centuries and an ironic assault upon ideas of racial purity. For many years afterwards, he identified his writings as being "By the Author of the True-Born Englishman." In 1702, Defoe got into severe trouble by impersonating the voice of a High Church bigot advocating the persecution of the Dissenters in England in a pamphlet with the title *The Shortest Way with the Dissenters*. Ian Watt suggested that Defoe was too much a writer of fiction to allow a break in the narrative that would have permitted the audience to recognize the irony of the text – to reveal the viciousness of the Anglican priest, whose genocidal attitude toward a religious minority should have shocked, and indeed did shock, its readers.[11] Certainly Defoe, the satiric writer of 1702, might have considered as too obvious the "concession" section of Jonathan Swift's ironic *Modest Proposal* (1729) in which Swift provided positive solutions for Ireland's problems. As contemporary readers would have had no trouble recognizing, there was enough in the extreme positions of Defoe's Churchman to reveal the irony, but it is also possible, as he maintained, that he wanted incompetent readers, those who felt a deep prejudice against the Dissenters, to take his High Churchman as a genuine figure.[12] Defoe created him with all his uncontrolled anger bursting out of him, wittily triumphing over his enemies, and violating all the rules that held society together. It showed a precocious ability to create character, but it also brought with it imprisonment, a large fine, and the pillory. It should have taught Defoe a lesson, but in 1713, he published three pamphlets with provocative titles written through the viewpoints of somewhat dim-witted narrators, who argued against (but just barely) bringing in the family of James II to rule England after Queen Anne's demise: "Reasons against the Succession of the House of Hanover," and "What if the Pretender Should Come? Or, some Considerations of the Advantages and real Consequences of the Pretender's Possessing the Crown of Great Britain," and "An Answer to a Question that No Body thinks of, viz. But what if the Queen should die?" At that time, he was rescued by his patron, Robert Harley, the Lord Treasurer, and by the Queen. But his enemies never let him forget it. The judge hearing the case said that a writer might hang for using such irony.

In 1704, Defoe put together a work called *The Storm*, a series of narratives about the storm of the previous year – a mixture of science, religion, and human interest – with a slight fictional interest, and in that year, he also started his journal, the *Review*, which will be discussed later in this chapter. But in 1705, he produced his first full-length work of fiction in the form of a voyage to the moon – what we would think of as science fiction. Defoe clearly read the early moon voyages with their mixture of satire and fantasy – the works of Bishop Francis Godwin (*The Man in the Moone* [1638]), Bishop John Wilkins (*Discovery of a World in the Moone* [1638]), and Cyrano de Bergerac (*Histoire comique* [1656]) – but his real influence was Jonathan Swift's *Tale of a Tub*, first published in 1704. Defoe read the narrative by Swift's half-insane advocate for modern thought as a rationale for frequently obscure allusions to contemporary politics. On the other hand, his account of the moon inventions is often clever enough, and his use of the relatively new Savery steam engine[13] as a space vehicle was in line with the way science fiction would use scientific inventions as a central device. That this "rocket ship" is also made an allegory for the British Parliament, however, only adds to the confusion. But Defoe never gave up on fantasy as a possible genre. He has Crusoe walking among the planets in *Serious Reflections*, the third volume of *Robinson Crusoe*.

After *The Consolidator*, Defoe concentrated on his political and economic journalism. But voyages, islands, and global geography were never far from his mind. In various works, he might lapse into speaking of how people who would be thrown on a desert island would establish government as their first act. Or, as in his *General History of Trade* (1713), he might contemplate the circulation of wealth, distribution of goods around the world, and the division of labor – economic themes that were to impact his thinking in writing *The Life and Strange Surprizing Adventures*. As mentioned earlier, he would occasionally employ allegory in describing economic, political, and social situations. And in several issues of his *Review* of June 21 and 23, 1711, he would engage in lengthy economic and political allegories to describe how society was constructed:

> NECESSITY – was a Female Bastard of an Ancient Family, Begotten in the earliest Ages of the World by Male *Pride*, upon the Body of Female *Sloth*, and having wasted a great Estate, which her Father *Pride* had got, a Legacy left by one of his Ancestors, called *Violence*, the Son of *Ambition*, she became very poor, for most of her Estate being got by *Rapin*, *War*, *Treachery*, and *Blood*, it therefore could not be expected to thrive much, *especially if our Proverb be true*, That what is gotten *over the Devil's Back*, will be spent *under his Belly* –.
>
> Being thus reduc'd, she fell in with a parcel of Beggars, and finding one nam'd *POVERTY*, A LIKELY Fellow, and able enough to Work for her, she Married him, and they had between them one only Son, call'd *Invention*, and a Daughter, call'd *Witt*.[14]

This account ends with the birth of the daughter, "CREDIT," valuable economic force, while all the children of Witt bring misery to the world.

The account of government is similar:

> *GOVERNMENT* was the Eldest Son of *Justice*, the Daughter of *Society*, which was the Son of *Invention*, which was the Son of *Necessity* – as aforesaid … the *Government* of Himself in Society, was left to his own Reason, to frame upon Foundations of Safety, Property, Defence, and publick Peace, circumstanced, extend, or restricted, as the Accidents of his Posterity should require – And as Justice and Wisdom directed – *Government* being thus discover'd to be Lineally descended from *Wisdom* and *Justice*, its immediate Parents, the Original of it is no more a Mystery, and its Divinity appears to be a Fiction only of the Moderns, Calculated for their private Designs, to carry on the Projects of Tyrants and oppressors, and support the Ambition of Men.[15]

I quote these passages not as examples of Defoe's ideology (though it is certainly interesting to see how much it suggests that ideological concepts were never far from the surface of Defoe's writing), but rather to demonstrate how bouncy and inventive he could be in his allegories – how he could make these abstract figures seem alive. The reason for this is that, in a sense, for Defoe, they were alive – were vitally connected to the economic and political world in which he lived. In his *Essay upon Projects* (1697), he had described how, in the real world, men driven to desperation by poverty would use their ingenuity to come up with projects that might rescue them from their condition and, in the process, not only benefit themselves but also enrich society. And as for his allegory of the true origin of government and the "Projects of Tyrants" in distorting its true end of government, Defoe had engaged in an attack upon tyranny and the very real monarchs who claimed divine sanction for their holding on to power in his long political poem, *Jure Divino* (1706).

Large parts of *Jure Divino* are historical – about individual tyrants and their roles in history. In considering Defoe's path toward *The Life and Strange Surprizing Adventures*, his involvement with historical narrative should not be forgotten. Indeed, "History," however fictional, was a term often used to describe contemporary novels, and as we have seen above, it was one of the terms he used in the preface to *Serious Reflections* in an effort to describe his particular kind of writing.[16] His journal, the *Review*, began with an historical consideration of the rise of French power in the world, and in that publication, he appeared to enjoy continually rehearsing historical cause and effect. In 1709, he brought out a large volume called *The History of the Union of Great Britain*, recounting the events involved in the union of England and Scotland. Defoe presents his account as someone who was deeply involved in the committee work that contributed to the ultimate success of the union. And this involved some fascinating passages in which Defoe described how in Glasgow and Edinburgh he was pursued by anti-Union mobs. At a time when the genuine truth value of history was viewed with skepticism, an account from a participant in an event such as the Union might be viewed as making a real contribution, even though it was sometimes thought that the narrator tended to exaggerate his role in the events. Defoe quite accurately presented himself as being in the middle of an important historical event. Detractors tended to attack it as first-person fiction.

This was hardly the only historical work Defoe engaged in before writing *The Life and Strange Surprizing Adventures*. His *General History of Trade* (1713) was an attempt at economic history; his *Secret History of the White Staff* (1715) belonged to the genre of "secret history," an account of political events by an insider; and his *Memoirs of the Church of Scotland* (1717) gave an historical account of the sufferings of the Covenanters in Scotland. This last work was particularly important because it described this persecuted religious group as "wandering about in Sheep-skins and Goat skins, in Dens, and Holes, and Caves of the Earth," after the defeat of their army in the battle of Bothwell Bridge in 1679.[17] Defoe also depicted sublime aspects of the Scottish landscape in this work, and these descriptive passages may have prepared him for situating Crusoe on his island. Crusoe is far from being persecuted for his religious beliefs, but the sufferings of the Covenanters and the landscape through which they moved may have stuck in Defoe's imagination.

In addition to his involvement in history, Defoe was also deeply involved in geography, particularly economic geography. In the *Life and Strange Surprizing Adventures*, Crusoe sails down the east coast of England, then goes to Africa, and in the second voyage ends up as a slave in Sallee, in North Africa, present-day Morocco. In escaping, he sails down the west coast of Africa, is rescued, and taken to Brazil. After several years spent working as a sugar and tobacco planter and manufacturer, he is shipwrecked on an island in the Caribbean off South America. Crusoe lives on the island for twenty-eight years, but after arriving in England, he travels to Portugal to visit the Portuguese Captain who befriended him. Then he travels over the Pyrenees to France and back to England. Crusoe's island experience is so central to Defoe's fiction that we may forget how much movement through other locales is involved. In *The Farther Adventures*, Crusoe's travels are indeed epic. He returns to his island, then voyages to Madagascar and to the Far East. He is abandoned at an outpost in the Bay of Bengal (present-day Bangladesh), engages as a merchant in the East Indies, travels through China and then crosses Asia through Siberia until his final return to England.

Travel became central to much of Defoe's work after the Crusoe volumes and is particularly noteworthy as an element within his fiction.[18] His Captain Singleton travels to Madagascar and then on land across Africa. In his career as a pirate, Singleton operates throughout the Caribbean and later in the Indian Ocean. The Cavalier of *Memoirs of a Cavalier* (1720) travels to France and Germany and ends up fighting throughout England during the wars of the Rebellion. Colonel Jack travels north from London to Scotland, to the North American Colonies, to France and Italy, and back to England and North America. Even the female protagonists engage in some adventurous travels. Moll does considerable traveling in England and becomes a plantation owner in America. Roxana travels to France and Italy, picks up a knowledge of Turkish manners and language from a maid, returns to England, and then goes to Holland with her husband. The narrator of *A New Voyage Round the World* (1724) visits what was thought to be Australia, lands in southern Chile and tells of a voyage across the Andes from the Pacific to the Atlantic Ocean. Even a work such as *A Journal of the Plague Year* (1722) has its narrator H. F. explore various parts of London, and the three workmen who escape from London to Epping Forest cross the city in a manner not very different from Captain Singleton's trip across an Africa haunted by ferocious, strange beasts.

Defoe seems to have been extremely knowledgeable about geography, particularly wherever economic matters were concerned. A scholar treating the sugar industry in Brazil during the seventeenth century maintained that the way in which Crusoe eventually becomes the owner of an *ingenio* or factory was precisely the process that most manufacturers pursued.[19] He read widely in travel accounts for the Crusoe volumes. And some of his knowledge may have been first-hand, at least from the standpoint of buying and selling goods, if not from that of actual travel. In his role as a young merchant, he had traded to North America and probably to Africa. In addition to extensive travel within Britain, he seems to have done some travel on the European Continent. Some of his willingness to invest so much time in researching this material may have been connected with a volume which William Taylor had contracted, *Atlas Maritimus & Commercialis*, for which Defoe wrote the section on economic geography. Although it was not published until 1728, Taylor had advertised a similar volume in the back of *The Farther Adventures* in 1719. At any rate, much of Defoe's output after 1719 had a geographical element, including his three-volume *Tour thro' the Whole Island of Great Britain* (1724–6) and *A Plan of the English Commerce* (1728; 1730).

Another form that Defoe practiced in the years prior to the publication of the *Life and Strange Surprizing Adventures* was the memoir. In 1715, fearing a backlash from his enemies after the George I's ascension to the throne and a shift from a Tory to a Whig administration, Defoe published *An Appeal to Honour and Justice, Tho' It Be of His Worst Enemies*, an account of his career as a writer, what amounted to a justification of his public life. Although he provided some interesting biographical details, the intent of this work was to place his actions in defense of the Tory ministry that dominated British politics from 1710 to 1714, the last four years of Queen Anne's reign, in the best light possible. He had not changed his political views, he argued, it was the times that had changed. He was always sincere in his beliefs.

If his enemies might have considered this work a form of fiction, it merely amounted to a degree of concealment and some bending of the truth. On the other hand, he produced a fictional political memoir in 1717, which showed how capable he could be in handling this form. *Minutes of the Negotiations of Mons. Mesnager* was the purported account of a diplomat sent over to Britain by Louis XIV in an effort to obtain a peace agreement. Mesnager was dead by 1717 and therefore in no position to refute the account of Defoe's fictional diplomat. In so far as one can see, the purpose of the entire fictitious account was a passage which showed that the former

Lord Treasurer, Robert Harley, Earl of Oxford, who had been imprisoned in the Tower since 1715, was innocent of any complicity in restoring the exiled Stuart dynasty to the throne of Great Britain. In Mesnager's version of events, although Harley was interested in making peace with France, he was entirely committed to the House of Hanover. Mesnager finds that Harley was extremely elusive – difficult to pin down about anything. Of Mesnager's character we learn little. He is a loyal servant to Louis XIV. He is Catholic. He views the English common people as "furious and brutal," lacking in "due subordination."[20] He tries to bribe a journalist (Defoe), who turns down his overtures. For the most part, Defoe makes Mesnager into a fairly typical Frenchman, given just enough elements of character to make him convincing. But after all, the memoir was supposed to be about external events. One of Defoe's less friendly fellow journalists quickly discovered this was by Defoe and complained about his "Forge of *Politicks* and *Scandal*."[21] This accusation that he was a forger of fictions might have pushed him into the possibilities of longer and more elaborate narrative fiction.

In 1715 and again in 1718, Defoe produced two volumes of religious dialogues, both entitled *The Family Instructor*. The first volume presents a fairly unified vision of a family, including a father who decides to turn toward firm Christian beliefs and his son who remains defiant and perishes miserably. Defoe showed an adept use of dialogue and developed his characters with considerable skill. Although these volumes purported to be based upon the lives of genuine families, they were generalized sufficiently to allow for the broad moral that Defoe wanted to convey. And they depicted the lives of his characters with seriousness and sympathy. Most eighteenth-century novels portrayed devout Dissenters as objects of comedy or satire. For example, in most of these works, it is impossible to imagine a serious scene such as that in which the daughter is sassy toward the mother, causing the mother to box her ears. Even in Samuel Richardson's *Pamela*, scenes of this kind border on the comic, and in Henry Fielding's novels, they tumble into farce. In the second volume, there is less unity, but the central figure – a man who finds himself unable to control his passions – brings up a theme that will become important in almost all of Defoe's fiction. These volumes, both of which continued to be reprinted during the nineteenth century, marked in their sharply rendered scenes and fully realized characters a flair for the dramatic in Defoe's writing. Nevertheless the scenes are set in a novelistic fashion, with considerable detail about the emotions of the characters. They are essentially dramatic fictions exploiting religious themes.[22]

As one critic suggested, at least the first volume in this series was probably suggested by the dangers posed by the Schism Act of 1714. That Act was essentially intended to end the existence of Dissenting schools or even

Dissenting tutors in private homes throughout England. Only the Church of England would be permitted to engage in religious education. A work such as the first volume of *The Family Instructor* was probably intended, in part, as a means of religious instruction for Dissenting families. Although the dangers inherent in the Act ended with the death of Queen Anne at the very time at which it was supposed to go into effect, it still provided the possibility of practicing home religious schooling.[23] Defoe's turn toward the evils of passion dominating domestic life in the second volume is probably an indication that the original target of his interests had shifted. But we should be aware that some of the subject matter in these volumes carried over to *The Life and Strange Surprizing Adventures.* From the first volume comes Crusoe's discovery of his Christian beliefs, not through the preachings of the Anglican Church, or any other church, but rather away from organized religion; from the second volume comes Crusoe's finding himself carried away by his passionate "Wandering Fancy" to throw himself upon the dangers of the sea. It should also be noted that the opening domestic scene of *The Life and Strange Surprizing Adventures* has some of the same ambience as the second volume of *The Family Instructor* – life among the middle orders with its typical conflict between parents and children.

In composing these volumes, Defoe grew as a writer. In the second volume of *The Family Instructor*, the bitter dialogue between the husband and the wife, with its witty allusion to the eclipse of 1715, is done brilliantly.

> the Husband tells her, that the Moon was like a cross Wife, that when she was out of Humour, could Thwart and Eclipse her Husband whenever she pleased; and that if an ill Wife stood in the Way, the brightest Husband could not shine.
>
> She flew into a Passion at this, and being of a sharp Wit, you do well, *says she*, To carry your Emblem to a suitable height; *I warrant*, you think a Wife, like the Moon, has no Light but what she borrows from her Husband, and that we can only shine by Reflection; it is necessary then you should know, she can Eclipse him when she pleases.
>
> Ay, ay, *says the Husband*, but you see when she does, she darkens the whole House, she can give no Light without him.
>
> [*Upon this she came closer to him.*]

> WIFE. I suppose you think you have been Eclips'd lately, we don't see the House is the darker for it.
>
> HUSB. That is because of your own Darkness; I think the House has been much the darker.[24]

And so the quarrel continues, with husband and wife becoming more enraged with each bitter, witty exchange. In such passages, Defoe showed an ability to render his characters with considerable psychological depth. Ian Watt credited Defoe with the importation of "formal" or "circumstantial" realism into the novel, singling out scenes such as that in which, going through the pockets of a drowned boy from a wreck, Crusoe could tell us: "He had on no clothes, but a seaman's wast-coat, a pair of open knee'd linnen drawers, and a blew linnen shirt, but nothing to direct me so much as to guess what nation he was of: He had nothing in his pocket, but two Pieces of Eight, and a tobacco pipe" (149). In order to make his paradigm fit, Watt had to deny Defoe what he called "psychological" realism, arguing that this particular aesthetic concept was an innovation of Samuel Richardson.[25] But Defoe was deeply involved in the psychology of his characters.[26] The realistic details of the boy's clothing and the contents of his pocket are intended to disguise the "affliction" (149) Crusoe feels at the sight of the boy's body. He has just had a kind of fit of uncontrollable emotion at contemplating the failed possibility that one person might have been saved out of the ship in distress he had heard during the night.

In making a claim to "novelty" in the second volume of *The Family Instructor*, Defoe instanced *The Turkish Spy* as being among those books that "have pleased and diverted the world, even to the seventh or eighth volumes." He was probably already at work on his *A Continuation of Letters Written by a Turkish Spy*, which was published on August 29, 1718, by William Taylor, the same publisher who was to bring out *The Life and Strange Surprizing Adventures of Robinson Crusoe* eight months later. There is indeed a strong possibility that Taylor was seeking to turn Defoe toward works of fiction. In writing his *Continuation* of the popular work by Giovanni Paolo Marana (1642–93), Defoe did more than bring Marana's device of having a Turkish spy in Paris comment on seventeenth-century political life in Europe. He transformed the character of the spy, Mahmut, into a more complex personality. Mahmut has grown old in the service of the Turkish government, and he longs to return to his native Arabia. The work begins in the year 1687; Mahmut has been in Europe for almost fifty years, passing as Titus the Moldavian. But he has grown tired of a life of disguise and of exile from his native land. He longs to "flie from this Exile."[27] When he learns of a plan to replace him and bring him back to a land where he feels he can practice his religious beliefs openly, he has a truly ecstatic moment in which he envisions himself back in his native land.

Robinson Crusoe, who is indeed exiled from the human race on his island, until his encounter with the cannibals and then with Friday, experiences a somewhat different kind of exile from that of Mahmut, but making the connection between the two had to be easy enough. And indeed Defoe, who at this time was working for the Whig government as a spy on the Tory and Jacobite press, probably felt a strong identification with Mahmut. Thanks to his former ties with Harley and the Tories, he now posed as a skilled journalist, only too willing to join in the political struggle against the Whig government. He wrote to the Under-secretary of State, Charles De la Faye, about his situation. Often, he noted, it was impossible for him to prevent anti-government material from appearing. Under such conditions, De la Faye would have to forgive him and indeed sympathize with him:

> I Beg leav to Observ Sir one Thing More to his Ldpp in my Own behalf, And without which Indeed I May one Time Or other Run the hazard of fatall Misconstructions: I am Sir for This Service, Posted among Papists, Jacobites, and Enraged High Torys, a Generation who I Profess My Very Soul abhors; I am Oblig'd to hear Trayterous Expressions, and Outrageous Words against his Majties Person, and Government, and his Most faithfull Servants; and Smile at it all as if I Approv'd it; I am Oblig'd to take all the Scandalous and Indeed Villainous papers that Come, and keep them by Me as if I Would gather Materialls from Them to Put them into the News; Nay I often Venture to let things pass which are a little shocking that I may not Render my Self Suspected.[28]

Defoe may have indeed experienced discomfort and alienation in having to converse with people he regarded as traitors, but there is a rhetorical element in this passage. It is only too reminiscent of a somewhat jaunty letter to Harley in which he saw himself as a spy among conflicting groups as he entered Scotland during the debate over the Union:

> I have Compass't my First and Main step happily Enough, in That I am Perfectly Unsuspected as Corresponding with anybody in England. I Converse with Presbyterian, Episcopall-Dissenter, papist and Non Juror, and I hope with Equall Circumspection ... I have faithfull Emissaries in Every Company And I Talk to Everybody in Their Own way. To the Merchants I am about to Settle here in Trade, Building ships &c. With the Glasgow Mutineers I am to be a fish Merchant, with the Aberdeen Men a woollen and with the Perth and western men a Linen Manufacturer, and still at the End of all Discourse the Union is the Essentiall and I am all to Every one that I may Gain some.[29]

And it is hardly surprising that he had mentioned Marana's Turkish spy to Harley just a few years earlier.[30]

Still functioning as a kind of spy, then, Defoe must have felt some kinship and sympathy for Mahmut. In the preface to the *Continuation*, Defoe expressed his intention to "make the Language plain, artless, and honest, suitable to the Story, and in a Stile easie and free, with as few exotick Phrases and obsolete words as possible," stating his intention to appeal to "the meanest Reader." Such an intention may well have spilled into *The Life and Strange Surprizing Adventures*. But the passage in the introduction that is most interesting has to do with the creation of character in a work of fiction:

> It was objected, I know to the former Volumes of this Work, that the *Turk* was brought in too much debasing the Christian Religion, extolling *Mahomet*,

and speaking disrespectfully of Jesus Christ, calling him the *Nazaren*, and the Son of *Mary*, and it is certain that the Continuation must fall into the same Method; but either Mahmut must be a *Turk* or no *Turk*, either he must speak his own Language, or other Peoples Language, and how must we represent Words spoken by him in the first Person of invincible *Mahmut* the *Arabian*, if we must not give his own Language the very Stile of the Original?[31]

Posing as the translator, Defoe states that wherever Mahmut wrote anything that might be offensive to Christian ears, he removed it. But dismissing "the nice Palates of a censorious Age," he insists that Mahmut must be "a *Turk* or no *Turk*," that he has to remain in character. With these statements on style and character, Defoe was offering a kind of manifesto for a new kind of fiction.

To a certain extent Mahmut fashions his character to suit the person to whom he is addressing his letters, but he shows a solid core of personality, along with his skepticism about Catholicism and his strong faith in own mystical religious beliefs. Nineteenth-century critics, such as Leslie Stephen, maintained that all of Defoe's characters were simple projections of the author; whether creating pirate or pickpocket, whore or soldier, Defoe simply wrote his own personal identity into these characters, asking himself, were I Roxana or Robinson Crusoe, what would I do next? Stephen's formulation was intended to suggest that Defoe had a limited imagination, an imagination Stephen may have associated with Defoe's status as a shopkeeper. In fact, when Defoe wanted to emphasize characterization (and sometimes, admittedly, he did not) he made them highly individualized. *Pace* Stephen, there is no confusing Robinson Crusoe with Daniel Defoe or Moll Flanders as Defoe in drag. In addition to a degree of snobbery toward Defoe as a person once engaged in trade, Stephen's and his period's conception of women probably made him consider both Moll Flanders and Roxana as too masculine to have been conceivable as fulfilling the character expected of women. Hence Stephen saw them as merely versions of Defoe himself.[32] Defoe had a more complicated mind and emotional range than Stephen imagined. Indeed there is a degree of truth in W. H. Davies' argument that Defoe wrote his fictions as if his characters had no author but themselves.[33]

In addition to all of these lines that lead directly to *The Life and Strange Surprizing Adventures*, there were economic and religious events in the year 1719 that have some relationship to Defoe's work. The economic bubble that became the South Sea Scandal was already creating considerable financial turmoil. There was talk about the possibility of the South Sea Company becoming involved in establishing a colony in South America not far from where Crusoe's island was located. Defoe, who was an enthusiastic supporter of new colonies in undeveloped areas and who wrote of such an adventurous exploration in his *A New Voyage Round the World* (1724), would have found such a prospect very exciting. But he looked on the financial speculation that would become the disastrous South Sea Bubble as just what it was. He watched John Law's experiment with paper money in France with considerable dismay, and feared the kind of speculation that would force up the price of stocks that had no intrinsic value. Shortly after the publication of *Robinson Crusoe*, Defoe published an economic tract with the title *The Anatomy of Exchange Alley* (1719), warning of what might happen: "Stock-Jobbing is Play; a Box and Dice may be less dangerous, the Nature of them are alike a Hazard."[34] And he blamed the Stock-Jobbers who were driving up prices – men who "will do anything for Money":

> The Truth is … that these Men by a Mass of Money, which they command of other Peoples, as well of their own, will, in time, ruin the Jobbing-Trade. But 'twill be only like a general Visitation, where all Distempers are swallow'd up in the Plague, like a common Calamity, that makes Enemies turn Friends and drowns lesser grievances in the general Deluge.[35]

One of the important lessons learned by Crusoe on his island has to do with the uselessness of gold on a desert island, and his address to the gold that he discovers on his wrecked ship is one of the best known passages in Defoe's work.

> I smil'd to my self at the sight of this money, O drug! said I aloud, what art thou good for? Thou art not worth to me, no not the taking off of the ground, one of those knives is worth all this heap, I have no manner of use for thee, e'en remain where thou art, and go to the bottom as a creature whose life is not worth saving.
>
> However, upon second thoughts, I took it away. (47)

Crusoe's self-conscious oration on the artificiality of money, though sound enough in theory, is ironically undercut by Crusoe's very civilized inability to resist the temptation of the gold before him. He is not the founder of a utopia (though there are moments such as this when he is aware enough of what that might mean) but a castaway from wealth-obsessed contemporary Europe. Nevertheless it is impossible to avoid the conclusion that Defoe's skepticism about this new world of rapacious finance had an influence on a work in which his hero finds himself in an economy without money, in which he has to become a farmer, a herdsman, and a maker of clay pots.

If economic matters were to loom large in 1719, almost equal in importance were the religious squabbles within the Church of England and among the Dissenters. As a writer of pamphlets, Defoe was to participate in both of these controversies. Benjamin Hoadly, Bishop of Bangor, preached a sermon in 1716, which essentially argued against the excessive interference of the Church of England in politics. The debate that ensued led to an end to Convocation – the gathering of the Church members that some members of the High Church party had hoped would become equal to the gathering of Parliament. In the debates, there was a great deal of criticism aimed at Hoadly's arguments about the sincerity of belief. If the High Church mocked "Bangorian Sincerity" as equivalent to no sincerity at all, sincerity emerged from the debates as a crucial concept for the period. As a Dissenter, Defoe would have always considered sincerity a crucial element in judging the validity of religious belief, but he tended to mock Hoadly, a staunch enemy of the Dissenters, more than he mocked Hoadly's enemies. The dispute among the Dissenters involved a debate over the Trinity. Meeting at Salters Hall[36] on February 19, 1719, a majority of those present would not vote to affirm a belief in the traditional concept of the Trinity, more from a dislike of being forced to take a position than from a doctrinal standpoint, but the meeting broke up in disarray. A staunch supporter of unity among the Dissenters as well as an equally staunch upholder of the Trinity, Defoe could not but be distressed at this development. That Crusoe comes to avow an orthodox position on Christianity on an island away from such controversies, suggests again how, for Defoe, life on an island away from civilization and its discontents might simplify religious belief.

I began my discussion with the suggestion that so far from being an "accident," *The Life and Strange Surprizing Adventures of Robinson Crusoe* might be viewed as the inevitable result of his interests as a writer. I have tried to trace some of the themes that would have stirred his imagination and some of the challenges in the writing of fiction that he had attempted to work through over many years as a writer. Questions involving exile, isolation, religious disputes, economic experiments, politics, considerations about European history, thoughts about the nature of reality and how humans experience it – it had to be all still fresh in his mind. And in experimenting with the creation of strong, independent character through dialogue and epistolary form, he had honed narrative techniques that he had been perfecting over the years. By 1719, Defoe already had an amazing ability to tell a story in a way that made everything seem real – an ability to combine a sense of a seemingly convincing environment with a character's response to that environment. Now he succeeded in creating fictions that seemed to open up worlds equivalent to those we might experience on a daily basis, even if one of those worlds might be an uninhabited island in the Caribbean. In *The Strange Surprizing Adventures of Robinson Crusoe* and to a certain extent in *The Farther Adventures*, he achieved something remarkable, even if critical opinion has sometimes been uncertain whether he could have been conscious of what he was doing – conscious as a writer, conscious as a thinker. Such uncertainties fail to pay serious attention to his achievements – both intellectual and writerly – during the period preceding the publication of his masterpiece.

NOTES

1 Anthony Trollope, "Novel Reading," *The Nineteenth Century* 23 (1879): 30.

2 Richard Altick, *The English Common Reader* (Chicago, IL: University of Chicago Press, 1957), 63.

3 By Charles Gildon's *The Life and Strange Surprising Adventures of Mr. D— De F—, of London, Hosier* (London, 1719). Gildon had his own version of Crusoe and Friday complain bitterly against their treatment by Defoe, waylaying him on the road to his home in Stoke Newington and tossing him in a blanket.

4 Defoe, *Serious Reflections during the Surprising Adventures of Robinson Crusoe* (London, 1720), sig. A6.

5 Ibid., sig. A5v.

6 Defoe, *The Life and Strange Surprizing Adventures of Robinson Crusoe*, ed. John Richetti (London: Penguin Books, 2001), 90. Subsequent citations from this work will be included within parentheses in my text.

7 This manuscript is located at the William Andrews Clark Memorial Library. The manuscript containing the "Meditations" is at the Henry E. Huntington Library.

8 For Defoe's use of an episode in *The English Rogue*, see Maximillian E. Novak, *Realism, Myth, and History in Defoe's Fiction* (Lincoln, NE: University of Nebraska Press, 1983), 114.

9 His *Memoires de M.L.C.R.* (the Count de Rochefort) had a strong influence on Defoe's novel of education, *Colonel Jack*.

10 One aspect of *An Essay upon Projects* has an interesting connection with *The Life and Strange Surprizing Adventures*; the one I have in mind has to do with Defoe's advocacy of strenuous exercise in connection with his proposal for a military academy. His suggestion about the importance of teaching swimming plays a role in Crusoe's saving himself from the shipwreck that throws him on his island as well as in his swimming out to the wrecked ship from the island to gather the supplies that will enable him to survive.

11 Ian Watt, *The Rise of the Novel* (Berkeley, CA: University of California Press, 1957), 126–7.

12 Defoe, *The Present State of the Parties* (London, 1712), 18–24.

13 A diagram of this engine, which was mainly intended to pump water from mines, was printed in John Harris's *Lexicon Technicum* (London, 1704). It is reproduced in *The Consolidator*, ed. Joyce Kennedy, Michael Seidel, and Maximillian Novak, Stoke Newington Edition of the Writings of Daniel Defoe (New York, NY: AMS Press, 2001), 42.

14 *Review*, ed. John McVeagh, 9 vols. (London: Pickering & Chatto, 2003–11), 8:193, Part 1, 1711–12 (originally 8:153–4).

15 *Review*, 8:198, Part 1, 1711–12 (originally 8:158).

16 As in Defoe's *The History and Remarkable Life of the truly Honourable Col. Jacque* (1722).

17 Defoe, *Memoirs of the Church of Scotland* (London, 1717), 231.

18 For a general discussion of the relationship between voyages and the novel, with frequent mentions of Robinson Crusoe and Defoe's other fictional characters, see

Percy G. Adams, *Travel Literature and the Evolution of the Novel* (Lexington, KY: The University Press of Kentucky, 1983), especially pp. 119–24.

19 Stuart B. Schwartz, *Sugar Plantations in the Formation of Brazilian Society: Bahia, 1550–1835* (Cambridge: Cambridge University Press, 1985), 211.

20 *Minutes of the Negotiations of Mons. Mesnager*, ed. P. N. Furbank, in *Satire and Writings on the Supernatural by Daniel Defoe*, ed. W. R. Owens and P. N. Furbank, 8 vols. (London: Pickering & Chatto, 2003), 4:56, 91. It is significant that Defoe made the supposed author of *The Great Law of Subordination Consider'd* (London, 1724), who complains of the lack of a sense of class difference, into a naturalized Frenchman.

21 See Abel Boyer, *The Political State* 13 (June 1717): 627–30.

22 Defoe published two other works using this format: *Religious Courtship* (1722); and *A New Family Instructor* (1727).

23 The third volume in the series, *A New Family Instructor* (1727), has a specific educational tendency with a father instructing his children. This is of interest considering the manner in which *The Life and Strange Surprizing Adventures* was adapted later in the eighteenth century and again in the nineteenth century for educational purposes.

24 *The Family Instructor, Volume II*, ed. P. N. Furbank, in *Religious and Didactic Writings of Daniel Defoe*, ed. W. R. Owens and P. N. Furbank, 10 vols. (London: Pickering & Chatto, 2006), 2:9–10.

25 Watt, *Rise of the Novel*, 29–34, 175–7, 188–9, 199, 232–8.

26 Commenting on reader expectation for relatively simple characterization, Kate Loveman notes how complex Defoe's characters were: "they are plausible enough to persuade their readers that they are capable not only of deception but also of self-deception." See *Reading Fictions, 1660–1740* (Aldershot: Ashgate, 2008), 49.

27 *A Continuation of Letters of a Turkish Spy*, ed. David Blewett, in *Satire, Fantasy and Writings on the Supernatural by Daniel Defoe*, ed. W. R. Owens and P. N. Furbank, 8 vols. (London: Pickering & Chatto, 2005), 5:109.

28 *Letters*, ed. George Healey (Oxford: Clarendon Press, 1955), 454.

29 Ibid., 158–9.

30 Ibid., 38.

31 *Continuation of Letters of a Turkish Spy*, 46.

32 Leslie Stephen, *Hours in a Library* (London: Smith, 1874), 24–5.

33 W. H. Davies, "Introduction," *Moll Flanders* ([New York, NY:] The Bibliophilist Society, 1931), xi–xii.

34 Defoe, *The Anatomy of Exchange Alley* (London, 1719), 43.

35 Ibid., 27, 44. As early as 1701, Defoe had attacked the manipulation of stocks in his *The Villainy of Stock-Jobbers Detected* (London, 1701).

36 The Salters were one of the twelve major livery companies in London. Their hall, rebuilt in 1668, after the London Fire of 1666, was often used as a general meeting place.

4

PAT ROGERS

Robinson Crusoe: Good Housekeeping, Gentility, and Property

A paradox lies at the heart of the novel. The hero is a trader, and his creator had once followed the same occupation, while commerce remained at the center of Defoe's concerns up to the end of his life. Among the books that display this interest (still blessedly immune from deattribution such as has happened in recent years to many anonymous works traditionally assigned to Defoe, some on very shaky grounds) are early works such as *An Essay upon Projects* (1697), many others from the mid-period such as *A General History of Trade* (1713), and a cluster of characteristic items from the author's last decade, most obviously *The Complete English Tradesman* (1726). To these we might add tracts for the times, such as the pamphlets Defoe wrote about the contentious commercial treaty with France in 1713, which did so much to hasten the dissolution of the Tory government led by Robert Harley. Plainly, the *Tour thro' the Whole Island of Great Britain* (1724–6) exhibits an obsessive preoccupation with the workings of domestic, and occasionally overseas, trade. We could also take into account other novels, especially *A New Voyage Round the World* (1724), with its nakedly colonialist aim to encourage a settlement on the Pacific coast to encourage exploitation of the South Sea, and its resemblance to both of the first two parts of *Crusoe* as regards setting and descriptive idiom. One of the threats faced by everyone engaged in business is failure and ultimately bankruptcy, something that Defoe had known at first hand, and that echoes through his writings, even more insistently after the great financial meltdown set off by the so-called South Sea Bubble in 1720. Crusoe does not technically endure such a fate, though his state as a castaway initially does involve a draining of all his resources (as in the collapse of traders reduced from riches to rags, a topic that floats to the surface of the text in the *English Tradesman* and elsewhere) and a kind of spiritual liquidation. All this would suggest that there is a close fit between the main character and the author, each centrally implicated in the business world, one as a day-to-day practitioner, the other as a lifelong commentator on the practices and values of the commercial community.

Yet in his island prison, Crusoe has absolutely no opportunity to engage in trade, or financial dealings of any kind. In *Das Kapital* (1867) Karl Marx was able to discount as mere side-issues his "prayers and the like," and to see his situation as an archetypal example of human labor as the prime determinant of value. However, as Diana Spearman pointed out long ago, it is nonsensical to think of Crusoe as an embodiment of economic man, when he is denied all the tools of capitalism.[1] He soon comes to the realization, in a famous passage, that gold has no place in a world without exchange currency: "O drug! said I aloud, what are thou good for?"[2] Robbed of this familiar resource, he tries instead to replicate many of the offsite activities of a gentleman trader, from keeping a daybook to improving his home and his putative country estate. He also follows standard patterns of husbandry and crop-growing. He aspires to a kind of genteel Western living while passing a solitary existence on a remote tropical isle. Unlike most of Defoe's fictional protagonists, Crusoe is not an out-and-out rogue, not even a criminal by the standards of the day – whatever we might think today of his proto-imperialist background. The conversion he undergoes over his years of exile is not from sinful money-maker to a naturally benevolent Cheeryble figure (Charles and Ned Cheeryble are lovably philanthropic identical twin brothers in Charles Dickens' novel, *Nicholas Nickleby* [1839]). Rather he discovers a God who will bless his seemingly blameless existence as a landed proprietor in an unpeopled landscape, until the arrival of other humans and his rescue ultimately return him to the moral dilemmas posed by the inhabited world.

This chapter will relate Crusoe's life on the island to contemporary practices in the areas of trading, domestic living, and property management. It will develop my earlier study of the hero as *Homo domesticus*, and revisit the issue of "middle class gentility," in light of much subsequent work by historians on British social structure

The Mercantile Vocation and Social Status

We learn at the outset that Robinson was told by his father that he should not attempt to quit "the middle state, or what might be called the upper station of *low life*, which he had found by long experience was the best state in the world, the most suited to human happiness, not exposed to the miseries and hardships, the labour and sufferings of the mechanick part of mankind, and not embarrass'd with the pride, luxury, ambition and envy of the upper part of mankind" (6). It has become a critical commonplace that the son's "original sin" lies in the hubris with which he disregarded his father's advice, a choice which he has to abrogate on the island. In his earlier career he has turned into an adventurer and an overreacher, denied the chance of contentment by his urge to rise in the world – a moral failing promoted by a category error in his social identity.

But what exactly is the middle station? Few historians today would equate this precisely with the middle class as that group would evolve in the next two centuries, and even fewer would want to invoke a concept of the bourgeoisie. People engaged in commerce covered a wide spread in the demographics of the time: Gregory King's celebrated breakdown of the population in 1688 recognized a considerable range within this category. King allots an annual family income of £400 to a large number of "merchants and traders by sea" and only half of this amount to a much larger number of "merchants and traders by land." Fully 180,000 persons belong to the families of "shop-keepers and traders," whose average income is put at a miserly £45. The next category in the list is named as "artisans and handi-craft," a capacious label that would include small journeymen who could be thought of engaged in trade. Their income is just £40, while their families amount to almost a quarter of a million people, something approaching 5 percent of the entire population.[3] It might be added that a good many in-dividuals higher up the social scale took an active role in business, whether as owners, investors, or managers. A few, like the great Duke of Chandos, had a huge slice of their capital at stake in these enterprises – more even than in their landed estates, extensive as these were. In the light of these facts, it is clearly inappropriate to look on the trading interest as a homogeneous entity, composed of a "middle class" with members allied by background, education, training, or interests.

This applies particularly to the City of London, where Defoe grew up and where the commercial life of Britain had its main engine. Here a caste of merchant princes had arisen, aristocrats in all but title. This is where the notion of the middle class becomes an exceedingly blunt tool. Unless we take the view that all merchants, all City financiers, all Whig MPs, all émigrés, and all Dissenters can be lumped together under a category of the bourgeoisie, on account of their activity or ideology, the expression offers little help. It makes no sense when applied to men who had headed the great corporations, had sat in Parliament for decades, had occupied roles in national government, had served as masters of the livery companies, had become Lord Mayor, had established durable commercial dynasties, had gained a knighthood or a baronetcy (ultimately even a peerage), had made rich marriages, had acquired vast fortunes, or had built their own sumptuous houses on spacious country estates. Not all were *nouveaux riches*: some used inherited money to support their business, to engage in charitable work, or to acquire objects of virtù. To insist that we regard such men as "middle class" betokens a retrospective snobbery. They had only a limited amount in common with those in the middle station, as the Crusoe family would have known that social position.

We are told in the second sentence of the novel that Crusoe *père* "got a good estate by merchandise, and leaving off his trade, lived afterwards at York" (5). He must have done very well: not only did he take early retirement, he married a woman of good family, Anglicized his surname, and moved to the more genteel York from workaday Hull. Moreover, Robinson had an elder brother, gone very early from the story, who became a lieutenant colonel in a regiment of foot. This was normally a matter of expensive purchase rather than promotion through the ranks. So the young man had a solid start, and understandably his father wishes to protect him from the vicissitudes of high life, especially after the eldest son has ignored parental advice and lost his life fighting in Flanders. But in spite of a decent education, which gave him "a competent share of learning" (5), Robinson turns down the respectable career as a lawyer that his father had planned, such was his burning desire to go to sea. It is worth noting two things here that often get overlooked. First, the elder Crusoe does not try to send his son into his own line of business – the quiet life in the middle station that he envisages for Robinson would involve a career in one of the learned professions, a fact that qualifies some of the interpretations that have been offered of the hero's original sin. Second, the warning about the "labour and sufferings of the mechanic part of mankind" takes on an ironic edge once Crusoe fetches up on the island. His hardships extend beyond mere isolation: he is forced to engage in some heavy-duty manual labour, which meant learning to perform practical tasks. Predictably he is quite clumsy at these to begin with, a measure of the distance he has travelled from his comfortable home. Many of these jobs would have been carried out in the Crusoe household of his boyhood by servants, who ranked among the almost three million people on the bottom rungs of King's ladder who depleted the wealth of the nation.

Gentility

Readers of *Moll Flanders* will recall her unsatisfactory husband, whom she terms "this amphibious creature, this *Land-water-thing*, call'd a *Gentleman-Tradesman*."[4] It was a recurrent theme in Defoe's writing. Peter Earle remarks in his excellent study of the English mercantile class that he "was warning his tradesman readers to stick to their trades and not let the dream of gentility bankrupt them."[5] In *The Compleat English Tradesman*, Defoe would insist that "to say a Gentleman-tradesman is not so much nonsense as some people would persuade us to reckon it." Indeed, he goes on, "as trade is now flourishing in *England,* and encreasing, and the wealth of our tradesmen is already so great; 'tis very probable, a few years will shew us still a greater race of trade-bred Gentlemen, than ever *England* yet had."[6] At some level the major characters in almost all of Defoe's fiction harbor what Earle calls "the dream of gentility." This implies economic security first of all, but it also connotes social respectability. How significant this notion was to Defoe throughout his life has been brought out by Michael Shinagel in a good book that has been unjustly neglected in recent years. Signs of the personal importance attaching to this concept, as Shinagel shows, were the gentrification of his own name from Foe to De Foe or Defoe; his adoption of a coat of arms; and his use of the form "Gentleman" as author and more widely as a citizen.[7]

It is noteworthy that Shinagel devotes separate chapters to *Moll Flanders, Colonel Jacque,* and *Roxana,* but not to *Robinson Crusoe.* The explanation is clear: the castaway spends most of the novel in solitary confinement, with no opportunity to acquire or demonstrate gentility, a standing which draws its meaning from interaction and behavior within society. Yet in particular ways Crusoe does take on some of the genteel qualities of a self-educated man, as set out in *The Compleat English Gentleman* (written *c.*1729, but not published until 1890). The manual tells us it is open to anyone, even without a background in the learned languages, to "store himself with all the learning necessary to make him a complete gentleman." Further:

> If he has not travell'd in his youth, has not made the grand tour of Italy and France, he may make the tour of the world in books, he may make himself master of the geography of the Universe in the maps, attlasses, and measurements of our mathematicians. He may travell by land with the historian, by sea with the navigators. He may go round the globe with Dampier and Rogers, and know' a thousand times more in doing it than all those illiterate sailors. He may make all distant places near to him in his reviewing the voiages of those that saw them, and all the past and remote accounts present to him by the historians that have written of them.[8]

Except for a few trading voyages in his early career, Defoe himself had to make do with this kind of second-hand acquaintance, gained by poring over maps and globes. He obviously identifies with the armchair student of world affairs, who is able to carry out this vicarious form of voyaging – "When armies march or fleets sail, he can trace them with his eye," and so on. It is not so with his creation, the world traveller Crusoe, and there may be some element of wish-fulfillment in the adventures that fall to the hero's lot.

Of course Robinson has traveled in his youth, but not on the aristocratic rite of passage known as the grand tour – the countries he has visited are of interest chiefly for their commercial links with Britain, not their ancient cultural capital. Far from an illiterate sailor, he had the advantage of a good basic education; but more important to his survival on the island are the practical skills he had observed on his travels (though in most cases he has no first-hand experience of these tasks). But he has obviously acquired the kind of geographic knowledge that Defoe desiderates, and he shows plenty of aptitude as a navigator. All that is lacking, when he begins his long exile from the world, is a religious sense. Otherwise he approaches the qualities that Defoe looks for in a gentleman "bred," as opposed to "born." In his deprived situation, he cannot pursue the course of reading that the manual recommends: even if a young man has missed out on a classical education, "he may master all the polite parts of learning; he is fully quallifyed for the study of Nature ... he may in a word be every thing which a gentleman need to be." Again: "The gentleman that reads will necessarily instruct himself, he needs only a tutor like a *Lexicon Technicum* to be at hand, to resolve difficultyes, explain terms, and state the world to him as it comes in his way."[9] How would Crusoe have done with a copy of John Harris' famous dictionary of arts and sciences! First published in 1704, it had gone into its third edition by this time, stuffed with astronomical tables and helpful illustrations of building, fortification, anatomy, and botany among other subjects.

Yet the hero did not start out as a seeker of social respectability: otherwise he would have settled for the cozy opportunities afforded by the legal profession. The wild life that Crusoe had led before he was cast away seems to have been aimed chiefly at the acquisition of wealth, with a dash of adventure thrown in. Paradoxically, it is only when he lands up on the island that he starts to take over some of the pretensions of the landed class. This is absurd: while he has enough land at his command to envisage himself in the role of a grand proprietor, as we have just seen he has to scrape a bare existence in an environment that is challenging both physically and psychologically. In other words, Crusoe starts to covet some of the attributes of gentility only when his route to such a status, trading activity, has been blocked off.

After his initial feelings of desolation in his place of exile, he is able to cheer up a little when he reflects "that I was king and lord of all this country indefeasibly, and had a right of possession; and if I could convey it, I might have it in inheritance, as compleatly as any lord of a manor in *England*" (80). The language here immediately recalls the debate over the rights of the sovereign in the period before and after the Revolution of 1688. Yet, even if he sees himself as monarch of all he surveys, his efforts to build a life appropriate to the leisured classes are largely a sham. Quite early on he finds a pleasant inland valley where he decides to set up a second home. At first he thinks of making this his principal habitation, but he then realizes that it would be better to remain in his cave above the coastline. The "Bower" he has created in the middle of the island becomes a place for rest and refreshment: he speaks of going "to my country-house, as I call'd it" (86). The merchant community of London had already started to acquire such a bolthole away from the city. Earle mentions a growing number of such men,

> who illustrated a developing trend by living in a villa or farm just outside the metropolis ... Nearly all these men were either rentiers or retired or, if they were still active, merchants. Men who reflected the truth of Defoe's remarks on the fine buildings of Tottenham, which generally belonged "to the middle sort of mankind, grown wealthy by trade, and who still taste of London; some of them live both in the city and in the country at the same time."[10]

Of course, this is more make-believe on the part of Crusoe. He can no longer take an active part in trade, and could be described as the uncommercial traveler. Unlike his father he has no way to live off retirement income. There is no metropolis where he conducts his daily work – rather, he must exist in a squalid cave. Still, his visits to the bower represent a coping mechanism and a consolatory fantasy that go back to the aspirational urges of his creator, and more specifically to Defoe's over-developed interest in members of the merchant class who made it big.

There is nothing very strange about this, and indeed the novel offers a believable picture of a man under stress finding an outlet for his inner needs in practical exertions. The comfort they afford comes in part from the fact that they can be construed mentally as satisfying the same desires as those of individuals "back home," on Crusoe's native shore. It matters little that his puny one-man efforts raise him to the top of a social hierarchy consisting of a single individual. At this point, after more than two years of solitude, his newfound religious convictions enable him to regard the state of his life in a much more favorable light, so that he can assert, "my very desires alter'd, my affections changed their gusts, and my delights were perfectly new" (90). Only at intermittent intervals now does he give way to despair, as the "Anguish of my Soul at my Condition" (82). In a way that might be familiar to students of the protestant ethic, this spiritual regeneration brings with it an increasing impulse to master his environment and reassert his agency as an autonomous performer on his limited stage.

Grinding It Out

The Crusoe that has been celebrated in literary and historical legend is a doer, a can-do person, a man who devises practical solutions in response to the demands made on him by a tropical ecology. For readers in Victorian Britain, he could be recast as a pioneer of colonial expansion, like the engineers who built railways across the African savannah (Cecil Rhodes, who wanted to construct a line from the Cape to Cairo, must surely have known the novel from an early age). Speculators would invoke the hallowed name: the Crusoe mine was registered at Menzies, east of Perth, during the Australian goldrush of the 1890s. In America, even before the west was won, the hero served as a model of hard work, independence, determination to fight against the odds and simple piety. The afterlife extended as far as Samuel B. Allison's *American Robinson Crusoe* (first presented in a teacher's version in 1910), which has had numerous editions up to the present and remains available across various media. The book, aimed explicitly at "American boys and girls," was written by a former teacher. It transposes Robinson's birthplace to New York, but in general the adaptation takes surprisingly few liberties with the text (obviously the Xury episode has to disappear).[11] The values that Allison wished to inculcate can be deduced from chapter headings: "Robinson as a hunter," "Robinson makes some furniture," "How Robinson lays up a store of food," and so on.

On the whole this construction of a mythical Crusoe has not done much violence to the book, though it isolates some features at the cost of neglecting others. When Ian Watt analysed the hero as one of the foundational "myths of modern individualism," along with Faust, Don Quixote, and Don Juan, he actually termed the book an "epic of the stiff upper lip."[12] That is too reductive, but it is not wholly without an element of truth. But there is one key issue that can easily be overlooked: Crusoe only starts to get things done after his physical and mental collapse, prior to the conversion sequence. It is then that he starts to venture out and about, finally deciding to undertake the overdue exploration of the island. As he conducts his new experiments with handicrafts, he begins to use the language of genteel social advancement.

The list of skills that Crusoe has to acquire is a long one, and these involve both domestic crafts and a variety of ancillary tasks to support his daily living. Some of the latter amount to light manufacturing; others take the form of small-scale projects in agriculture or husbandry. It hardly needs to be said that the household tasks would not have come naturally to him. They meant the expenditure of hard manual labor. As noted earlier, this lay outside the responsibility of persons of the middle station, male ones at least. When it came to activities demanding elbow grease, people in the status group of the Crusoe family, just like Villiers de l'Isle-Adam's Axël,[13] had servants to do it for them. Most household management fell to the lot of women, and if Robinson's parents employed a cook, sometimes amalgamated with the role of housekeeper, this would have been a woman. If we think back to Gregory King's estimates, female domestics would have constituted a majority within the 10 percent of the population classified as serving within the home. The boy would not of course have been exposed to any kind of domestic science in his education, and though he took up a maritime career he would have had no need to equip himself in this area. The smallest commercial craft tended to employ a specialist cook – someone on the fringe of this with his pirate background is the most famous sea cook in literature, Long John Silver (in Robert Louis Stevenson's *Treasure Island* [1883]).

Crusoe does not make much of his kitchen skills, so that after he has retrieved a considerable quantity of provisions from the shipwrecked vessels he chooses not to dilate about the way he prepared, or ate, these. A typically brief comment goes, "I went out with my gun and kill'd two fowls like ducks, which were very good food" (58). Perhaps we have another sign here of the radically English nature of his character, which has often been observed: for the British people as a whole have never – until very recently – been noted for culinary skills. It is a stronger clue than the "sexual apathy" detected in the hero by James Joyce in a 1911 lecture in Italian that he gave in Trieste ("Verismo ed idealismo nella letteratura inglese"). Some consolation for Crusoe may have lain in the fact that he did not have to clean up a lot of kitchen implements, and generally he was spared much of the sweeping, brushing, and polishing that fell to so many women in his society. When salvaging the ship, he looked for tools and armaments, but left aside any brooms or mops that might possibly have survived. Nor does laundering figure strongly.

The reasons that Joyce saw in Crusoe "the true prototype of the British colonist" had little to do with the aggressive imperialist urges commonly attributed to the project today. Rather, he served as a symbol of "the British conquest" on account of more personal activities: "Cast away on a desert island, in his pocket a knife and a pipe, [he] becomes an architect, a carpenter, a knife grinder, an astronomer, a baker, a shipwright, a potter, a saddler, a farmer, a tailor, an umbrella-maker, and a clergyman."[14]

Benjamin Franklin may have been right that man is a tool-making animal, but Crusoe is more of a tool-user and he has to survive with whatever implements he could lay his hands on. He constantly bemoans the fact that when he set out to improve his living conditions, "The want of tools made every work I did go on heavily" (53). In particular he regrets the lack of conventional props of civilization: as well as a store of ink which dries up in time, he instances "also spade, pick-axe and shovel to dig or remove the earth; needles, pins, and thread; as for linnen, I soon learn'd to want that without much difficulty" (53). Some of these implements are useful for him later on. But he was not as totally bereft of materials as this passage suggests, for he was able to salvage from the carpenter's stores on the ship "two or three bags full of nails and spikes, a great skrew-jack, a dozen or two of hatchets, and above all, that most useful thing call'd a grind-stone," not to mention clothes and bedding (44–5). How many of those who occupied the middle station back in England would have had access to a tool-kit as ample as this? It follows that Rousseau's description of his condition as a pure state of nature, deprived of all artificial aids, is not completely accurate. What Crusoe stands for is something more than *unaccommodated man*, "such a poor, *bare*, forked animal" as in Shakespeare's *King Lear* the ragged Edgar appeared to Lear. Rather, he comes briefly quite close to the primitive capitalist, able to take advantage of human contrivances to exploit the bounty of nature. So far is he from subsistence living, once he has finished pillaging goods from the wreck, that he can boast, "I had the biggest magazine of all kinds now that ever were laid up, I believe, for one man" (45). The point of the story for Defoe is less that you can survive with very little than that you can improve what you have been given through industry, thought, and resolution.

At first Crusoe is preoccupied by the need to make sure he has adequate shelter for himself – he adds an extension to house his large store of goods safely. At this stage he is not so much an architect as a jobbing builder. Subsequently he turns his attention to interior features, starting with a chair and table, to provide "the few comforts I had in the world" (55). A key passage occurs at this point, which deserves more notice than it usually gets:

> So I went to work; and here I must needs observe, that as reason is the substance and original of the mathematicks, so by stating and squaring every thing by reason, and by making the most rational judgment of things, every man may be in time master of every mechanick art. I had never handled a tool in my life, and yet in time by labour, application, and contrivance, I found at last that I wanted nothing but I could have made it, especially if I had had tools; however, I made abundance of things, even without tools; and some with no more tools than an adze and a hatchet, which perhaps were never made that way before, and that with infinite labour: For example, If I wanted a board, I had no other way but to cut down a tree, set it on an edge before me, and hew it flat on either side with my axe, till I had brought it to be thin as a plank, and then dubb it smooth with my adze. It is true, by this method I could make but one board out of a whole tree, but this I had no remedy for but patience, any more than I had for the prodigious deal of time and labour which it took me up to make a plank or board: But my time or labour was little worth, and so it was as well employ'd one way as another. (55–6)

Defoe lived in an era when humble artisan trades were starting to shade into technological pursuits, as had happened before with clock-making and now with instrument-making more generally. He himself had no great manual skills that we are aware of. As for building, the one career that might have proved useful to someone in Crusoe's situation was the manufacture of bricks and tiles, a business in which Defoe was once engaged at Tilbury along the Thames estuary. He claimed that it employed a hundred poor people, and made him a profit of £600 a year generally, allowing him to set himself up as a gentleman for the first time, before a series of reverses brought him down.[15] Unfortunately there was, of course, no market for bricks on the island, even if there had been clay suitable for their manufacture.

Denied his ambition to rise in the world as a kind of gentleman trader, Crusoe has to retrain himself as an artisan. It is scarcely an accident that the British rise to power over the next century was fueled in part by the achievements of humble craftsmen. More widely, we think of the Enlightenment as underpinned by developments in basic science. So it was: but a glance at the volumes of illustrations to the *Encyclopédie* of d'Alembert and Diderot (1751–72) will show us the fuller picture – hundreds of plates exhibiting a huge variety of emerging technologies, some of them exploited by small businesses or even one-man operations at home. With his "useful" grindstone on hand, Crusoe is able to extend his activity to grinding tools, a key part of the project. This involves some characteristic home-spun improvement worthy of Ben Franklin:

> I had three large axes and abundance of hatchets, (for we carried the hatchets for traffick with the *Indians*) but with much chopping and cutting knotty hard wood, they were all full of notches and dull, and tho' I had a grindstone, I could not turn it and grind my tools too; this cost me as much thought as a statesman would have bestow'd upon a grand point of politicks, or a judge upon the life and death of a man. At length I contriv'd a wheel with a string, to turn it with my foot, that I might have both my hands at liberty: *Note*, I had never seen any such thing in *England*, or at least not to take notice how it was done, tho' since I have observ'd it is very common there; besides that, my grindstone was very large and heavy. This machine cost me a full week's work to bring it to perfection. (67)

At such moments it becomes obvious that the story is not about the state of nature. Crusoe does not re-enact the whole history of mankind from prehistoric times. The way he goes about surviving resembles more closely the progress of early modern manufacturing.

This point could be illustrated in another way. Two years before the novel appeared, a relatively obscure individual, Abraham Darby, died at the age of thirty-eight. His coke-fired blast furnace to produce iron, developed around

1709, is now commonly cited as the first step to making Britain the first industrial nation: it was set up at Coalbrookdale, close to what would be the crucible of the revolution later in the century. Before he set up his business there, Darby had been apprenticed to a fellow-Quaker in brass manufacture at Birmingham. Then he moved to Bristol, where he became a leading light in the Bristol Brass Company from 1702. Another of the founders of this company was a merchant named Benjamin Coole, prominent like his colleagues in the local Quaker community. It turns out that when Defoe made a political trip around the country in 1706 on behalf of his patron Robert Harley, one of his two contacts in Bristol was "Benja Cool, Quaker." He claimed in a letter to Harley that in a stay of four days in the city he had gained "an Exact scale of the people, their Trade, and Magistracy."[16] Since Darby was still working there, it is by no means unlikely that Defoe came to hear something of the enterprising young man. Of course, he could not have foreseen what was to come. But he was always on the lookout for innovations in the commercial world. When he described the town of Derby in the third volume of his *Tour*, he made much of the new silk-throwing machinery introduced by John Lombe (aided by the engineer George Sorocold) in 1718. As Wikipedia notes, this "may have been the first instance [in England] of workers being gathered under one roof to work machinery driven by an inanimate power source." Once again we have a development crucial to industrial progress, observed by Defoe (even if not on the spot) at the time that *Robinson Crusoe* came out.

Mechanic Exercises

Robinson acquires all the skills he wants for his own protection and comfort. He spends a great deal of time on a fort and stockade to insulate his dwelling against attacks by wild animals or possible human invaders. It is worth recalling here that engineers were by origin the people who carried out military fortifications and sapping techniques. When he makes one of his most serviceable tools, it is of course not something that he could market or mass-produce:

> The excessive hardness of the wood, and having no other way, made me a long while upon this machine, for I work'd it effectually by little and little into the form of a shovel or spade, the handle exactly shap'd like ours in *England*, only that the broad part having no iron shod upon it at bottom, it would not last me so long, however it serv'd well enough for the uses which I had occasion to put it to; but never was a shovel, I believe, made after that fashion, or so long a making. (59–60)

We notice once more that Crusoe is trying to *copy* with the primitive means to hand some existing technologies. Similarly when he takes up potting, and manages to bake some loaves, it is far from a hobbyist pursuit: he says that he had "no notion of a kiln, such as the potters burn in, or of glazing them [the pots] with lead." But he finds a method to achieve what he desires: "I must needs say, as to the shapes of them, they were very indifferent, as any one may suppose, when I had no way of making them; but as the children make dirt-pies, or as a woman would make Pies, that never learn'd to raise paste" (97). The thing to notice here is that though Crusoe makes light of his efforts he is fully aware of what skillful potters were able to do with the current technology. His bread-making has greater success, although the work comes to a halt for several months because he does not have a sieve to sort the wheat from the chaff. Eventually he overcomes this problem, and "thus, as well as in the best oven in the world, I bak'd my barley-loaves, and became in little time a meer pastry-cook into the bargain" (98).

Along with his crudely fashioned goat-skin garments and umbrella (the latter constructed to mimic those he had seen in Brazil), the best known of Crusoe's endeavors concerns his attempt to build a boat. This is forestalled at first by his inability to move the heavy vessel to the water, but later crowned with success when he makes a smaller piragua. In all these operations he stresses the time and labor involved, but despite the ingenuity he displays it remains true that the raw materials he needs are conveniently to hand – if he had been stranded in the middle of the Sahara, his opportunities would have been far fewer. His situation improves further when a ship is wrecked on rocks at the south side of the island. As well as guns, clothes, and liquor, he finds several more domestic implements. Meanwhile, he has gradually made advances in his workmanship across a number of different crafts: "I improv'd my self in this time in all the mechanick exercises which my necessities put me upon applying my self to, and I believe cou'd, upon occasion, have made a very good *carpenter*, especially considering how few tools I had" (114).[17]

In addition the castaway has to master some of the basics of planting and animal husbandry. He discovers by accident that some barley and rice seeds have started growing; after digging out and manuring the ground, he is able to sow more for a regular harvest. With typical resourcefulness, he reaps his crop with an old cutlass, in the absence of a proper sickle. He gives himself the semblance of a domestic garden and adorns his country bower with a double hedge. He plants trees, a behavior of cultural significance in Britain at this period. At the same time he learns to harness the stock of wild goats that populate his island. At first the animals serve as meat and clothing material, but as time goes on Crusoe finds other uses:

> For now I set up my dairy, and had sometimes a gallon or two of milk in a day. And as Nature, who gives supplies of food to every creature, dictates even

naturally how to make use of it; so I that had never milk'd a cow, much less a goat, or seen butter or cheese made, very readily and handily, tho' after a great many essays and miscarriages, made me both butter and cheese at last, and never wanted it afterwards. (117)

Eventually he catches and tames enough animals to have a flock of twelve. As with the other crafts mentioned, there was an extensive literature on topics such as stock-breeding, although in England this would normally concern horses and cows. As for planting and gardening, books flowed off the press every year with helpful advice. Crusoe could not quite imagine himself as "the gentleman farmer," to quote the title of a work by Roger North that was issued by the publisher Edmund Curll in 1726. Still, he would have been aware that landownership went hand in hand with agricultural and horticultural developments. On the most favorable showing, the hero's efforts represent a parody of what was being done on the finest estates, and even on the modest suburban boxes to which some city folk could retreat. When he sets up his goat-pen he chooses a stretch of meadow, constructs hedges, and adds gates like some eighteenth-century grandee enclosing the neighboring properties.

In spite of the multifarious ways that Defoe found to make – and lose – money, he lacked first-hand experience as a farmer when the novel was written. He did own a number of properties, including substantial houses in London, and he had once conceived himself as a developer, when he negotiated together with a bricklayer to build some new tenements in Westminster, very close to the Abbey and Houses of Parliament. Then, three years after *Robinson Crusoe* came out, he moved into rural property and took a long lease on hundreds of acres of land outside Colchester in Essex. The holding was currently occupied by many tenants, who were apparently small farmers for the most part. The parcels brought with them the rights to plant and fell timber. Defoe intended "to use his rich farm lands to breed cattle and raise corn; he could sell some of the corn and market cheese, butter, veal, and beef, all established Colchester products."[18] (He also thought of setting up another brick and tile factory at nearby Earl's Colne.) Moreover, no one could read works such as the *Tour* or *A Plan of English Commerce* (1728) without noticing just how closely the author observed the patterns of agriculture across the nation. In the *Plan* he pays particular attention to the wool industry, specifying the areas of the country that provide "the best and richest kid of Sheep Ground."[19] In the *Tour* he often comments on the quality of arable land, as well as on the breeding of cattle in a particular district. Probably like Crusoe with his goats he would have made some sort of shift if required to work his own farms.

Neither the complete English tradesman nor the complete English gentleman, Crusoe labors to reproduce some of their accomplishments in a hostile and incongruous setting. There is something comic about his attempts, as with the rituals of tea-taking that were preserved by Anglo-Indians under the Raj. But he has the excuse that he is not doing this in the midst of an uncomprehending native population.

Good Housekeeping

More generally, Crusoe quite naturally seeks to recreate familiar routines in desperately unfamiliar terrain. Far from an epic of economic man, his story should be seen as the story of *Homo domesticus*, since so much of the narrative is to do with setting up and organizing a personal space. The evidence for this case lies in his reluctance to stray far, and his feelings of a mighty exploration when he eventually conducts a survey of the island after five years – Jim Hawkins, the boy hero of Stevenson's *Treasure Island*, would have undertaken this in five hours. He wanders about the island now and then, but never more than two miles a day. Psychologically, the hero beds down within the narrow compass afforded by his cave and his bower. His sense of scale has shrunk over the period of his lonely sojourn. He takes on the mantle of one pursuing philosophic retirement, as against the *vita activa* that had characterized his youth. When Friday arrives, the new-comer is consigned to a kind of granny annexe, a special tent erected within the stockade. Naturally his wanderlust reappears once he is off the island and travel becomes a possibility once more. When he returns to England he tries to settle down, but after his wife dies he will head off on his farther adventures round the globe, as the last sentence of the first part promises.

Two paragraphs can summarize how Crusoe's assimilation into a world of quiet regularity and dutiful housekeeping connects with his desire to emulate the gentleman trader and his need to turn himself into a competent artisan. First, there is an awkward point which perhaps seems too obvious to be often made. *Robinson Crusoe* may owe much to travel-books, but its hero spends twenty-eight years virtually standing on the spot. Whatever Crusoe's inclinations might be (overseas trader, explorer, adventurer, tamer of a continent), he is forced by circumstances to be what is now called a home-maker. And though he is allowed briefly to play up to his self-image as colonial governor, this is a belated, short-lived, and histrionic episode, and we do not suppose that he seriously believes it. For most of his sojourn on the island, Crusoe is less the pioneer than the proprietor. He cannot conquer jungles; he can only plant an exotic version of the kitchen-garden. He cannot civilize barbaric tribes; he can merely train a house-boy. In all sorts of ways, his experience relates to the domestic life of Augustan England. Quite a lot of it, like his home-brewing, basket-making, and potting, almost suggest the modern handicrafts class or the Do-It-Yourself movement – and though some of these activities were masculine vocations, other tasks such as bread-making were even at that period characteristically women's occupations when carried out in the household.

It has become common to emphasize Crusoe's quasi-economic way of living. The other side of his existence on the island has received less attention, perhaps because it squares less obviously with the Crusoe we see at the start and finish of the book. But Crusoe is a householder of sorts, with peculiarly limited chances of escape. In this context it is significant that among the most popular of Defoe's books in the eighteenth century, along with the first part of *Robinson Crusoe*, were the domestic manuals, *The Family Instructor* (1715) and *Religious Courtship* (1722). Courtship on the island is not in question, but in some respects, Crusoe does keep up a simulacrum of family life. Even before Friday enters the story, the narrator describes sitting down for dinner with his "little family," that is a dog and two cats, and Poll, his parrot, "the only person permitted to talk to me" (118). In few ways does the hero seem more of a normal British citizen than in his devotion to his pets.

It is when Defoe's narrative reaches the island that the theme emerges fully. On finding himself cast up on the shore, Crusoe turns his mind first to a safe harbor for the night. He climbs up into a tree, and passes his first hours in a deep sleep. Crusoe's actual phrase is that he "took up [his] lodging" in this place. The next day he climbs down "from [his] apartment in the tree" (40), and only then turns his attention to salvaging operations. Home-making, even just finding a home, is naturally his first urge. He then constructs a raft and goes out to see what he can rescue from the ship. Having decided what he most wanted, he starts by bringing back provisions; after this he looks out some clothes, some tools, and then arms. Critical attention is most commonly fixed on the tools, and it is often implied that Crusoe acts as a capitalist entrepreneur in his choice of salvage material. In fact, he behaves more like a good household manager – starting, that is, with food, drink, and clothing. It is true that he tends to itemize his stores rather in the fashion of a warehouse inventory; but it should be remembered that domestic manuals advised just such an approach to housewifery. Defoe's own contributions to this genre are not just moral tracts; they include proper lessons in the care of one's home. They are not only conduct books but also early documents in the discipline of Household Sciences. Defoe was constantly preoccupied by the problem of servants, as a work like *The Great Law of Subordination Consider'd* (1724) indicates. He was interested, that is, in the efficient running of the home as well as its virtuous management. It is not only the complete English tradesman who must enter his ledgers punctually: his wife must keep her books carefully, too. In the absence of a companion, Crusoe himself must take over domestic management.

Viewed in the light of the foregoing facts, Crusoe emerges as a much more diversely interesting figure than the proto-capitalist described by Marx. During his years of solitude, he has no skin in the commercial game. Rather, he aspires, so far as his cramped condition allows, to imitate the activities of a respectable member of the middle station. Whether in the guise of domestic craftsman, patient husbandman, assiduous improver of property, kindly pet owner, or spiritual bookkeeper, he clings to the norms of this caste. As long as he remains stuck on the island, the globetrotter turns into a reluctant expat.

NOTES

1   Diana Spearman, *The Novel and Society* (London: Routledge & Kegan Paul, 1966), 162–72.
2   *Robinson Crusoe*, ed. John Richetti (London: Penguin Books, 2001), 47. All further page references in the text are to this edition.
3   King's estimates can be found in *Two Tracts by Gregory King. (a) Natural and Political Observations and Conclusions upon the State and Condition of England, (b) Of the Naval Trade of England and the National Profit Then Arising thereby*, ed. George E. Barnett (Baltimore, MD: Johns Hopkins University Press, 1936).
4   *Moll Flanders*, ed. G. A. Starr (London: Oxford University Press, 1971), 60.
5   Peter Earle, *The Making of the English Middle Class: Business, Society and Family Life in London 1660–1730* (Berkeley and Los Angeles, CA: University of California Press, 1989), 12.
6   Daniel Defoe, *The Complete English Tradesman*, 2 vols. (London: Rivington), 1, 380.
7   Michael Shinagel, *Daniel Defoe and Middle-Class Gentility* (Cambridge, MA: Harvard University Press, 1968), 73–4 and *passim*.
8   Daniel Defoe, *The Compleat English Gentleman*, ed. Karl D. Bülbring (London: D. Nutt, 1890), 225.
9   Ibid., 228–30.
10 Earle, *The Making of the English Middle Class*, 206.
11 In the introduction Allison singles out one principal departure from the original: the fact that Crusoe gets nothing from the stranded ship and has no tools ready to hand for some years. This was presumably to reduce him further to a state of nature. See Samuel B. Allison, *American Robinson Crusoe* (Boston, MA: Educational Publishing Company, 1910), 7.
12 Ian Watt, *Myths of Modern Individualism: Faust, Don Quixote, Don Juan, Robinson Crusoe* (Cambridge: Cambridge University Press, 1996), 144.
13 Jean Marie Mathias Philippe Auguste, comte de Villiers de l'Isle-Adam (1838–89) was a French Symbolist writer whose play, *Axel* (1890), features the remark by the hero, Axel, "Vivre? les serviteurs feront cela pour nous" ("Living? Our servants will do that for us").
14 Joyce's 1912 lecture, translated by Joseph Prescott, and reproduced in Michael Shinagel, *Norton Critical Edition: Robinson Crusoe* (New York, NY: W. W. Norton, 1994), 321.

15 Maximillian E. Novak, *Daniel Defoe: Master of Fictions: His Life and Ideas* (Oxford: Oxford University Press, 2001), 139–40, drawing on *The Letters of Daniel Defoe*, ed. George Harris Healey (Oxford: Clarendon Press, 1955), 17.

16 *Letters*, 116, 111.

17 Defoe would certainly have known a book by Joseph Moxon, *Mechanick Exercises* (1703). Moxon is remembered today for his contributions to printing history, but the scope of his 1703 book emerges from its full title: *Mechanick Exercises: Or, The Doctrine of Handy-works. Applied to the Arts of Smithing, Joinery, Carpentry, Turning, Bricklayery. To which is Added, Mechanick Dyalling: Shewing how to Draw a True Sun-Dyal on Any Given Plane, however Scituated; Only with the Help of a Straight Ruler and a Pair of Compasses, and without any Arithmetical Calculation.* Crusoe could have made good use of the volume on his island. Moxon's main interests included geography, travel, navigation, and exploration – a precise match for those of Defoe.

18 Paula Backscheider, *Daniel Defoe: His Life* (Baltimore, MD: Johns Hopkins University Press, 1989), 467–9, is the fullest account of the transaction.

19 Defoe, *A Plan of the English Commerce*, 2nd edn (London: Rivington, 1730), 157–62.

5

G. A. STARR

Robinson Crusoe and Its Sequels: The Farther Adventures and Serious Reflections

Despite its marked differences, *The Farther Adventures of Robinson Crusoe* is a legitimate and worthy sequel to *Robinson Crusoe*. Many of its passages nearly match the first volume in narrative, rhetorical, and psychological interest. It begins (almost as *Robinson Crusoe* had begun) with Crusoe at loose ends in England, obsessed with venturing abroad – this time, to revisit his island. The opportunity arises when his nephew invites him to join a voyage to the East Indies. On route, they rescue survivors from a burning ship, and from a second ship disabled in a storm (13–26). Reaching the island, they find the English and Spanish settlers at loggerheads, and in the course of three weeks manage to establish greater harmony, prosperity, and religiosity among them (27–119). Proceeding on their journey, they encounter a fleet of native war-canoes on the Brazilian coast, and Friday is killed (119–23). Heading eastward, they stop at Madagascar, where the ship's crew massacres a native community; Crusoe's outspoken criticism of this barbarity leads to a virtual mutiny, and to his being put ashore in India (129–40). There he makes friends with an English merchant, whom he accompanies on a successful trading voyage to Sumatra and Siam; on their second voyage they are in danger of being captured and mistakenly executed as pirates, so they leave their ship at a port in China (144–72). Crusoe travels overland first to Beijing, then across Tartary and Siberia; he winters in Tobolsk in the company of an exiled Russian prince, continues westward to Archangel, and finally returns (after nearly eleven years) to England (172–217).

Of the three volumes, *Serious Reflections* has been reprinted, read, and discussed the least. In the earlier volumes, Crusoe's proposition that "the life of man" is a "strange … chequer work of Providence" (124) is firmly grounded in his actual vicissitudes. In the third volume, similar principles are put forward, and the resulting *Serious Reflections* are interesting and effective as moral and religious essays, but they have rather little to do with the experiences or character of Crusoe as set forth in the preceding volumes, and they are bound to disappoint readers craving a new series of far-flung adventures. *Serious Reflections* presents itself as a further sequel, yet its connections with the earlier volumes are more tenuous and problematic than the links between the first and second parts of Crusoe's story. *Serious Reflections* does deal extensively, however, with long-standing concerns and beliefs of Defoe himself, which extend backward and forward to his writings in various genres from the 1690s until his death in 1731.

A typical thematic continuity between these two books is Defoe's fondness for paradox, which can impart extra strangeness and surprise to "Strange Surprising Adventures" but also to the unfolding of arguments on social, political, economic, and religious topics. Among the paradoxes posed in *Farther Adventures* are that sudden joy can be as upsetting and as dangerous as sudden grief (17–19); that when groups of ordinary Englishmen and Spaniards are thrown together, Englishmen may prove to be the more selfish, slothful, irascible, and irrational, Spaniards the more generous, industrious, patient, and judicious (31–9); that Roman Catholic priests, far from being obsessed with converting everyone they meet, can work actively and sincerely for the spiritual welfare of non-Catholics without trying to seduce or dragoon them to Rome (83–92). And Crusoe sees the paradox in his own "Wild Goose Chase" when he observes, "how easily Heaven can gorge us with our own Desires; make the strongest of our Wishes, be our Affliction, and punish us most severely with those very Things, which we think, it would be our utmost Happiness to be allow'd in" (126). Other paradoxes seek to debunk mistaken assumptions, pretensions, and evaluations of all kinds; thus Defoe tries to show that China is actually a sorry place, despite the prestige its religion, government, economy, and exports like tea and porcelain enjoy in Europe (173–7; see *Serious Reflections*, 138–43). In *Farther Adventures*, he develops the paradox that a prince can be a happier and better man as an innocent exile in Siberia than enjoying power and prestige at the Russian court.[1]

In *Serious Reflections* as well there are numerous paradoxes: that one can become devout and contemplative within an active life by cultivating meditative habits, more than by withdrawing from the world into ascetic seclusion ("Of Solitude," 57–66); that slander can be as vicious, cause as much pain, and be as hard to counteract or punish, as bodily assault;[2] that Europeans who sin against the light afforded them by the Gospel may fare worse at the last judgment than benighted natives of other continents who live virtuously ("An Essay on the Present State of Religion in the World," 133–4). This last paradox is quite somber, but others are distinctly carnivalesque, and turn the world upside down with a clear satiric purpose. For instance, there is a long and amusing account of the Thanksgiving ceremony at St. Paul's for Marlborough's great victory at Blenheim: the point is that contrary to its ostensible function – to thank God for blessing the English arms and nation – gratitude and religion are wholly absent, with vanity and worldliness taking their place (155–8). To a degree unusual in *Serious Reflections*, this passage consists of lively narration, but here as often elsewhere, Defoe is telling a story to support an argument, not for its own sake.

Other contexts bring out similarly sardonic humor. The Aztecs, Defoe holds, were totally under the sway of the devil in practicing their hideous rites of human sacrifice. Provoked by their crimes, God used the Spaniards as instruments of his punishment. The conquistadores were thus executing a divinely ordained mission, yet they themselves had no justification for invading and massacring the natives. They were doing God's work, but in killing fellow humans who had done them no harm, they were as bad or worse than the Aztecs. That Providence sometimes uses unworthy tools to bring about desirable ends is a recurring paradox. Elsewhere (210–11) Defoe argues that "the Invasion of the Romans was an unjust, bloody, tyrannical Assault upon the poor Britains ... yet God was pleased to make this Violence be the kindest Thing that could have befallen the British Nation," which would otherwise have "layn above 300 Years longer in Ignorance and Paganism, than they did."

The grim and morally perplexing interactions of native Americans, Spaniards, and Providence would not seem to make for comedy, yet Defoe springs this joke:

> The poor Wretches the Indians in America ... when they were talked to of the Future State, the Resurrection of the Dead, Eternal Felicity in Heaven, and the like, enquir'd where the Spaniards went after Death, and if any of them went to Heaven? And being answered in the Affirmative, shook their Heads, and desired they might go to Hell then, for that they were afraid to think of being in Heaven, if the Spaniards were there. (217)

Here too everything turns on a paradoxical inversion: rejecting a heaven inhabited by Spaniards, the natives choose hell, because only there could they be free of their oppressors.

The Farther Adventures and *Serious Reflections* have their xenophobic moments, but at various points Defoe enters sympathetically into the frame of mind of alien figures. Elsewhere he stereotypes the French as frivolous, and in *A New Family Instructor* (1727), he deprecates the sinister machinations of Roman Catholic priests, intent on seducing naïve Englishmen to popery.[3] But in *Farther Adventures* a French Benedictine priest works selflessly for the spiritual welfare of Crusoe's colony, and his devout religiosity is untainted by sectarian rigidity or intolerance. In a similar vein, Defoe contrasts the "black legend" of Spanish violence in the New World with the dignity and self-restraint of the Spaniards on his island, who show generosity and forbearance toward dangerous Englishmen and savages, and refuse to take native women as paramours.[4]

Nor is Defoe's pursuit of paradox simply a matter of redeeming from their bad reputations those ordinarily seen as England's religious or political enemies or rivals – a pattern Gildon castigated as disloyalty to England and Protestantism. Crusoe has often been seen as epitomizing Englishness, but this judgment is based chiefly on his original island experience. He interacts much more with his fellow-countrymen in *Farther Adventures*, and the picture of them that emerges is highly critical of the English national character. The cannibals had sickened and appalled him, but he could distance himself from a form of violence practiced only by benighted savages. In *Farther Adventures* Crusoe cannot simply disavow kinship with his brutal shipmates, yet by refusing to participate in wanton killing or to condone it, he can stop short of total identification with their beastliness. He expresses horror and revulsion at the initial "Massacre of Madagascar" – which he antagonizes the perpetrators by refusing to call by any other name (140) – but after witnessing similar episodes, his shock and loathing give way to a melancholy resignation.[5] Crusoe knows that cruelty, violence, tumult, and suffering occur everywhere, and that nature or Providence is somehow responsible, but he cannot fathom their purpose. This depresses him, and in the second and third volumes, he is low-spirited over various theological or metaphysical problems that he finds insoluble. The resilience, determination, and optimism about finding solutions that Defoe's heroes and heroines (including the Crusoe of the original volume) usually bring to their practical difficulties are much less in evidence.

In *Robinson Crusoe*, the most memorable scenes are not overtly violent ones, but the prosaic domestic labors of this unheroic hero. Crusoe does not commit or suffer much actual violence, yet it is often on his mind.[6] He feels vulnerable to it, and dreads it, but also resists one major temptation to inflict it, and at other times minimizes the violence he himself must use for self-preservation.[7] More of the violence in this book is threatened or plotted than carried out, and more is in the hero's head than in the outward events of the story.

This pattern is reversed in *Farther Adventures*, which in this respect is more akin to *Captain Singleton* (1720) and *Col. Jacque* (1722). The world may not be inherently more dangerous than in *Robinson Crusoe*, but these narratives consist much more of people inflicting or suffering palpable and often lethal violence. Nevertheless they share one significant pattern with *Robinson Crusoe*: in all three works, the hero-narrator tends to be a reluctant or resistant spectator of violence rather than an initiator or supporter of it. In *Farther Adventures* Crusoe reports in detail on conflict and carnage, and one might question whether this points to imaginative complicity on his part. Yet he is at pains to distance himself from responsibility for such enormities, not only by regretting or condemning them in his role as retrospective narrator, but also by trying to thwart, restrain, or rebuke the bloodthirstiness and brutality of his colleagues at the time.

In *Farther Adventures*, most violence is initiated by Europeans, who are represented as impulsive and rash. Crusoe shares these traits, but his natural "inclinations" and "propensities" are never toward sex, drink, or gluttony. According to Defoe's view of the passions, he is thus at less risk than his fellow-countrymen of sinking into sheer animality, which he is intent on avoiding.[8] Impulse provokes others to violence, but leads Crusoe to imprudent adventures. Defoe's religious and didactic writings, such as *The Family Instructor* (1715–18), show that vehement passions like anger can border on madness and cause great suffering. Yet from his perspective, inertia and vacancy seem almost worse than inordinate passions. The best example is probably Crusoe at the beginning of *Farther Adventures*. In *Robinson Crusoe* his original story (like Captain Singleton's) ends but scarcely culminates in marriage; he had not needed a wife to achieve domesticity, and for faithful service and companionship, Friday and William Walters greatly surpass the wives that Defoe finds for these two heroes, just as Amy and Mother Midnight outdo Roxana's and Moll's husbands and lovers. In Defoe's fictional writings, fratrimony and sororimony definitely outshine matrimony.[9]

Considering all that Crusoe had seen and done, we might expect his serious reflections to consist of locomotion recollected in tranquility. His past had been anything but calm, not only when he was gadding about, but even when he was least mobile and least anxious on the island: he could seldom sit still, bodily or mentally, but was obsessively active. In *Serious Reflections*, however, the former restless bustle does not give way to static repose. Whether it is Crusoe's or Defoe's voice we hear, its tone is as intense and urgent as ever. Defoe alludes to Crusoe's latter end, like Job's, being better than his beginning, and in material terms this is true.[10] But to be placid and sedate is never Crusoe's reward. Defoe may have thought tranquility borders too closely on idleness to be desirable, let alone ideal; better anxious exertion than languid quietude.

Once Crusoe is back in his native land, prosperity and security are not enough to withstand renewed bouts of restlessness. For Defoe, idleness is perhaps the deadliest of sins, but not one that any of his heroes or heroines can be charged with. So great is their dread of apathy or inertia that they often act rashly to escape it. One instance is H. F. the saddler venturing out of the safety of his house to see what is happening in plague-stricken London.[11] The same impulse sets Crusoe in motion in *Farther Adventures*, not only driving him abroad again at the outset, but pushing him yet farther afield at later points when he has the option of staying put. This compulsion is in fact a major link between the first and second volumes: it makes Crusoe's motivation consistent and plausible, and it generates a peripatetic action that is in principle interminable. As in the picaresque, which is similarly resistant to immobility and finality, there is no real stopping-point, no sense of an ending, dictated either by the structure of the action or by the psychology of the hero. Crusoe returns to London after the death of his wife:

> but I had no Relish to the Place, no Employment in it, nothing to do but to saunter about like an idle Person, of whom it may be said, he is perfectly useless in God's Creation ... This also was the Life, which of all Circumstances of Life was the most my Aversion, who had been all my Days used to an active Life; and I would often say to my self, A State of Idleness is the very Dregs of Life; and indeed I thought I was much more suitably employ'd, when I was 26 Days a making me a Deal Board.
>
> (*FARC*, 10)

He has nothing to do, and his sense of emptiness and purposelessness nearly drives him mad, as if he were confined to the Happy Valley in Samuel Johnson's Abyssinia in his moral fable, *Rasselas* (1759). Any passion, however questionable in itself, seems better than none at all. To be affectless is to be lifeless, and to deliberately seek or cultivate such a state, like ascetic "Solitaires" in the "Desarts of Arabia and Lybia," strikes Defoe as foolish and perverse.[12] True, Defoe's characters often draw the line at this or that passion they disapprove of. Nevertheless it is by moving about in a world of passions that they come to life, and that their stories have stayed alive. And by obeying desires that Defoe and his characters acknowledge are irrational, they manage to avoid what he and they regard as worse, namely lethargy and inertia.

Defoe probably would not have agreed that love of fame is "The Universal Passion";[13] his view seems to have been that restlessness is the paramount stimulus to human action, at least in response to stasis or idleness.[14] He did recognize that staying put and sticking to gainful routines was probably the safest path to prosperity and contentment. For an ordinary merchant, this makes sense; thus Crusoe reports that "My new Friend ... would have been content to have gone like a Carrier's Horse, always to the same Inn, backward and forward, provided he could, as he call'd it, find his Account in it" (*FARC*, 146).

Crusoe had this orderly procedure preached to him by his father as most likely to secure him a respectable place in the "middle Station of Life" (*RC*, 6). But years later, in the middle of the second volume, he feels no more drawn to prudent, profitable monotony than he had been at the beginning of the first volume. Contrary to the merchant's principle, "mine was the Notion of a mad rambling Boy, that never cares to see a Thing twice over" (*FARC*, 146). This is not nearly as harsh, of course, as labeling the earlier running off to sea his "Original Sin" (*RC*, 154), and a note of amused self-irony seems to have crept into his self-criticism. All the same, whether he is judging himself severely or indulgently, he is prompted to "ramble" once again by passion rather than reason.

We can call this passion "wanderlust," but to say that he is driven to wander by a lust for wandering is circumlocution, not explanation. It seems more constructive to think about what he wants and needs to get away from; and this, as I have suggested, is an oppressive sense of immobility and purposelessness, from which he has to break out. Eventually, Crusoe and Defoe's other traveler-trespassers belie the pattern recommended by Crusoe's father, and embodied by Crusoe's merchant-companion: they end up better off than if they had stuck to proven, safe routine, and obeyed reason rather than passion. But Defoe may not want us to infer that we too should abandon reason for passion. On the contrary, he probably regards the merchant's submission to prosaic but profitable routine, like that of the "Carrier's Horse," as a prudent pattern. By following it, we ought to be able to lead lucrative but listless lives. This in turn should pay off for Defoe as author: prosperous leisure will provoke in us the same restlessness that drives Crusoe to ramble, but it will make us merely buy and read Defoe's books, in which we too can escape ennui and experience strange surprising adventures.

* * *

Deliberative rhetoric is a prominent feature of Defoe's so-called novels. To take an uncontroversial example, the long dialogue between Col. Jack and his servant-tutor in Virginia brings out interesting analogies and paradoxes in the respective situations of servant and master, but also serves to dramatize social, economic, and legal contentions: that being transported to a new life in Virginia represents a splendid opportunity for condemned criminals, an excellent alternative to the wasteful practice of hanging them, a fine way to lessen crime at home and increase population in the colonies, and so on. The tutor's account of himself does little to advance the picaresque hero's own story, but provides an apposite case-history to support Defoe's arguments in behalf of the policy of transporting felons to the New World.[15]

In Defoe's writings throughout the 1720s, there was to be a productive tension, already present in *Farther Adventures* and *Serious Reflections*, between storytelling on the one hand and persuasion on the other. Over a century ago George Aitken, one of Defoe's most sensible editors and critics, observed that the difference between the conduct manuals and what he called the romances was one of proportion rather than kind, depending on whether instruction or narration happened to be uppermost.[16] This theory may not pass muster with sophisticated modern critics, but has a lot to be said for it – not as an all-purpose generic litmus test, but as a reminder that the writings of Defoe's last decade are mixed rather than pure, and that we should try to do justice to their multiple intentions and effects, instead of striving for taxonomic rigor. They can be ranged between poles of narration and persuasion; in practice, the two usually occur together, although the proportions vary from one book to another and even within single works. *Serious Reflections* is close to the persuasive end of the scale, and devotes little space or emphasis to narrative. Why, then, did it present itself as a sequel to the first two volumes? The simplest answer is that *Serious Reflections* exploits the success of the earlier volumes by packaging, as if it were Crusoe's, a rather miscellaneous batch of literary merchandise, some of which Defoe brazenly acknowledges he had had on hand for nearly two decades.[17]

Serious Reflections displays an objective that is present in all of Defoe's writing of the 1720s, but seldom in such undiluted form, namely a determination to persuade us. The prefaces to several of the fictional works contain protestations that what matters is not the fable but the moral, not the story but its "application" or "improvement," that is, the edifying interpretations that we can and should draw from the narrative, and from the hero's or heroine's own comments on it. Some readers have dismissed such claims as meretricious gestures designed to assure squeamish bourgeois readers that imaginative participation in whoring and thieving is actually good for them. But *Serious Reflections* tends to bear out Defoe's repeated contention that beyond mere amusement, stories can be worthwhile for giving rise to Serious Reflections. Elsewhere he sometimes spells out what these useful inferences consist of. Some are mundane and crass: reading *Moll Flanders* teaches ladies to keep their watches secure if they insist on wearing them to church. Others, however, add substantial religious and metaphysical implications to practical advice. A notable instance is a chapter entitled "Of listning to the Voice of Providence" (180–200), a practice Defoe continues to advocate throughout the 1720s. By listening to the voice of Providence we acknowledge God's ongoing government of the world he has created, and we also enable ourselves to benefit from the useful hints and warnings Providence constantly sends our way.

The difference between Defoe as an essayist intent on persuasion and most of his predecessors in that genre can be seen clearly in the opening chapter of *Serious Reflections*, "Of Solitude." Earlier writers on the subject usually enjoyed an option: should they remain in active, responsible roles within society, or give them up for the advantages of a return to the countryside? They tended to treat solitude and retirement as more or less interchangeable terms: some marshaled pastoral and georgic commonplaces to justify withdrawal from the compromised gratifications of urban life, while others repudiated retirement in the interest of civic obligation and culture, or of avoiding rustic boorishness and sloth.

In any case, the element of choice had always been a key factor in essays on retirement or solitude: the author could renounce society or not, as he saw fit (it was almost always a man who had this power and chose to write about it). So the subject of these essays was voluntary retirement or voluntary solitude – a deliberate retreat into a more or less hermitlike state – whereas the solitude Crusoe experienced in the first volume of the trilogy had been entirely involuntary. You might suppose this would cause Defoe to write a new and different kind of essay, based on Crusoe's special qualifications as a veteran of imposed rather than chosen isolation. In fact, the twenty-eight-plus years Crusoe spent alone supply a mere pretext or occasion for Defoe to hold forth about solitude. No effort is made to have these serious reflections grow out of Crusoe's unique predicament, or the thoughts and sensations it could plausibly have given rise to. Once he has set the essay in motion, Defoe does not bother keeping it in character, and this is the case throughout much of the book. The opinions expressed, and the voice uttering them, seldom violate jarringly those we associate with Crusoe. Yet they scarcely build on Crusoe's character or situation, once we are past the Preface. The Crusoe of this third volume is not a fully realized persona, with a distinctive voice of his own, who now happens to be reflecting on his life rather than living it. Instead, the voice we hear more nearly matches Defoe's, and at certain moments it is so much Defoe's that it cannot be Crusoe's.

What the essay "Of Solitude" offers, at any rate, is not a series of genteel, even-handed ruminations on the pros and cons of giving up the urban hubbub for bucolic peace, but rather a series of emphatic contentions, sometimes amply argued and illustrated, sometimes peremptorily asserted. All are designed to discredit traditional notions about the desirability of solitude, traditional legends about the value (and even the sheer possibility) of ascetic renunciation of the secular world by hermits, and traditional beliefs that spiritual self-assessment and self-improvement can be achieved only by separating oneself bodily from the distractions of society. To Defoe, the blandishments of isolation are not mere myths or fantasies, but pernicious delusions. They fly in the face of human nature, which depends upon society for bare existence, mutual support, and the possibility of genuine happiness. They enshrine rank selfishness as if it were saintly. Worst of all, they fail to recognize that the kind of retirement that is truly valuable and necessary, the periodic scrutiny of one's own spiritual and moral welfare, is just as possible within society as outside it, for those willing and able to turn their attention from secular affairs to higher concerns. "Of Solitude" thus takes on a tone and spirit that are not merely didactic but homiletic. The essayist, like a preacher, has the task of weaning people away from what he sees as the illusory attraction of literal solitude and retirement. In place of this, he advocates the cultivation of a kind of figurative, mental retirement, which he believes can and should take place at intervals amidst worldly demands and distractions.

When he set out to write about solitude, Defoe evidently had in mind various ideas he wanted readers to accept. Unlike many essayists before and since, he does not adopt the form as a method of discovery, of finding and weighing various possible meanings and values that solitude (for example) might have. In some hands, the essay can function as a heuristic tool, a search process in which the reader can follow the writer and arrive at the same goal; the writer may not know (or may pretend not to know) from the outset where the path may lead. In this case, persuasion may be the ultimate object, but it is pursued indirectly. Such obliqueness, however, is not characteristic of Defoe. He introduces rival positions chiefly to explode them before laying out his own, not as partial truths pointing the way toward a higher or fuller truth. In this respect, Defoe's essays in *Serious Reflections* and after retain much of the combativeness of his earlier pamphleteering and journalism.

The argumentativeness of *Serious Reflections* may be at once its greatest strength and its greatest weakness. Some traditional essayists give the impression that they are content to meander wherever the current of their thought carries them. In *Serious Reflections* there is little of this indeterminacy. Even at their most improvisatory, Defoe's paragraphs usually move toward definite goals. At best, this can give these essays a bracing sense of purpose sometimes missing in the more relaxed, urbane lucubrations of a Montaigne or Shaftesbury. Intent on making a point, Defoe's prose is in no danger of seeming a mere leisure pastime for genteel, unencumbered writers and readers. But this purposefulness runs a different risk: entertaining us, which can be a way of lowering our resistance to persuasion, is liable to be abandoned for tendentious arm-twisting. Defoe recognizes this danger, and evidently thinks he has avoided it by joking about it, and by twitting his readers for wanting amusement rather than edification. Nevertheless he sometimes succumbs to it.

Defoe's fictional characters are prone to invoke big concepts like necessity to justify or palliate their misdeeds. When such concepts seem genuinely relevant to their circumstances and motives, as they sometimes are, we call such casuistry legitimate, and respond sympathetically. When such concepts seem far-fetched or inapplicable, we call this bad casuistry or special pleading, and react skeptically. In "An Essay upon Honesty," the speaker argues – in a manner familiar to readers of *Moll Flanders* and *Roxana* – that honesty is a matter not of overt deeds but of motives and intentions; that people should not presume to pronounce on such matters, let alone condemn anyone for dishonesty, unless they themselves have been subjected to extreme pressures and temptations; that momentary lapses should not brand one as dishonest if one usually wishes and tries to be honest, and so on (*SR*, 67–101). The implication is that one's legal accountability and one's moral status may be quite different, and that committing dishonest acts does not necessarily make one a dishonest person.

The problem is not that these arguments are unsound, but rather that their supposed author, Crusoe himself, really has no occasion for them. There are various missteps and misjudgments that he can reproach himself with, but dishonesty is not one of them. Indeed, in *Farther Adventures*, when he dreads being wrongfully seized and hanged as a pirate, he says, "I was now very uneasy, and thought myself … to have been in the most dangerous Condition that ever I was in thro' all my past Life; for whatever ill Circumstances I had been in, I was never pursu'd for a Thief before; nor had I ever done any Thing that merited the Name of *Dishonest* or Fraudulent, much less, Thievish" (154, italics added). An intricate casuistical discussion of honesty is thus put in the mouth of someone who has no need to defend himself against imputations of dishonesty, and who has been treated not only honestly but remarkably generously by others. For Crusoe, then, this entire essay is curiously out of character; yet it is totally in character for Defoe. For him the topic is not merely of abstract or theoretical interest, but is acutely personal and pressing. His bankruptcies were blemishes on his integrity that he could never live down. Five years later, in *The Compleat English Tradesman* (1725–7), he was still struggling to free himself from the stigma of dishonesty; and once again, it was by redefining honesty that he tried to do so. There are sporadic gestures toward Crusoefying these reflections. In the essay "Of Honesty," there is an amusing comparison between Yorkshire honesty, Scottish honesty, and New England honesty: the farther from London you go, the shakier honesty becomes, so that New England honesty is a virtual oxymoron. This is followed by the contention that Turks are more scrupulous about keeping their word, and then by the essayist saying, "but I never went there," in a voice that we are no doubt meant to identify as Crusoe's. There are other such moments, but they are too isolated and infrequent to make up a sustained dramatic impersonation of a reflective Crusoe (*SR*, 76).

Tonally, if not generically, the third volume would seem a more plausible sequel to its predecessors if its serious reflections were clearly and consistently those of Crusoe himself, looking back over his own life. If they
were more in keeping with the personage supposedly expressing them, and
thus obeyed what was known as decorum, the title-page pretense that they
were Crusoe's would have been better kept up, even if most readers in 1720
already shared Charles Gildon's awareness that Defoe was behind the whole
enterprise. As I have indicated, various reflections have little to do with
Crusoe's past, and sound odd coming from him, but they do grow naturally out of Defoe's past. From this we might infer that the voice we hear is
really his rather than Crusoe's. Yet it is not a simple either/or matter, because
from the Preface onward, Defoe deliberately obfuscates the source of these
reflections. He suggests that he is and is not Crusoe, and that he and Crusoe
are and are not speaking for one another. Instead of trying to establish and
sustain a clear distinction between editor and supposititious autobiographical author, as he had done at the beginning of the first volume and was to
do again in various works of the early 1720s, Defoe here turns the tables
on Gildon by seizing upon and exploiting the very overlap and blurring
between himself and his creation that Gildon had satirized as a moral and
artistic absurdity. Half in jest and half in earnest, Defoe sets up his own
version of the equivalence and interplay between author and character. His
strategy, I believe, is to pretend that Crusoe wishes to write a life of Defoe,
because of Defoe's virtues and example as a teacher, but does not want
to identify Defoe as the subject, because of popular prejudice against him;
therefore he has published a made-up story, which nevertheless corresponds
allegorically to Defoe's real life. This interpretation seems supported by
prefatory paragraphs such as this (*SR*, 53):

> Had the common Way of Writing a Mans private History been taken, and I had
> given you the Conduct or Life of a Man you knew, and whose Misfortunes
> and Infirmities, perhaps you had sometimes unjustly triumph'd over; all
> I could have said would have yielded no Diversion, and perhaps scarce have
> obtained a Reading, or at best no Attention; the Teacher, like a greater, having
> no Honour in his own Country. Facts that are form'd to touch the Mind, must
> be done a great Way off, and by somebody never heard of: Even the Miracles
> of the Blessed Saviour of the World suffered Scorn and Contempt, when it was
> reflected, that they were done by the Carpenter's Son; one whose Family and
> Original they had a mean Opinion of, and whose Brothers and Sisters were
> ordinary People like themselves.

The role of *Serious Reflections* as a bridge between Defoe's earlier
and later writings is particularly striking in the latter part of the book.
Its long concluding section, "A Vision of the Angelick World" (221–73),

harks back to the imaginary lunar voyage of *The Consolidator* (1705) and shorter passages involving space travel elsewhere. But it also looks forward to the extraterrestrial visions in several major works on the supernatural, including *A Political History of the Devil* (1726), *A System of Magick* (1727), and *An Essay on the History and Reality of Apparitions* (1727). Once again, however, the subject matter is not as important to Defoe as its usefulness as a vehicle for satire or some other ulterior purpose. In *The Consolidator*, for example, he had scarcely concerned himself with the possibilities for fantasy afforded by the established genre of the lunar voyage. Yet much of the authority of his critical commentary on British political and religious life in *The Consolidator* derives from the supposedly detached, elevated perspective of a lunar observer: space travel yields very little of mimetic or narrative interest, but affords Defoe a new stick for beating old enemies. These priorities remain true of "A Vision of the Angelick World" and the works of the 1720s that employ similar devices. The chief difference is that the objects of attack are no longer hostile political parties or public figures, but religious or irreligious groups Defoe opposes. His chief targets are beliefs he deems idolatrous, fanatical, or superstitious, such as Roman Catholicism, "Mahometanism," and Asian polytheism. He also attacks various shades of skepticism, heresy, and disbelief. In these works, his discussions of the devil, magic, apparitions, and other supernatural entities and phenomena vary widely in tone, from the playful and witty to the earnest and grave. What connects them all, without fully unifying them, is their common, sustained rhetorical thrust, in behalf of what Defoe regards as sound belief, or against what he takes to be threats to it. Whether defending or attacking, each polemical passage is a skirmish or battle in a larger, ongoing war.

These three works (*Political History of the Devil, System of Magick, Essay on the History and Reality of Apparitions*) are grouped appropriately (in the Furbank and Owens edition) among Defoe's satirical and supernatural writings, but they could just as well be classified as religious and didactic writings, along with books that obviously belong in that category like *Religious Courtship* (1722) and *A New Family Instructor*. What these works have in common is that they are all arguing for the same set of beliefs, and arguing against the same versions of unbelief. True, amidst the moral and theological preoccupations that run through them all, some are more prominent than others at a given moment or in a given work. But Defoe treats his positive values and concerns as interdependent, and he sees the same connectedness among the objects of his hostility: thus he does not simply identify Deism, freethinking, and skepticism, but he does regard them all as leading to (if not disguises for) atheism.

Earlier I brought out Defoe's conviction that to benefit from retirement you need not absent yourself bodily from the world, but should instead try to reflect seriously during moments of mental or spiritual withdrawal from the cares and pleasures of ordinary life. This turns out to be equally true in the final section of *Serious Reflections*. To achieve "A Vision of the Angelick World" you do not have to become a space traveler. Defoe quickly drops that narrative device, and proceeds to make a case analogous to the one in "Of Solitude": you are not obliged to go anywhere at all, but you must try to cultivate an openness and responsiveness to the guidance sent us from the "angelick" or "invisible" world by the benevolent spirits who inhabit it. As in the essay "Of Listning to the Voice of Providence," Defoe's rhetoric seeks to persuade us on two different levels. One is metaphysical or theological: we should acknowledge that God exists (as even pagans and savages do) and that he also actively governs his creation through his benign Providence. The other level is more applied or practical, and has both hortatory and monitory elements: if we believe that divine Providence promotes our welfare here and hereafter by sending us messages, then piety and prudence alike oblige us to be attentive and responsive to the voices, hints, dreams, visions, etc., by which directions of divine origin are communicated to us. Such beliefs may seem hard to place within latter-day Calvinism, or Protestantism, or even Christianity, and the three books on the devil, magic, and apparitions in which Defoe discusses these matters at greatest length are sometimes referred to as treatises on the occult. But Defoe resisted seeing them in that light. In writing on the supernatural, in *Serious Reflections* and other works of the 1720s, he tried hard to distance himself from enthusiasm and occultism, as well as from materialism and skepticism. Since Dissent had long been stigmatized as naively or fanatically credulous, Defoe was at pains to distinguish his own position, which he regarded as moderate and orthodox, from the irrational excesses of sectarian zealots. To a modern reader, however, his conceptions of angelic or invisible worlds – indeed, his very belief in their existence – are liable to smack of superstition.[18]

NOTES

In this chapter, all quotations from *Farther Adventures of Robinson Crusoe* and *Serious Reflections during the Life and Surprising Adventures of Robinson Crusoe: with his Vision of the Angelick World* are from the forty-four-volume edition of *The Works of Daniel Defoe*, of which P. N. Furbank and W. R. Owens are the general editors (London: Pickering & Chatto, 2000–10); this edition is available (and fully searchable) electronically in the InteLex Past Masters series: http://pm.nlx.com/xtf/view?docId=defoe/defoe.oo.xml;chunk .id=div.defoe .pmpreface.1;toc.depth=2;toc.id=div.defoe.pmpreface.1;hit .rank=0;brand=default. *Farther Adventures of Robinson Crusoe* appeared as volume 2 of the Novels, edited by W. R. Owens, *Serious Reflections of Robinson Crusoe* as volume 3, edited by G. A. Starr (2008), and are cited by page numbers; throughout, the place of publication is London. *Robinson Crusoe* is cited from the Penguin edition, edited by John Richetti (London, 2001).

1 See *Farther Adventures*, 209–11. Col. Jack's slave-tutor in Virginia similarly demonstrates that virtuous self-esteem in lowly circumstances is better than unmerited worldly prosperity; see *The History and Remarkable Life of the Truly Honourable Col. Jacque* (1723), in *Novels*, vol. 8, ed. Maurice Hindle (2009), 157. Defoe may have been attracted to this paradox by a belief that his own situation was analogous.

2 See *Serious Reflections*, 73–4. In *An Appeal to Honour and Justice, tho' it be of his Worst Enemies* (1715), Defoe likens his predicament to that of Jeremiah, taunted by the Israelites: "Come and *let us smite him with the* Tongue, *and let us not give heed to any of his* Words" (Jeremiah 18:18; see title-page and p. 55). In *Serious Reflections* he says one can withstand "the general Slander of a prejudic'd Age, and a State of universal Calumny, where the Mind is free from the Guilt they charge: Such a Man, tho' the World spits upon and despises him, looks in with Comfort, and looks up with Hope" (167). Much of *Serious Reflections* represents a further installment in Defoe's unending campaign to parry the malice of "his Worst Enemies," by presenting himself as a maligned but upright defender of sound social, economic, and religious values.

3 See *A New Family Instructor*, ed. W. R. Owens (2006), in *Religious and Didactic Writings*, vol. 3, 90–132.

4 See *Farther Adventures*, 46–58; "let the Accounts of Spanish Cruelty in Mexico and Peru, be what they will, I never met with seventeen Men of any Nation whatsoever … who were so universally Modest, Temperate, Virtuous, so very good Humour'd, and so Courteous as these Spaniards; and as to Cruelty, they had nothing of it in their very Nature, no Inhumanity, no Barbarity, no outrageous Passions, and yet all of them Men of great Courage and Spirit" (58).

5 Near the "Bay of Tonquin," Crusoe's ship is attacked by a large group of "the Cochinchinesses," but they are driven away: "we got this Victory without any Blood shed, except of that Man the Fellow kill'd with his naked Hands, and which I was very much concern'd at; for I was sick of killing such poor Savage Wretches, even tho' it was in my own Defence, knowing they came on Errands which they thought just, and knew no better; and that tho' it may be a just Thing, because necessary, for there is no necessary Wickedness in Nature, yet I thought it was a sad Life, which we must be always oblig'd to be killing our Fellow-Creatures to preserve, and indeed I think so still; and I would even now suffer a great deal, rather than I would take away the Life, even of that Person injuring me" (158).

6 Crusoe ponders killing cannibals, and fears being devoured by them, or swallowed by the sea, by wild animals, by collapse of his dwelling during an earthquake, or by wolves in the Pyrenees. Other anxieties arise from the unstated but unsettling possibility of violence, as when he comes upon the single footprint in the sand, or the glowing eyes in the dark cave. Once the menace is made quite explicit, by the man in his dream-vision who brandishes a spear and threatens to kill him.

7 Crusoe throws a Moor overboard near the port of Sallee as he makes his escape from captivity there, but insists that he "swam like a cork"; Ismael heads for shore, "and I make no doubt but he reach'd it with ease, for he was an excellent swimmer" (20). If Crusoe had supposed his life was in danger from either Xury or Friday, he probably would have thought it necessary to kill them, and that the law of self-preservation would justify him in doing so.

8 The passions that most worry Defoe are the ones that turn men into beasts: "That was a good Story, whether real or invented, of the Devil tempting a young Man to murder his Father. No, he said, that was un-natural. Why, then says the Devil, Go and lye with your Mother: No, says he, That is abominable. Well, Then, says the Devil, If you will do nothing else to oblige me, go and get Drunk; Ay, ay, says the Fellow, I'll do that, so he went and made himself Drunk as a Swine; and when he was Drunk, he murdered his Father, and lay with his Mother." See *Col. Jacque*, in *Novels*, vol. 8, 213.

9 "Fratrimony" is an excellent coinage of Georg Christian Lichtenberg (1742–99): see his *Sudelbücher I*, in *Schriften und Briefe*, ed. Wolfgang Promies, 4 vols. (Frankfurt: Zweitausendeins, 2000), vol. 1, 515 ("In Fratrimonio leben"), kindly traced by Alessa Johns; Lichtenberg is not responsible for "sororimony."

10 See Job 42:12, "So the Lord blessed the latter end of Job more than his beginning: for he had fourteen thousand sheep, and six thousand camels, and a thousand yoke of oxen, and a thousand she asses." For Defoe's application of the phrase to Crusoe, see *Robinson Crusoe*, 224; it occurs again in *Serious Reflections*, 230; *Col. Jacque*, in *Novels*, 32.

11 See *A Journal of the Plague Year* (1722), ed. John Mullan (2009), in *Novels*, vol. 7, 85, 103.

12 See *Serious Reflections*, 64. Defoe is harsh toward these early Christian hermits, whose chief fault seems to have been that they were sluggards, dependent on angels for their victuals and drink. Not one to praise fugitive or cloistered virtue on the part of monkish layabouts, Defoe evidently deems the desert fathers guilty of accidia or sloth; his implicit ideal is "Up and be doing, and God will prosper." This motto, placed by Sir William Spencer at the entrance to a wood of oaks and beeches he planted at Althorp in 1624, is a variant of David exhorting Solomon to get on with building the temple in 1 Chronicles 22:16, "Arise therefore, and be doing, and the Lord be with you": see Thomas Frognall Dibdin, *Aedes Althorpianae; or An Account of the Mansion, Books, and Pictures, at Althorp* (1822), ix.

13 See Edward Young's popular poem, *The Universal Passion* (1725–8).

14 Crusoe's merchant friend in Bengal asks, "what should we stand still for? The whole World is in Motion, rouling round and round; all the Creatures of God, heavenly Bodies and earthly are busy and diligent, Why should we be idle? There are no Drones in the World but Men, Why should we be of that Number?" (*FARC*, 144); after a successful trading voyage, Crusoe declares that "stirring about and trading ... had more Pleasure in it, and more Satisfaction to the Mind than sitting still, which to me especially, was the unhappiest Part of Life" (*FARC*, 146). That Defoe shares these views is indicated by his writing a few years later, "A Life of Sloth and Idleness, is not Happiness or Comfort; Employment is Life, Sloth and Indolence is Death; to be busy, is to be chearful, to be pleasant; to have nothing to do, is all Dejection, dispiriting, and in a word, to be fit for nothing

but Mischief and the Devil": see *A Plan of the English Commerce* (1728), ed. John McVeagh (2000), in *Political and Economic Writings*, vol. 7, 160.

15 See *Col. Jacque*, in *Novels*, vol. 8, 155–7.

16 See *Romances and Narratives by Daniel Defoe*, ed. George A. Aitken, 16 vols. (1895), vol. 1, xxix.

17 See footnote on p. 112 of *Serious Reflections*, "*This was all Written in King William's Reign and refers to that Time.*"

18 On these topics, see my Introductions to *An Essay on the History and Reality of Apparitions, in Satire, Fantasy, and Writings on the Supernatural*, vol. 8 (2005), and to *Christianity Not as Old as the Creation: The Last of Defoe's Performances* (2012).

6

REBECCA BULLARD

Politics, History, and the *Robinson Crusoe* Story

In a defense of *Robinson Crusoe* published the year after his ground-breaking novel, Defoe faced down his literary opponents who had accused him of publishing a pack of lies. He denied penning an "Invention scandalous in Design, and false in Fact," affirming "that the Story, though Allegorical, is also Historical."[1] By "Historical," Defoe may mean that the adventures he describes have an independent, verifiable basis outside the text.[2] But the novel can be seen as historical in another sense. Defoe puts dates on Crusoe's journey: he arrived on his island in 1658 and returned to England in 1687. The three decades Crusoe spent in exile were among the most tumultuous in British political history. Defoe, born in 1660, grew up during these years and took a direct part in some of their political upheavals.[3] In 1719, the year of *Robinson Crusoe*'s publication, Britain was still feeling the aftershocks of seismic political events that had taken place within the living memory of a whole generation of older readers. Defoe's decision to set his first long work of fiction in the recent past seems a provocative act. He asks his readers to cast their minds back to the troubled years of the mid-seventeenth century, to read through the lens of a familiar but frightening past. If we are to understand the originality of Defoe's achievement in *Robinson Crusoe*, we need to do the same.

When Crusoe left home, England was experiencing the only brief moment of republican rule in its history. Its last monarch – Charles I – had been executed in 1649 as a tyrant and a traitor to his country's constitution. His death had followed more than half a decade of civil war between supporters of the Crown on the one hand and of Parliament on the other. Although less bloody, the decade after Charles' death brought yet more political upheaval. The radical changes to Church and state that took place under parliamentary rule and Oliver Cromwell's protectorate government aimed to turn the country into a godly (or Puritan) commonwealth. Such was the England that Crusoe left behind him.

Shortly after Crusoe's departure, England experienced another political sea-change. In 1660, the year of Defoe's birth, Charles II was restored to the throne – King of England and head of the newly reinstated Church of England. Not all Protestants were willing to be subsumed back into this national Church, however. Protestant Dissenters, including Defoe's Presbyterian family, were no longer powerful stakeholders in a godly form of government; rather, they became second-class citizens, unable to hold public office or attend university, in a state that put significant pressure on them to conform to the new religious settlement. King and Parliament – notionally sharers in power under a "mixed" or "limited" monarchy – continued to grapple with one another for an increased share of constitutional sway. In 1685, the death of Charles II and the accession of his brother, James, to the throne inflamed an already volatile situation. James II was a Roman Catholic and an ally of England's long-time political enemy, France. His opponents regarded him as a threat both to the Church of England (of which, in spite of his own beliefs, he was head) and to the political liberties that English people had fought a bloody civil war to protect. Since Crusoe tells us that he returned to England in June 1687, he would have arrived in a country once more riven by religious and political faction. By the end of the following year, 1688, James II had been ousted by his nephew and son-in-law, William of Orange, in a sequence of events known, by its supporters at least, as the Glorious Revolution. Like many of his compatriots Defoe, an ardent admirer of William III, supported and celebrated this revolution as the fight-back of the Protestant people of England against popery and arbitrary government.

Crusoe's silence about the political ferment by which his homeland was gripped during the period of his "life and strange surprizing adventures" is, in some ways, itself surprising. By 1719, Daniel Defoe had spent more than two decades writing pamphlets, periodicals, and longer tracts, in verse and prose, on political topics as diverse as the foundations of political sovereignty, the use of a "standing army" in peacetime, England's relationship with France and the progress of wars between these two nations, the political union between Scotland and England, matters of fiscal policy such as taxation and national debt, and religious toleration, especially the social, political, and economic position of Protestant Dissenters. He had been employed by the government for over a decade as an intelligencer, a role that included not only gathering information on persons or groups who might have been hostile to government policy but also writing and distributing propaganda on the government's behalf.[4] Defoe's periodical, *The Review*, which he wrote single-handedly from 1705 to 1713, served as a mouthpiece for government foreign policy for nearly a decade. Even after his primary political patron, Robert Harley, Earl of Oxford, fell from power in 1714, Defoe continued to intervene in public affairs – sometimes openly, as in his attempts to defend Harley during his impeachment, and sometimes more surreptitiously, as when he wrote for opposition journals in order, as he claimed, to neutralize the more extreme aspects of their politics.[5]

But although Crusoe remains silent about the particular political circumstances of the England that he left in the late 1650s and to which he returned three decades later, his story nonetheless offers itself up to political interpretation – it is, after all, "Allegorical'"as well as "Historical."[6] Island narratives like *Robinson Crusoe* had long been vehicles for political commentary. In the century before the publication of Defoe's novel, Francis Bacon's *New Atlantis* (1627), *A Description of the Famous Kingdome of Macaria* (1641) by Gabriel Plattes, James Harrington's *The Commonwealth of Oceana* (1656), Henry Neville's *Isle of Pines* (1668), the anonymous tracts *Antiquity Reviv'd; or The Government of a Certain Island Antiently call'd Astreada* (1693), and *The Free State of Noland* (1696), developed the literary tradition instigated by Thomas More's *Utopia* (1516), using the island motif to investigate apparently ideal societies and to explore ideas about power, control, and political sovereignty. Other more recent texts, including Delarivier Manley's *Secret Manners and Memoirs of Several Persons of Quality of both Sexes, from the New ATALANTIS, an Island in the Mediteranean* [sic.] (1709) and Defoe's own prose fiction, *The Consolidator* (1705), offer more overtly aggressive, satirical depictions of thinly veiled versions of contemporary Britain, which expose the political corruption of its ruling elites.[7] The island motif provides an opportunity to isolate (from the Latin *insula*, or island) aspects of social and political life and hold them up to particular scrutiny. While not every island that features in seventeenth- and eighteenth-century political texts represents Britain in a straightforward way, the literally isolated position that this country occupies off the Atlantic coast of mainland Europe perhaps made island fantasies a particularly effective vehicle for political reflection. Even when the island in a given text is explicitly not a northern European one, there can be little question that readers compared the political circumstances that pertained on the islands encountered in fantastic voyages of discovery with those they experienced in their own island nation.

If the generic framework of *Robinson Crusoe* invites a politicized approach toward this novel, Crusoe's description of his period in exile as a "reign" (109) and of himself as a "king, or emperor" (102–3) offers further encouragement to politically minded readers. But although Crusoe's language often resonates with contemporary political ideas, it is by no means easy to discern a clear and consistent ideological message in the novel. *Robinson*

Crusoe evokes political debates that endured during the seven decades between the 1650s, when Crusoe left England, and the time of the novel's publication in 1719. What we find in Defoe's novel is not, however, the articulation of any single, particular political doctrine, but rather a polyphony of political ideas, which sometimes combine harmoniously but more often clash dissonantly with one another.

Crusoe's descriptions of his island abound in language that modern readers may not recognize immediately as political but which, to Defoe's contemporaries, would have been instantly recognizable as such. Take, for example, his account of the first journey that he makes to the center of his island:

> I came to an opening, where the country seem'd to descend to the west, and a little spring of fresh water, which issued out of the side of the hill by me, run the other way, that is due east; and the country appear'd so fresh, so green, so flourishing, every thing being in a constant verdure, or flourish of *Spring*, that it look'd like a planted garden.
>
> I descended a little on the side of that delicious vale, surveying it with a secret kind of pleasure, (tho' mixt with my other afflicting thoughts) to think that this was all my own, that I was king and lord of all this country indefeasibly, and had a right of possession; and if I could convey it, I might have it in inheritance, as compleatly as any lord of a manor in *England*. I saw here abundance of cocoa trees, orange, and lemon, and citron trees; but all wild, and very few bearing any fruit, at least not then. (80)

At a high point on his island, with land falling away to both east and west, Crusoe arrives at both a literal and metaphorical watershed. The island which until now has been Crusoe's prison begins to seem like a version of paradise. Crusoe's phrase, "a planted garden," recalls Genesis 2:8, which tells us that "the Lord God planted a garden eastward in Eden; and there he put the man whom he had formed." Crusoe resembles the Adam of John Milton's *Paradise Lost*, who stands on the "verdurous wall of Paradise" to survey "his nether empire neighbouring round."[8] The greenness of the "delicious vale" and "constant verdure" of the island reflect the "enclosure green" of Milton's "delicious Paradise."[9] Defoe had made his deep respect for Milton clear in his long poetic satire, *Jure Divino* (1706).[10] It is hardly surprising, then, that when Crusoe wants to represent his island as a version of Eden, he should deliberately deploy language that evokes *Paradise Lost*.

There is, however, trouble in Crusoe's paradise – trouble felt through an overtly political strain of language. When Crusoe asserts "that I was king and lord of all this country indefeasibly, and had a right of possession; and if I could convey it, I might have it in inheritance, as compleatly as any lord of a manor in *England*," he reworks a linguistic formula that was closely associated in the early-eighteenth-century popular press with Jacobitism, or support for the ousted monarch, James II, and his direct descendants. Pamphlets such as *The History of Hereditary-Right* (1711) attack *"the Indefeasibleness, and All Other Such Late Doctrines Concerning the Absolute Power of Princes."*[11] This text, like others written by supporters of the Glorious Revolution and Protestant monarchy in Britain, vilified Jacobite efforts to re-establish not only the Roman Catholic branch of the Stuart family as monarchs, but also the political ideals that they espoused – including indefeasible (or unconquerable) hereditary succession. Crusoe's Jacobite language casts his self-presentation as a version of Adam in a new light. Supporters of the Stuarts in exile grounded their political beliefs on the work of a mid-seventeenth-century theorist, Sir Robert Filmer. In *Patriarcha, or, The Natural Power of Kings* (published in 1680, but written around 1640), Filmer argued that legitimate government is based not on the consent of the people to be ruled, but rather on God's gift to Adam of total dominion over all the earth – a gift passed on to the present through inheritance. When Crusoe presents himself as an Adamic asserter of indefeasible hereditary right, then, he closely resembles the kind of Filmerian, absolutist monarch that eighteenth-century Jacobites wished to see restored to their own throne.

Defoe's decision to put Filmerian, Jacobite language in Crusoe's mouth is strange to say the least, since he had spent much of the early part of his writing career combating precisely this political position. In *Jure Divino* he paraphrased, in verse, the political arguments of John Locke, whose *Two Treatises of Government* (1689) lambasted Filmer, ridiculed his arguments in favor of the divine right of monarchs to absolute power, and promoted the consent of the people as the only legitimate basis of sovereign power. And in *Queries to the New Hereditary Right-Men* (1710) Defoe attacks the Jacobites, who promoted the hereditary succession of the Roman Catholic Stuarts to the throne after Queen Anne's death. So why would a defender of the Glorious Revolution and the Protestant succession turn the heroic protagonist of his first novel into a Filmerian "hereditary right-man"? How might we approach this political crux?

Crusoe's description of the Edenic center of his island gives us some clues. His references to the "delicious vale" that he "survey[s] ... with a secret kind of pleasure" are, for Crusoe, unusually sexualized, and seem to represent a prelude to his thoughts about passing on his estate to an heir. Crusoe imagines himself as a patriarchal ruler, head of both a family and a nation. In the context of a passage preoccupied by sexual reproduction and inheritance, however, the fruitlessness of the trees at the center of the island is disquieting. Part of the problem seems to be a lack of husbandry on the island. In Genesis God put Adam in Eden "to dress it and to keep it" (Genesis 2:15), and Milton's Adam and Eve wish for children because Eden requires "More hands than ours" to control its abundant growth.[12] In his more Filmerian moments, Crusoe, it seems, misunderstands the relationship between fertility, the land, and political power. If they are not improved by human labor, God's gifts remain fruitless: the gift itself is not enough to guarantee prosperity. The passivity of the Filmerian model of government, in which dominion (that is, land and power) is bestowed from above and simply devolves from one generation to the next, has a stultifying effect on those who live under it. Significantly, Crusoe decides not to stay in his version of Eden because he realizes that "to enclose my self among the hills and woods, in the center of the island, was to anticipate my Bondage" (81). Unlike Adam, Crusoe leaves his paradise voluntarily and goes back to the coast to work in hope of redemption.

After moving back to his cave house, Crusoe continues his series of reflections on the relationship between labor and political power in language that, once again, would have been much more recognizably political to Defoe's contemporaries than it is to modern readers. This time, however, the political intertext is not Filmer's *Patriarcha* but, rather, its most celebrated antagonist: John Locke's *Second Treatise of Government*.[13] After Crusoe discovers European barley growing on his Caribbean island – a mystery explained when Crusoe remembers that he had once shaken out a sack of chicken feed in the spot where the barley appeared – he decides to attempt to bake bread:

> It might be truly said, that now I work'd for my bread; 'tis a little wonderful, and what I believe few people have thought much upon, (*viz.*) the strange multitude of little things necessary in the providing, producing, curing, dressing, making and finishing this one article of bread.
>
> I that was reduced to a meer state of nature, found this to my daily discouragement, and was made more and more sensible of it every hour, even after I had got the first handful of seed-corn, which, as I have said, came up unexpectedly, and indeed to a surprise. (94)

Crusoe's reflections in part take us back to Genesis and to God's punishment of the fallen Adam: "in the sweat of thy face shalt thou eat bread" (Genesis 3:19). But when he suggests that "few people have thought much upon" the extensive network of labor that produces each loaf of bread in the fallen world, Crusoe's irony is easy for modern readers to miss. His reflections on bread are in no way original; rather they allude directly to one of the most striking passages of Locke's *Second Treatise*, in which Locke argues that the foundation of all property is labor.

In his baking, Crusoe acts out a version of Locke's analysis of the complex human processes that produce bread:

> [N]ot barely the Plough-man's Pains, the Reaper's and Thresher's toil, and the Bakers Sweat, is to be counted into the *Bread* we eat; the Labour of those who broke the Oxen, who digged and wrought the Iron and Stones, who felled and framed the Timber imployed about the Plough, Mill, Oven, or any other Utensils, which are a vast Number, requisite to this Corn, from its being seed to be sown to its being made Bread, must all be *charged on* the account of *Labour,* and received as an effect of that: Nature and the Earth furnished only the almost worthless materials, as in themselves.[14]

The stalks of barley on Crusoe's island are "almost worthless materials, as in themselves." The catalogue of verbs with which Crusoe describes his own bread-making ("providing, producing, curing, dressing, making and finishing") echo at a rhetorical level the lists of verbs ("broke ... digged and wrought ... felled and framed") and nouns ("oxen ... iron and stones ... timber ... plough, mill, oven ... utensils") by which Locke affirms that the natural world becomes valuable property only through human labor. In part, Crusoe's Lockean meditation on bread seems designed to draw attention to his solitary condition: the complex social orchestra of laborers in Locke is reduced, on Crusoe's island, to a one-man-band. But Crusoe's bread-making also acquires political connotations through its association with Locke. Having undermined Filmer's argument that true sovereignty proceeds from God's gift of dominion to Adam in his *First Treatise of Government*, Locke uses his *Second Treatise* to outline an alternative theory of the origins of government. In a state of nature, Locke contends, all men are free and equal but, because men can be wicked and threaten the property of others, property owners give up some of their God-given freedom and equality in exchange for the protection offered by a sovereign power. When he turns barley into bread, Crusoe becomes a laboring property owner and, therefore, a potential stakeholder in a political system based on popular consent. His rejection of a Jacobite/Filmerian account of the origins of government appears to be complete.

This narrative of political conversion which witnesses Crusoe the Filmerian Adamic monarch turn into Crusoe the Lockean property owner is attractively neat, but it is by no means the whole story of Crusoe's engagement with contemporary ideas about sovereignty. Indeed, in the midst of his apparently Lockean reflections on bread-making, Crusoe strikes a dissonant note when he reflects that he "was reduced to a meer state of nature." Crusoe's "discouragement" in this condition is not necessarily at odds with Locke's assertion that the state of nature is one defined by freedom and equality, but it brings the tone of this passage closer to the pessimistic outlook of an earlier seventeenth-century political theorist: Thomas Hobbes.[15] Locke's vision of the state of nature as a condition of freedom and equality challenges not only Filmer's belief that all humanity is born under subjection to a monarch, but also Hobbes' characterization, in *Leviathan* (1651), of "the condition of mere Nature" as "a condition of Warre of every man against every man."[16] Hobbes' influence on Defoe's writing becomes particularly pronounced when Crusoe discovers that his island is not as uninhabited as he had, at first, assumed. If in his bread-making Crusoe adapts and performs Locke's theories, then in describing the impact of the cannibals from the mainland on his own life, he enacts a key aspect of Hobbes' political vision.

Shortly after describing, with horror, his discovery of the human remains of a cannibal feast on the far shore of his island, Crusoe's reflections take an unexpected turn:

> the frights I had been in about these savage wretches, and the concern I had been in for my own preservation, had taken off the edge of my invention for my own conveniences; and I had droppt a good design, which I had once bent my thoughts too much upon; and that was, to try if I could not make some of my barley into malt, and then try to brew my self some beer ... I verily believe, had not these things interven'd, I mean the frights and terrors I was in about the savages, I had undertaken it, and perhaps brought it to pass too; for I seldom gave any thing over without accomplishing it, when I once had it in my head enough to begin it.
>
> But my invention now run quite another way; for night and day, I could think of nothing but how I might destroy some of these monsters in their cruel bloody entertainment. (133)

Crusoe's mental excursion into the world of brewing creates a glitch or rumple in the texture of his prose. His optimistic, self-important reflections upon the possibility of turning the barley that formed his bread into an even more complex product – beer – sit awkwardly between the "horrid spectacle" (131) of the cannibal feast that fills him with "frights and terrors" and his violent expressions of bloodthirsty intent. How can we account for Crusoe's odd narrative digression away from a world of blood, flesh, and horror to one of craft and industry? Understanding the Hobbesian context for Crusoe's meditations helps to turn what appears to be a tonal peculiarity into a political observation.

In *Leviathan*, Hobbes outlines what it might be like to live in the state of nature:

> In such condition there is no place for Industry; because the fruit thereof is uncertain: and consequently no Culture of the Earth; no Navigation, nor use of the commodities that may be imported by Sea; no commodious Building; no Instruments of moving and removing such things as require much force; no

Knowledge of the face of the Earth; no account of Time; no Arts; no Letters; no Society; and which is worst of all, continuall feare, and danger of violent death; And the life of man, solitary, poor, nasty, brutish, and short."[17]

The bleak, spare asyndeton of the final clause of this passage is probably more familiar to readers now than the relentlessly negative anaphora of the clauses that precede it, in which Hobbes rhetorically strips away the arts and industries until only the state of nature remains. Crusoe's meditations on brewing, however, respond to this whole passage. Crusoe's desire to attack the cannibals puts him in a state of war with them since, according to Hobbes, war "consisteth not in actuall fighting; but in the known disposition thereto."[18] In this state, he loses his capacity for what Hobbes calls "industry," "culture," and "knowledge of the face of the earth," or, as Crusoe himself puts it, "invention." One of his remedies for this condition is, likewise, indebted to Hobbes. Before offering to rescue a group of marooned Spanish sailors, Crusoe makes them swear that they "would be entirely under and subjected to his commands; and that this should be put in writing, and sign'd with their hands" (195). His proposed contract is distinctively Hobbesian in flavor: in a state of nature, the Spaniards are free to make a contract with Crusoe but, having done so, they lose their political freedom, ceding their personal, political power to an absolute ruler. If this contract makes Crusoe seem too cut-and-dried a proponent of Hobbesian absolutism, though, Defoe introduces an element of absurdity into proceedings that challenges, without altogether undermining, Crusoe's sense of his own power.[19] Just after he has insisted that the Spaniards sign the contract that will deprive them of all political liberties, Crusoe muses, "How we were to have this done, when I knew they had neither pen or ink … was a question which we never ask'd" (195).

An overview of Defoe's engagement with political writings of the mid- to late-seventeenth century reveals several key, distinctive characteristics. *Robinson Crusoe* addresses texts written from a wide range of political positions, including Robert Filmer's expressions of faith in monarchical rule by divine right, John Locke's promotion of the rights of liberty and property, Thomas Hobbes' averment of the necessity of both government by consent and absolute sovereign power, and others that lie beyond the scope of this chapter.[20] Crusoe alludes to these writings not in an overt way – he never names thinkers explicitly – but rather through verbal echoes that form a polyphony of often antithetic voices rather than a coherent and univocal political philosophy. The tone of his allusions is invariably unstable, sometimes disturbingly so. Fruitless trees trouble his evocation of Filmer's patriarchal philosophy; the "state of nature" in a Lockean passage about property seems to belong more to Hobbes than Locke; and at the height of his Hobbesian power, Crusoe bathetically reflects that he has no paper or ink with which to make a contract. Readers who spot these allusions might reasonably be left wondering how to interpret their incongruities – if, that is, they notice the allusions at all. To modern eyes, references to Filmer, Locke, and Hobbes can seem almost invisible because they are invariably expressed with reference to the crafts and trades (husbandry, baking, brewing, etc.) that Crusoe practices on his island in order to survive.

One way of connecting these distinctive characteristics of *Robinson Crusoe's* engagement with politics is through the biography of their author. Defoe began his working life as a tradesman dealing in, among other things, stockings, bricks, and tiles, before becoming a political writer who espoused a wide range of causes (not all of them consistent with one another) and, finally, a novelist. His roots in trade and industry and his apparent political infidelity provided easy targets for his literary opponents. Charles Gildon's vituperative pamphlet, *The Life and Strange Surprizing Adventures of Mr D— De F—, of London, Hosier* (1719), argues that both the plot of *Robinson Crusoe* and its protagonist-narrator are just as incoherent as the contemptible hosier (or stocking-dealer) who created them. In this narrative, Gildon's fictionalized version of Daniel Defoe declares to Robinson Crusoe, "I have been all my Life that Rambling, Inconsistent Creature, which I have made thee."[21] To Gildon, the wide range of Defoe's political references, their unstable tone, and their focus on craft and trade are all connected to the money-grubbing, unprincipled character of their mercantile, hack author. I want to suggest, however, that there are ways of connecting the range, tone, and focus of Crusoe's political reflections other than those suggested by Charles Gildon – ways that illuminate not so much the author Daniel Defoe as the extraordinary new genre that he helped to create.

In order to make these connections, we need to focus not on Defoe the hosier, but on Crusoe the craftsman. On his island, Crusoe practices a remarkable number and range of crafts and trades. Having arrived on the island as a merchant experienced only in trade, plantations, and maritime navigation, he quickly becomes a baker, a potter, a carpenter, a basket-weaver, a shipwright, a tailor, and even an umbrella maker. Some of these skills he learns as a consequence of applying old-world knowledge in new-world contexts. When he comes to make baskets with the willow-like twigs that he finds on the island, for instance, he observes that "it prov'd of excellent advantage to me now, that when I was a boy, I used to take great delight in standing at a *basket-makers* in the town where my father liv'd, to see them make their *wicker-ware*" (86). He learns to practice carpentry without even this degree of external help, asserting that "I had never handled a tool in my life, and yet in time by labour, application and contrivance, I found at last that I wanted nothing but I could have made it" (55). In his craftsmanship, Crusoe's is optimistic, self-reliant, and, above all, pragmatic rather than idealistic.²² His creations are functional rather than aesthetically pleasing: his wicker ware is "not very handsome" but it is "handy and convenient" (115); his "great ugly clumsy goat-skin umbrella ... was the most necessary thing I had about me" (119). Crusoe is not the kind of character to aim at perfect consistency, whether in the texture of his manufactured goods, the quality of his ideas (remember, he denounces the "drug" that is money only to pocket the gold "upon second thoughts" [47]), or the structure of his narrative, with its unnerving shifts in topic and tone, repetitions and déjà vu, narrative cruxes and impasses.²³ For him, survival is all.

It is in the context of this broader set of ideas about craft practice that we might seek to situate Crusoe's craft-oriented political reflections. His engagement with Filmer, Locke, and Hobbes not only is expressed through the language of trade and industry but also resembles, in terms of its method, the other crafts that Crusoe practices on the island. Crusoe metaphorically tacks, weaves, or hammers together scraps and fragments of old-world political ideas in a new-world setting. He is self-conscious about the aesthetic ugliness of the results, just as he acknowledges the imperfections of his pots, baskets, and clothes. Between a long description of his ugly earthenware and wickerwork and his ugly goat-skin clothes and umbrella, Crusoe reflects:

> It would have made a Stoick smile to have seen me and my little family sit down to dinner; there was my majesty the prince and lord of the whole island; I had the lives of all my subjects at my absolute command. I could hang, draw, give liberty, and take it away, and no rebels among all my subjects. (118)

This self-deprecating pen portrait is overtly ironic not only because of its tone (even the most emotionless of philosophers, Crusoe suggests, might feel its humorous force) but because of its position in the narrative. This monarch with limitless power spends his days making imperfect pots, pipes, baskets, and clothes. His "majesty" is as improvised as "all the mechanick exercises which my necessities put me upon applying myself to" (114).

Robinson Crusoe resembles the literary tradition of utopian island narratives that had proved so popular in the preceding century, but ultimately it belongs to a very different species of writing. This long fictional work is set at a tumultuous period in British political history and alludes to some of the most controversial recent theorists of sovereignty, but it refuses to submit to coherent and consistent political interpretation. Rather than using his literary works to influence the reading public's ideas about the recent political past as he had in satires like *The Consolidator* and *Jure Divino*, Defoe draws on that past to illuminate the peculiarities and complexities of a literary character: Robinson Crusoe. By connecting Crusoe's political ideas with his craft practices, Defoe turns utopia into a novel.

NOTES

1 Daniel Defoe, *Serious Reflections during the Life and Surprising Adventures of Robinson Crusoe* (London, 1720) sig. A2v.

2 The germ out of which Crusoe's adventures grew can be found in early eighteenth-century accounts of a Scottish sailor, Alexander Selkirk, who was stranded in the South Pacific for four years. See Daniel Defoe, *Robinson Crusoe*, ed. John Richetti (Harmondsworth: Penguin, 2001), xiv. All further page references in the text are to this edition.

3 In particular, Defoe was involved with the Duke of Monmouth's unsuccessful rebellion in 1685, which led to the execution of more than 300 rebels. Maximillian E. Novak, *Daniel Defoe: Master of Fictions* (Oxford: Oxford University Press, 2001), 82–90.

4 J. A. Downie, *Robert Harley and the Press: Propaganda and Public Opinion in the Age of Swift and Defoe* (Cambridge: Cambridge University Press, 1979).

5 Paula Backscheider, *Daniel Defoe: Ambition & Innovation* (Lexington, KY: University Press of Kentucky, 1986), 352–6, 430–4.

6 For an interpretation of Crusoe's adventures as a direct, allegorical reflection of mid-seventeenth century British political history, see Michael Seidel, "Crusoe in Exile," *PMLA* 96.3 (1981): 363–74; Tom Paulin analyses *Robinson Crusoe* as a symbolic, allegorical reflection upon Defoe's own experience of political events in his essay, "Crusoe's Secret: Daniel Defoe," in *Crusoe's Secret: The Aesthetics of Dissent* (London: Faber & Faber, 2005), 80–104.

7 Strictly speaking, *The Consolidator* depicts a voyage to the moon rather than to an island. The isolated position of the fictional moon relative to the earth (and the close connection of fictional moon voyages such as Cyrano de Bergerac's *L'Autre monde ou les états et empires de la Lune* (1657) with the tradition of utopian writing) nonetheless situates Defoe's text on the fringes of the allegorical island narrative tradition. On early modern moon voyages, see Mary Baine Campbell, "Impossible Voyages: Seventeenth-Century Space Travel and the Impulse of Ethnology," *Literature and History* 6.2 (1997): 1–17.

8 John Milton, *Paradise Lost*, ed. Alastair Fowler (Harlow: Pearson Education Limited, 2nd edn, 2007), 4.143, 145.

9 Ibid., 4.132–3.

10 In *Jure Divino* (London, 1706) Defoe observes that "I cannot do too much Honour to the Memory of so Masterly a Genius" as Milton (p. 226).

11 Robert Fleming, *The History of Hereditary Right* (London, 1711), title page.

12 Milton, *Paradise Lost*, 4.629.

13 Readings of *Robinson Crusoe* which emphasize Defoe's debt to Locke include Ian A. Bell, "King Crusoe: Locke's Political Theory in *Robinson Crusoe*," *English Studies* 69.1 (1988): 27–36 and Maximillian E. Novak, "Crusoe the King and the Political Evolution of His Island," *Studies in English Literature, 1500–1900* 2.3 (1962): 337–50.

14 John Locke, *Two Treatises of Government*, ed. Peter Laslett (Cambridge: Cambridge University Press, 1960; rev. edn 1992), 299.

15 For an interpretation of Defoe's writings which emphasizes their debt to Hobbes, see Carol Kay, *Political Constructions: Defoe, Richardson, and Sterne in Relation to Hobbes, Hume, and Burke* (Ithaca, NY: Cornell University Press, 1988).

16 Thomas Hobbes, *Leviathan*, ed. Richard Tuck (Cambridge: Cambridge University Press, 1991), 96.

17 Ibid., 89.

18 Ibid., 88–9.

19 Rachel Carnell argues that political instruction in *Robinson Crusoe* depends upon readers repeatedly questioning and challenging the political ideas that Crusoe himself articulates and appears to embody (see Rachel Carnell, *Partisan Politics, Narrative Realism, and the Rise of the British Novel* (Basingstoke: Palgrave Macmillan, 2006), pp. 85–90).

20 Maximillian E. Novak in *Defoe and the Nature of Man* (London: Oxford University Press, 1963) explores Defoe's engagement with continental natural law theorists Hugo Grotius and Samuel Pufendorf; Coby Dowdell demonstrates his engagement with Whig political theory in "'A Living Law to Himself and Others': Daniel Defoe, Algernon Sidney, and the Politics of Self-Interest in *Robinson Crusoe* and *Farther Adventures*," *Eighteenth-Century Fiction* 22.3 (2010): 415–42; and in *Defoe's Politics: Parliament, Power, Kingship, and Robinson Crusoe* (Cambridge: Cambridge University Press, 1991), Manuel Schonhorn depicts Defoe as a committed royalist wedded to Old Testament-inspired ideas of the warrior king.

21 Charles Gildon, *The Life and Strange Surprizing Adventures of Mr. D— De F—, of London, Hosier* (London, 1719), x.

22 His attitude is very different from that of modern theorists of craftsmanship such as the sociologist Richard Sennett, who defines this quality as "an enduring, basic human impulse, the desire to do a job well for its own sake" (Richard Sennett, *The Craftsman* (London: Penguin, 2008), 9). An excellent account of Defoe's more pragmatic, contingent concept of craftsmanship can be found in Margaret Cohen, *The Novel and the Sea* (Princeton: Princeton University Press, 2010).

23 For an insightful analysis of the structure of *Robinson Crusoe*, see Michael Seidel, "*Robinson Crusoe*: Varieties of Fictional Experience," in *The Cambridge Companion to Daniel Defoe*, ed. John Richetti (Cambridge: Cambridge University Press, 2009), 182–99.

PART II

Robinson Crusoe in the Wider World

7

CARL FISHER

Innovation and Imitation in the Eighteenth-Century Robinsonade

The Origins of a Genre

Few narratives have proven as immediately impactful and yet continually enduring as Defoe's *Robinson Crusoe*. Alongside many editions and almost immediate translation, myriad adaptations of the Crusoe story appeared. The Robinsonade became a recognizable eighteenth-century genre, as many authors took Crusoe's "Strange Surprizing Adventures" as a starting point for an array of narrative possibilities. Of course, Defoe did not create the story in a vacuum; he had mastered many genres that come together in his novel from a writing life that included travel narratives, pirate tales, journalism, political pamphlets, and other contemporary forms. Just as *Robinson Crusoe* distilled many of these elements in an intricate balance, the Robinsonade refers to its source by directing readers to the narrative line of the novel but strikes out anew with each iteration. As the Russian critic, Mikhail Bakhtin, put it, "A genre is always the same and yet not the same, always old and new simultaneously. Genre is reborn and renewed at every new stage in the development of literature and in every individual work of a given genre … A genre lives in the present, but always *remembers* its past, its beginning."[1]

The Robinsonade's archetypal dimension resonates with its eighteenth-century audience while incorporating recognizable realistic elements for an era in which sea travel was understood to be extremely dangerous. The main character was the subject of identification, whether the shipwrecked sailor, the castaway islander, the isolated individual, the pragmatic realist, the questioning soul, the utopian visionary, the damned rebel, or the saved pilgrim. The Robinsonade weaves together many disparate elements and creates a genre which can be traced to Defoe's novel from which it takes its name and which in every variation remembers its origins.

The Robinsonade employs quintessential elements of the novel from which it springs, sometimes directly and sometimes obliquely, to rewrite the

Crusoe story, utilizing many of the narrative techniques of Defoe's broad writing tool-kit. Although Robinsonades were published within the same year of the initial publication of *Robinson Crusoe*, the first published use of the term "Robinsonade" (the standard English term for describing the genre) comes from a 1731 German novel, Johann Gottfried Schnabel's *Der Insel Felsenburg*.[2] Extensive bibliographies show how the Robinsonade has become a place both for referring to the original and for remarkable generic hybridity and interfacing. The Crusoe motif and design variously entertains children, emphasizes educational models, highlights female heroines, creates utopian or dystopian worlds, and goes beyond the novel to film, television, even video games adaptation, online apps, and interactive gaming.

Centered on one of the most versatile narrative archetypes, the Robinsonade's history after *Robinson Crusoe* initially begins as a travel and adventure story – and there were many similar stories before Defoe, now often known as pre-Robinsonades (like Henry Neville's *The Isle of Pines* [1668]) – but the richness and uniqueness of Defoe's novel is really the best starting point. There are an infinite number of ways to adapt the details of the original so that a Robinsonade can be about nature or human nature, explore economics and social relations, or switch genders. It synchronically remembers the past, accentuates the present, and anticipates the future. It is prone to intended and unintended ideologies, and as many possible interpretations. *Robinson Crusoe* fits within Bakhtin's concept of "the novel of ordeal," in which the hero is constantly tested, but succeeding Robinsonades are often much more like the *Bildungsroman*.[3] For authors and audiences, the great durability of the Robinsonade is rooted in the expectation that any Crusoe-inspired tale requires resilience and projects a blank tableau, almost literally, which allows variation on a primary motif: the main character is not named Robinson (usually), is shipwrecked (usually), and must undergo trials and tribulations (always) in order to survive (usually). Bibliographers have wrestled with how to define the parameters of the Robinsonade since the late eighteenth century, and often include proto-Robinsonades (precursors to the actual novel) and pseudo-Robinsonades (which avoid the island solitude but incorporate Crusoe themes), and the attempt to identify and list has developed a new life on the internet. The Crusoe archetype continues to be used as a plot device and character trope. Robinsonades may be derivative, some are absurd, but the genre is simultaneously recognizable and relatable in its central narrative concept and unique in its many imaginative possibilities in virtually any age. The focus in this chapter is on the Robinsonade as a novel – the longer form that allows exposition – but there were many chapbook titles in the eighteenth century and children's books beginning in the nineteenth century, and the original character and novel are noted in innumerable contemporary news stories, poems, and other genres. The references are not always to the novel but to the enduring qualities of the novel that center the many adaptations.

Robinson Crusoe's Resonance in Eighteenth-Century Anglo-American Adaptations

For literary historians and critics, identifying, cataloguing, and interpreting the Robinsonade is ongoing. From the narrowest variations found in translations to the broadest imaginative possibilities, eighteenth-century writers recognized the market-value of the Crusoe story, and used the adventure tale as a core concept to ride the commercial coattails of the original novel. Sometimes a travel story is just that, an attempt to capitalize on the rage for fictionalized escape or *terra incognita*. But more often than not appropriations and adaptations of the Crusoe story explore ideas, camouflaged by the adventure story, to delve into relevant social issues, political ideologies, religious beliefs, concepts of human nature, and the need to define and maintain societal order.

The Robinsonade became so popular in the eighteenth century because it fulfilled a number of expectations for the growing reading public. The main character had to live by his or her wits, working indefatigably to survive in a world in which they were the agents of their own survival. Despite Crusoe's self-sufficiency, with which a reader might identify, there was always a tension with the environment and a sense that isolation was cruel and unusual. Crusoe and his successors in the genre would learn to make the best of a bad situation, but would always long for a more recognizable, more connected, more comforting reality. Far from being an ideal, isolation was an imposed state. Crusoe accumulates because that is both a means to an end and an imbedded principle. He controls what he can of his environment, and does his best to foresee problems ahead. He stays as sane as he can, under the circumstances, but his longing for companionship and community is constant. The tension that the narrative creates, of the isolated human both within and against the environment, of the desire for agency in the world, of the evocation of the survival instinct, does not require the island isolation of *Robinson Crusoe*, but the narrative resonates because it encouraged identification with the striving impulse that typified the age.

The first Crusoe imitations were published within months of the original novel, and *Robinson Crusoe* remained a consistent model throughout the century. The first direct imitation meant to capitalize on the success of the original was probably *The Adventures, and Surprizing Deliverances, Of James Dubourdieu*, published along with *The Adventures of Alexander*

Vendchurch in 1719, the same year in which *Crusoe* is published. Like many succeeding Robinsonades, the title announces the premise of travel and an isolating incident (an island is most often involved) from which there is an escape. Many Robinsonades such as these attempt to capitalize on the popularity of *Robinson Crusoe*. Not very memorable, they still have many paradigmatic elements. Whether a Robinsonade is still read today or remains part of eighteenth-century ephemera often rests on a number of factors, including the variability from the original, the quality of prose, the complexity of the narrative, the believability of the main character(s), and sometimes simply changes in audience through time. In part, Defoe's Crusoe was so popular a character because an audience in that time (and perhaps any time) could identify with his anxieties, doubts, travails, and desires. Scenes became memorable, helped by iconic images that accompanied many editions (for example, illustrations of the goat-skin hat and clothing, the umbrella, the footprint, Friday's gesture). Lesser works remain relevant because while they may lack the complexity of the original, they engage topics of contemporary resonance for cultural studies, often dealing with gendered depictions or colonial tendencies or sexual mores.[4] Even almost 300 years after publication, these works can provide deep background on what was read and thought in the eighteenth century.

Two British examples are paradigmatic of the hold the Robinsonade had on the eighteenth-century reading public – Peter Longueville's *The Hermit* (1727) and Robert Paltock's *The Life and Adventures of Peter Wilkins* (1750) – both for how they reshape the Crusoe story and for how they diverge from it. *The Hermit* follows the Robinsonade formula closely, but like most Robinsonades, the text has enough variations to pique interest and encourage readership. The main character, Philip Quarll, resembles Crusoe in types of experience, including conflicts with natives and continuing self-analysis. However, the narrative is written in the third person, so it loses much of the immediacy of *Robinson Crusoe*, and Quarll idealizes his sufferings, heightening his Christian devotion to critique the world he left. When he is "discovered" at eighty-eight years old, Quarll refuses the opportunity to leave the island. He is, literally, a hermit by choice, and has no interest in returning to society.

By contrast, *Peter Wilkins* is like an odd mashup of *Robinson Crusoe* and *Gulliver's Travels*. The novel features a voyage to Africa, and a shipwreck forces Wilkins to live like Crusoe for a time, near Antarctica. But he finds an escape route to hidden caves that lead him to a mysterious land of "Glumms" and "Gawrys," who have learned to fly with mechanical wings. Wilkins marries one of the native people, and he tries to teach the people how to live well (i.e., by eighteenth-century standards). He attempts to return home when he is widowed but dies within sight of the British shore at Plymouth. The novel is certainly a Robinsonade, but the tonal emphasis is on the odd experiences rather than the character's struggles. Peter Wilkins is uncritical of the world he left, or of the one he found, and except for the pathos of the ending leans toward fantasy. In fact, when the novel is reprinted and reaches new popularity in the early nineteenth century, it is hailed for its imagination and is now seen as a forerunner of science fiction (for example, Jules Verne's 1874 novel *Mysterious Island*). In addition to the isolated island, like so many utopian/dystopian narratives Robinsonades emphasize the disconnect between the existence which readers would take for granted, their own historical daily contexts of living, and use a form of estrangement to show that things could be different than they are. By showing what could be better, or worse, it allows analysis of the present.

Eighteenth-century authors quickly saw the potential of creating female versions of *Robinson Crusoe*; while *Crusoe* is so masculinist in its characters and plot, the reading audience was increasingly female, and wanted to see women in leading roles. Penelope Aubin (1679–1738), in *The Strange Adventures of the Count de Vinevil* (1721), highlights the adventures of a daughter, Ardelisa, who is shipwrecked on an island, as the long title tells us, "with Violetta, a Venetian Lady, the Captain of the Ship, a Priest, and five Sailors." In other words, not a solitary figure but enough people for a communal society. In her preface to the novel, Aubin explains her purpose: "As for the truth of what this Narrative contains, since Robinson Cruso [*sic*] has been so well received, which is more improbable, I know no Reason why this should be thought a Fiction." Aubin plays on the common dynamic of the time in which authors want fiction to be read as real, in a publishing/reading world where histories and news have a constant market, but she also puts the focus on shipwrecked women among men.[5]

Many female Robinsonades have been reclaimed by recent critical studies, and so has the transatlantic tale, which is tailor-made for Crusoe rewritings. Within the Anglo-American tradition there are dozens of eighteenth-century Robinsonades which incorporate object lessons on morality, especially for an American colonial audience. For example, John Barnard's *Ashton's Memorial* (1725), in which Philip Ashton escapes from pirates to live on a desolate island for sixteen months, has a sermon attached that is designed as an afterword for shaping readers' view on what they have seen in the story. The transatlantic tale would be appreciated on either side of the Atlantic, and was often available in both Britain and the colonies (this novel is published in Boston first and reprinted in London in 1726). These adventure stories stress the presumably civilizing influence of Western thought and practice, but when they are read now it is usually through postcolonial criticism of colonialist ideology.

Eighteenth-century Crusoes were almost all "Extraordinary" or "Astonishing," "Surprising" or "Surprizing." Despite their spectacle, most eighteenth-century Robinsonades are best understood historically within their context of production. Jeanine Blackwell, writing about the female Robinsonade, points out that the picaresque-influenced heroines of earlier eighteenth-century Robinsonades give way to weaker, weeping versions as the century goes on, following the trends of literary and cultural history. The same is true for male-dominated versions. And context matters, because sometimes the Robinsonade goes in a contrapuntal direction. In 1782, for example, Thomas Spence, a well-known English radical, claims to bring the original novel up to date in *A Supplement to the History of Robinson Crusoe, being the History of Crusonia, or Robinson Crusoe's Island, Down to the Present Time*. His polemical pamphlet highlights common ownership of land and communal living, and is a precursor to his own imagined utopian republic, Spensonia. Elements of the utopian archetype mingle with Spence's political views to create an ideal world of equality that would not have been shared by many readers in his time. So while the Robinsonade adapts always to its historical contexts, these contexts continue to play a role in the ebb and flow of Robinsonade production and reception as the original and its adaptations are interpreted. In a sense, each age replicates the central elements of the genre, or interprets it differently, but always reveals the Robinsonade that best fits its needs.

The French Embrace Robinson: From Adventure Tale to Educational Narrative

The concept of Crusoe clearly captures the public imagination in a way that permeates European culture and encourages imitation and invention beyond eighteenth-century British examples. Defoe's unique narrative was translated and published quickly on the continent, and had numerous imitators abroad, including Swiss, Dutch, and Spanish variations on the Crusoe theme. France and Germany provide the most fertile ground for the development of the Robinsonade and adapt their models fittingly for each national context.

Early French Robinsonades capture the spirit of the French novel to that time, emphasizing the imaginary voyage and the adventure story, including islands inhabited only by lovers, Greek shepherds, or prehistoric humans. French writers incorporated and developed the Robinsonade because it was such a common literary plot from at least the mid-seventeenth century as to require little enhancement; the publication and dissemination of the novel in English and French translation added resonance to an existing genre.

The biggest paradigm shift in the eighteenth-century Robinsonade, not just in France but throughout Europe, comes with Jean-Jacques Rousseau's idealization of the original novel as an educational tool in *Émile* (1762). Rousseau's principle of training the sentiments as well as the mind and body extended the sensibility of the novel, while maintaining that learning the lessons and passing the tests of self-sufficiency are considered essential to well-being.

Rousseau's influence can be seen especially in a number of French Robinsonades in which men and women together are castaways. To take one example, Grivel's *L'Ile inconnue* [The Unknown Island] (1783–7, 6 volumes) openly acknowledges its resemblance to *Robinson Crusoe* and purposefully gives his castaway a female companion, which is designed to emphasize the civilizing possibilities of a sentimental education in which emotional development plays a role along with intellectual insight and survival skills. But while the novel may embody liberal bourgeois ideology, it has striking scenes of violence, including torturing cannibals. Adult readers might be open to narrative influence, but often maintain the habits of mind they bring with them to a text. Novels for and about younger people, who are still in the developmental process, start to be written more often and castaway tales involving children and teenagers became more common. Bernardin de Saint-Pierre's *Paul et Virginie* (1788) creates a sentimental island paradise where young lovers learn virtue. It is set in Mauritius and has much praise for the communal life there, and critiques French social inequality in a prelude to French Revolutionary thought. After the French Revolution, in *Histoire de Sudmer; ou Robinson Crusoé rétabli dans son intégrité* (1802) the author rewrites the story presumably to return integrity to the Crusoe story, and implicitly to critique what is seen as a corrupt, unstable, and violent political culture. It tells of a castaway who never returns, like Peter Wilkins, but his refusal to return to civil society has a different force in a post-French Revolutionary era. The island is seen as more hospitable than the world at home. Like Spence's updated supplemental "history" of Crusonia, which can be understood best in context of the development of British radical thought, this novel can best be understood by seeing it as a rejection of the values of the French Revolutionary era.

German Literature Adopts and Adapts
Robinson Crusoe: The Kreutznauer Connection

While *Robinson Crusoe* has a strong impact on French letters, it is even more influential on German literary production. The novel, through immediate translation and wide dissemination, provided a model that was particularly timely for German literary culture. The first German Robinsonade is usually considered *Der Teutsche Robinson oder Bernhard Creutz* (1722), but there are dozens of Crusoe imitations throughout Germany in the eighteenth century, including many female heroines and some that had specific regional qualities. German authors and readers found in *Robinson Crusoe* a kindred spirit, a departure from adventure-oriented *romans* and a movement toward the rational and realistic. To say that German audiences embraced the Robinsonade concept puts the case mildly. Defoe's Crusoe speaks to the German imagination and was adopted by German writers as one of their own; after all, Defoe highlights the German origins of the character's family, Kreutznauer, with his father from Bremen, and the many virtues of his personal behavior as being in the Germanic tradition. While French Robinsonades highlight their own national tradition, first the adventure story and then the affinity for nature, the German Robinsonade immediately emphasizes the genre's educational potential, and highlights social elements as an opportunity to question, critique, reform, or recreate society. Not that there is a single monolithic French or German Robinsonade, but these are the broad strokes of how the novels diverge in each cultural setting.

Some of the most extensive bibliographical work on the Robinsonade has been in German, in part because there were so many German Robinsonades. There is as much social history in the popularity of the Robinsonade as there is a developing literary aesthetic, as German audiences embraced the work ethic and self-sufficiency as a model of individual redefinition. Since most German readers would be expected to know *Robinson Crusoe*, at least in translation, there was a probable market for more, and German writers embracing the Robinsonade genre take advantage of this background knowledge to actively engage in a dialogue with the novel. The most original early version is Schnabel's *Die Insel Felsenburg* (mentioned above for the first use of the term "Robinsonade"). It is about a ship wrecked on the coast of an island, during the Thirty Years War, where the main character marries and starts a family of 300. It is in the social utopian strain of the Robinsonade, creating a world apart from violence. It was so popular in its time that German author Arno Schmidt wrote in a review to a 1960 reissue of the book that, in 1750, anyone who had the ability to read and the means to own two books would have a copy of *The Bible* and *Die Insel Felsenburg*. The novel's title was extremely long, and in the tradition of many eighteenth-century novels it summarized much of the plot and introduced the main characters. It went through many editions and reprintings, but only became known as *Die Insel Felsenburg* when Ludwig Tieck abridged, retitled, and republished it in 1828.

The same audience that read Schnabel found the narrative of Bachstrom's *Land der Inquiraner* (1736) relevant, and for similar reasons. The main plot has prisoners persecuted by the Inquisition escape and sail toward freedom. They are shipwrecked and scattered on a number of islands, eventually to be reunited on a central island. However, the survivors decide that to escape the long arm of the Spanish Inquisition, and the threat to their beliefs, they must sail to Africa to create an ideal community. As in Schnabel's novel, threats to personal integrity, whether from physical violence or religious persecution, are resolved by utopian impulses.

Later eighteenth-century German Robinsonades remain in dialogue with *Robinson Crusoe*, even when they stray in terms of plot and character. Two works from around 1780 show the continuing grip of Defoe's themes, Joachim Heinrich Campe's *Robinson der Jüngere* (1779–80) and Johann Karl Wezel's *Robinson Krusoe: Neu bearbeitet* (1779–80). The former takes the Crusoe experience as developmentally formative. Rather than a story of sea travel or shipwreck, however, it features a father who takes his family to an idyllic, isolated area outside Hamburg to create an artificial island, so that they can learn how to live well apart from the corrupting influences of society. The novel is structured as a pedagogical exercise, a dialogue in which the father describes elements of Robinson's life as an educational tool and the children ask questions. It incorporates Rousseauian ideas about human development, although it is not entirely in concord with either Defoe or Rousseau. It argues for communal good over the individual will, critiques slavery, and insists that any value added to survivor development only has use when returned to society.

By contrast with the moral idealization of Campe's text, Wezel's novel creates a colony that goes through the stages of civilization. It has elements that create parallelism and direct contrasts with Crusoe, but it emphasizes issues of power, governance, slavery, and the meaning of civilization over pedagogy or plot development, as a set of philosophical conflicts. Wezel, in fact, takes the Robinsonade in a direction that suggests that the way humanity conducts itself is destructive, and that the Enlightenment has not led to a kinder, gentler world. In the novel, competing forces, internal and external, ultimately lead not to a happy ending, whether a return to the world or the creation of an ideal community, but to the destruction of the colony.

The trajectory continues through the eighteenth century, and the influence of *Robinson Crusoe* filtered through the German rewritings can be seen in Goethe's *Sorrows of Young Werther*, a novel of education in which Goethe dramatizes the logical endpoint of a world of sentimental education, and highlights the dilemma of an individual influenced by Rousseauian concepts. Goethe acknowledged that *Robinson Crusoe* influenced his writing of *Wilhelm Meisters Lehrjahre* (1795–6), considered a paradigmatic *Bildungsroman* about the formation of character from experience and the desire to give meaning to life.

Publishing history and bibliographies provide evidence that *Robinson Crusoe* and the German Robinsonade were popular and influential not only in the eighteenth century but beyond. For example, few eighteenth-century Robinsonades are as beloved as Johann David Wyss's 1812 novel *Der Schweizerische Robinson* (Anglicized to *The Swiss Family Robinson*), which Jill Campbell deals with extensively in Chapter 12 of this volume. Given the overwhelming success of the Robinsonade in Germany, and the utopian element of German Robinsonades that focus on community values, it is understandable why Karl Marx in *Das Kapital* points to *Robinson Crusoe* as an example of economic formation, where the critical concept is use value and labor value, not accumulation. German writers populate their imagined islands with communities and families, meant to show industrious solidarity as an ideal, a means to a fairer world. Marx also argues in *Grundrisse* that the most important element of many eighteenth-century Robinsonades – even the fact that he mentions the many adaptations shows their resonance – is not the isolated individual, but the way in which the story prefigures the development of civil society after the French Revolution as an antidote to capitalist individualism. He sees in the novel a Hegelian dialectic, action and reaction, and he projects that through the constant ebb and flow humanity can reach new and perhaps better historical realities.

From Monologue to Dialogue: Crusoe's Continuing Afterlife in the Robinsonade

The primary developments of the eighteenth-century Robinsonade occur in Britain, France, and Germany, with wide circulation and adaptation. Like all works with mythic substructures, *Robinson Crusoe* is eminently adaptable to different times and spaces. Like the novel itself, the Robinsonade's dueling concepts of entertainment and enlightenment remain central to its appeal. While my emphasis in this chapter is the eighteenth-century triangulation of the novel in British, French, and German contexts, every literary period produces Robinsonades written for specific social and national contexts and the audience of its own time and space. Almost every culture has its own Crusoe story, a Robinsonade which reshapes the character and often revises the plot drastically, sometimes with just a core or a kernel or a reference to the original story and character. The connection to *Robinson Crusoe*, even in contrapuntal relationship, renders a kind of authenticity and testifies to the influence and endurance of the original.

There are innumerable literary and other cultural texts which find their originary idea in Defoe's novel. Cultural history shows that there are nodes to Crusoe crazes, but Crusoe is rarely absent since 1719 and Robinsonades are produced consistently. Many of these works are ephemeral, mere footnotes to the prevailing taste of their time, market-driven imitations meant to exploit commercial possibility, and commentators often critique the "non-literary" aspects of many Robinsonades, but each Robinsonade has a culturally and temporally specific quality. Some of these works are groundbreaking reimaginings or retellings. Others are pale imitations. Sometimes the reference is shallow but it spins off in many directions, like a meme that is imaginatively appropriated, reclaimed, reconstructed, and sent off on its own to unknown audiences. Increased critical attention reinterprets the original novel but also highlights the many adaptations in literary history. The use of the Robinsonade as postcolonial reality (i.e., Tournier's *Friday* or Coetzee's *Foe*) may speak back to the original text, but it also encourages rereading the original, and popular culture adaptations remain a staple (*Cast Away*; *Survivor*; *Lost*), but all these appropriations continue a cultural dialogue with the original *Robinson Crusoe*. Conceptually, the narrative speaks forcefully to every generation. The Robinsonade hero (or heroine, or heroes) must manage difficult transitions to a world they did not create, often hostile to their existence, and survive through intelligence, industry, and improvisation to overcome isolation.

Robinsonades fulfill the requisites of what Bakhtin describes as "the novel of ordeal" and influence the development of the *Bildungsroman*. As a genre, the Robinsonade embraces contradictions, many of the same ones with which Crusoe grapples, precisely because ideas and ideals are often at odds with physical realities. Robinsonades try to find tenable solutions to the complications and paradoxes of life: can there be reward without risk, redemption without sin, homecoming without exile? Is being isolated a form of purgatory, or is hell other people? Is home really heaven, or is the goal elsewhere or always out of reach? Robinsonades can alter the physical details of the novel – the food, dress, number of castaways, construction of living environment – and there are infinite variations and permutations to the original storyline, such as the shipwreck, the exotic setting, the taming of nature, the available resources, the length of isolation, their reason/purpose/rationale for travel, their adventures before and after their shipwreck, or their reabsorption into the world, as well as their unique thoughts and perspectives.

Both the story (and the character) are known almost everywhere. *Robinson Crusoe* and Robinsonades engage audiences precisely because either forces readers to put themselves in that spot, to project themselves in that situation, to walk in those shoes (or without any). Complex Robinsonades go beyond incorporating discernible tropes to explore the psychological and emotional stress of survival, solitude, and contact with others. Readers might imagine a Robinsonade as a form of entertainment, but they also use it as a measure of how they would handle the obstacles and challenges of similar situations. The realism that carries the novel forward, the depiction of an ordinary person in an unexpected environment, is an ongoing inheritance.

In this sense, Robinsonades call into question the essence of the human condition, the competing interests of individual need and social inter-action. The educational, economic, and interpersonal underpinnings of these texts keep them relevant, and create an ongoing, multidirectional dia-logue. Robinsonades go beyond the spectacle of sheer survival but show how an individual or community can capitalize on what is available and create something habitable, safe, and sustainable. The Robinsonade keeps Crusoe a dialogical figure, always involved in multiple conversations, endlessly reincarnated, reliving the same or similar situations in different contexts, which allows Defoe's text to maintain resonance long past 1719. Interestingly, perhaps a bit dismissively, an 1860 French novel was entitled *Le dernier Robinson* [The Last Robinson, E. de La Bedolliere]. The irony of this title is delicious, for while the eighteenth-century was a hotbed for the genre, there will probably never be an end to the Robinsonade. What began in England became a Europe-wide phenomenon, a durable story type which is still being written today.

NOTES

1 Mikhail Bakhtin, *Problems of Dostoevsky's Poetics*, ed. and trans. Caryl Emerson (Minneapolis, MN: University of Minnesota Press, 1984), 106.
2 The term *Robinsonade* has multiple variations. In German, *Robinsoniade* is sometimes used, in French, the term is *Robinsonnade*, and in literary criticism it is common to find *Robinsoniad*.
3 Mikhail Bakhtin, *Speech Genres and Other Late Essays*, ed. Michael Holquist and Caryl Emerson, trans. Vern McGee (Austin, TX: University of Texas Press, 1986). Bakhtin distinguishes between the typical travel tale and "the novel of ordeal" in the essay "The *Bildungsroman* and Its Significance in the History of Realism (Toward a Historical Typology of the Novel)" (pp. 10–19).
4 See *The Authentic Relation of the many Hardships and Sufferings Of a Dutch Sailor* (1728), included as a castaway narrative in Evan Davis's Broadview edition of *Robinson Crusoe* (2010). Presumably based on a journal found on an island by a British captain and published anonymously, it tells the first-person story of a sailor left on an island by his ship for committing sodomy. It had multiple editions, and led to a moralizing response pamphlet entitled *The Just Vengeance of Heaven Exemplify'd* (1730).

5 Evan Davis includes a selection from Aubin's novel in an appendix to the Broadview edition of *Robinson Crusoe*, including the preface selection quoted here, to highlight the ways in which Crusoe quickly influenced literary production. Female Robinsonades, including *The Female American; or, The Adventures of Unca Eliza Winkfield* (1767) and Charles Dibdin's *Hannah Hewit; Or, The Female Crusoe* (1792), have had a great deal of scholarly interest, especially for their transgressive qualities, or for how they complicate contemporary views of gender and race in the eighteenth century.

8

HELEN THOMPSON

The Crusoe Story: Philosophical and Psychological Implications

In his influential account of Daniel Defoe's *Robinson Crusoe*, Ian Watt defines the novel's relation to "[t]he division of labour."[1] By splitting productive work into increasingly specialized tasks, Watt suggests, the division of labor jeopardizes "our completeness as men."[2] For Watt, *Robinson Crusoe* reverses the breakdown of holistic self-sustenance into remunerative work by offering "substitute experiences" in the medium of print. Watt evokes the significance of the imaginative panacea provided by Crusoe's solitary attempt at survival, an attempt "which the reader can share vicariously":[3]

> The appeal of these efforts is surely a measure of the depth of the deprivations involved by economic specialisation, deprivations whose far-reaching nature is suggested by the way our civilisation has reintroduced some of the basic economic processes as therapeutic recreations: in gardening, home-weaving, pottery, camping, woodwork and keeping pets.[4]

Whether he undertakes "therapeutic recreations" or reads *Robinson Crusoe*, the individual who occupies an age of economic specialization can reconstitute work's lost completeness. Aligned with crafts like "home-weaving," *Robinson Crusoe*'s popular appeal testifies to the novel's success as a purveyor of traditional experience. When, in his third year on the island, Crusoe decides that he will try to "botch up some such pot"[5] to hold his grains, *Crusoe*'s reader partakes in the restorative therapy delivered, Watt argues, by hobbies like pottery as well as by a literary genre – the novel – whose rise salves the deprivations attendant on economic modernity.

To frame the philosophical and psychological implications of *Robinson Crusoe*, however, I will suggest that the mandate and conditions for Crusoe's achievement of productive competence on the island depart from those of contemporary hobbyists. Most notably, Crusoe lacks instruction. While present-day DIY crafters take classes and watch YouTube, the castaway Crusoe enacts the strictly solitary acquisition of technical proficiency. All by himself, Crusoe arrives at the mechanical or artisanal competence also designated *scientia*, a word that historically implicates not just learned practice but, as Jole Shackelford explains, "knowledge of a process."[6] Shipwrecked on September 30, 1659, Crusoe records his first foray into productive work, his attempt to build a table and chair, on November 4 of the same year. Having taken a month to retrieve an arsenal of materials and instruments from his grounded ship, Crusoe voices the premise that justifies his ensuing achievement of *scientia*: "So I went to work; and here I must needs observe, that ... by stating and squaring every thing by reason, and by making the most rational judgment of things, every man may be in time master of every mechanick art" (55). With neither expert guidance nor previously inculcated skills – as he notes of his lack of specialized training, "I had never handled a tool in my life" (55) – Crusoe will make himself "master of every mechanick art" by deploying his own "judgment" and "reason." His anticipated mastery marks Defoe's claim for the sufficiency of inductive understanding. Alone on the island, lacking theoretical and practical schematics, Crusoe recapitulates the progress of artisanal knowledge as he grapples with the making of things.

Crusoe's inductive arrival at mechanical mastery does not, of course, reinvent anything. Midway through his months-long "experiment" (97) botching pots, when he changes the "end" (96) of his efforts from dry to wet storage, Crusoe stipulates that "to hold what was liquid," he must "order my fire to make it burn me some pots" (96). At this juncture, Crusoe exhibits knowledge acquired in advance: although he has never handled a tool in his life, he understands that to contain fluids, clay must be glazed and fired. When he prefaces this portion of the pottery experiment by announcing that "I had no notion of a kiln" (96), Crusoe balances between an inductive pretense to unassisted mechanical mastery and a deductive foreknowledge that glazing requires intense heat. Crusoe's "no notion of a kiln" denies his awareness of the technical specifics of oven-building, but Crusoe deploys an advance understanding of chemical cookery when, having placed his raw vessels in the "embers" (96) of a fire, he observes that "the sand which was mixed with the clay melted by the violence of the heat, and would have run into glass if I had gone on" (97).

Crusoe re-enacts *scientia* already realized by artisans and chemists: his induction is bounded by knowledge already vindicated by experiments he desists from replicating. By divesting Crusoe of training or guidance while arming him with some scientific and technical postulates – which enable him to name sand mixed inside clay as what fuses in the fire to seal his pots – Defoe accommodates inductive and deductive modes of reasoning. Crusoe reconciles inductively achieved manual competence (even if, historically, such technical artistry was indebted to collective sources of wisdom like guilds) and already proven experimental knowledge that enables him to reproduce the object world he has left. *Robinson Crusoe* thus has it both ways: Crusoe recapitulates the reason of already proven practices, but his radical ineptitude affirms the blankness of a mind which could almost be inventing them all anew.

To trace the philosophical import of *Crusoe*'s recombination of inductive and deductive forms of knowledge, we can note the emphasis Defoe places on Crusoe's peculiarly regressive experience of induction:

> It would make the reader pity me, or rather laugh at me, to tell how many awkward ways I took to raise this paste, what odd mishapen ugly things I made, how many of them fell in, and how many fell out, the clay not being stiff enough to bear its own weight ... and in a word, how after having laboured hard to find the clay, to dig it, to temper it, to bring it home and work it, I could not make above two large earthen ugly things, I cannot call them jars. (96)

This paragraph occurs early in the pottery experiment, when Crusoe attempts to make pots suitable for grain by drying hand-molded clay in the sun. As such, it marks the novel's most ludic depiction of his practical liabilities, solicited perhaps by the most recognizably childish activity he undertakes on the island. Of course, the theological resonance of Crusoe's effort "to raise this paste" is unmistakable. Defoe echoes an apostrophe penned by the Old Testament prophet Isaiah: "you are our Father; we are the clay, and you are our potter; we are all the work of your hand."[7] But the humor of the novel's passage derives from Crusoe's comparably restricted creative agency: he fathers "odd mishapen ugly things."

Defoe sustains the regressive momentum of the pottery-making episode when Crusoe later concludes with an equivocal appraisal of its success:

> I wanted no sort of earthen ware for my use; but I must needs say, as to the shapes of them, they were very indifferent, as any one may suppose, when I had no way of making them; but as the children make dirt-pies, or as a woman would make pies, that never learn'd to raise paste. (97)

This synopsis exposes the paradox involved in Defoe's effort to reconcile induction and deduction, for by the close of the pottery experiment, Crusoe has demonstrated a quite sophisticated ability to make his pots watertight. But Defoe summarizes the enterprise with a countervailing emphasis, because at this moment Crusoe is far from resembling either the divine father or the master of every mechanic art. Lacking a wheel to perfect his pots' shapes, Crusoe instead claims as his avatars a woman who cannot bake and children who make dirt-pies. Even though Crusoe deploys chemical wisdom to answer the primary end of use, Defoe closes this scene by amplifying the likeness of Crusoe's productions to juvenile botches. However, by leveling Crusoe's pottery-making and that of a child, Defoe does more than underscore his castaway's incompetence or naïve zeal. Crusoe's resemblance to an untutored woman or child reflects the revolutionary criterion for learning advanced by seventeenth-century empirical scientists and Puritan revolutionaries as well as Dissenting educational reformers of Defoe's day.

In *An Essay upon Projects* (1697), Defoe advances his defense of "An Academy for Women" by insisting that for women as well as men, "as the Rational Soul distinguishes us from Brutes, so Education carries on the distinction, and makes some less brutish than others."[8] Defoe compares Crusoe to an ignorant woman not because she is innately inept, but because neither she nor he has acquired facility in the raising of paste. As testimony to his schooling at the experimental scientist and Dissenting minister Charles Morton's academy at Newington Green, Defoe claims externally imparted education as the primary adjudicator of human distinction, even the distinction of sex. Following both Morton and the empirical philosopher John Locke, Defoe's "Academy for Women" denies essential difference to assert that men and women alike are shaped from the outside in. When he stresses Crusoe's likeness to a child, Defoe rehearses this developmental narrative, whose egalitarian promise is based on a preliminary state of mental emptiness: the infant whose mind Locke's *An Essay concerning Human Understanding* (1690) depicts as an "empty Cabinet"[9] or blank sheet of paper is unencumbered by prejudice, jargon, and arcane scholastic logic. In his *Essay* and elsewhere, Locke claims this initially empty mind as the precondition for renovated understanding that adults must strive to approximate by jettisoning their old ideas: "he that begins to have any doubt of any of his tenets … ought as much as he can to put himself wholly into this state of ignorance in reference to that question and throwing wholly by all his former notions … examin with a perfect indifferency the question."[10] Only the man who "throw[s] wholly by all his former notions" achieves the regression to epistemological childhood that restores his mind to a state of "perfect indifferency." By downplaying Crusoe's retention of some experimental principles, Defoe stages this return in both a material and a geophysical register. Crusoe re-enacts the mandate for empirical learning as he strives to make dirt-pies on a deserted island off the coast of present-day Venezuela.

Charles Webster has shown that a Puritan movement for epistemological reform flourished in the decades between Francis Bacon's early seventeenth-century championing of inductive experimental method and the Restoration of Charles II to the English throne in 1660, the year of Defoe's birth.[11] Defoe's biographical connection to this strand of reformist pedagogy resides in his tutelage under the Dissenting academician Morton from 1674 until "late 1679 or early 1680."[12] Morton, the gist of whose modernizing text-book *Compendium Physicae* (1687) Defoe avers he saved in manuscript for decades,[13] promulgated the new experimental methods endorsed by scientists like Robert Boyle and Isaac Newton rather than, Morton writes, "the Dullheads of the universities."[14] More precisely, Morton's *Compendium* replaces the systems of Aristotelian or scholastic "Dullheads" with English vernacular instruction whose familiarizing treatment of nature relies heavily on the corpuscular or mechanical philosophy of the experimental chemist Boyle. When Morton teaches that the "Elasticity or Springiness" of air may be "Illustrated by a pound of wool which is capable of being thrust into a Quart pot; but when freed of the compression, will of its self expaciate to its former bulck,"[15] he echoes Boyle's influential air-pump trials of atmospheric and hydrostatic pressure, *New Experiments Physico-Mechanicall, Touching the Spring of the Air and its Effects* (1660). Morton's likeness of particles of air to "any Curled hair of wool, [which] may be drawn out to a greater length"[16] and recoil, adopts the claim to superior intelligibility promoted by Boyle's chemical matter theory, which grants particles or corpuscles the causal lucidity entailed by mechanical attributes such as springiness. Crusoe's shipwreck compels him to reprise the Puritans' and Dissenters' reformist epistemology, which is allied at its core with the ambition of empirical science to reinvest language – even language that refers to minuscule parts – with experiential meaning.

Locke's insistence that words refer to sensory impressions is pre-dated by what Webster designates Bacon's "sociology of knowledge" or Bacon's assault, in *The Advancement of Learning* (1605) and elsewhere, on "ideological obstacles"[17] to so-called universal or democratic systems of sense-based understanding. Such impediments had historically been sustained, Bacon writes, by "fantastical learning ... contentious learning ... delicate learning; vain imaginations, vain altercations, and vain affectations."[18] Throughout the Civil War and commonwealth, Puritan reformers like the Czech refugee John Amos Comenius furthered Bacon's attack on abstract scholastic logic and metaphysics because, Webster suggests, "Baconian science was basically anti-authoritarian; its criteria of proof rested on an appeal to experiment which was seen as analogous to personal revelation."[19] As Comenius declares in *A Patterne of Universal Knowledge* (1651), "if the mindes of all men be brought into the open field of things themselves, and there [sic] prejudices being layd aside, freely view not opinions of things but things themselves."[20] According to Comenius, men who are permitted to freely view will not misapprehend: "the matter it selfe instructs us." As evidence for the pedagogical force of things themselves, Comenius reiterates Bacon's valuation of practical as opposed to elite knowledge: "we see it every day in the example of Mechanick Arts, which as it were endued with a vitall spirit, increase dayly, and come to perfection."[21] Alone on the island, Crusoe dramatizes Comenius' example. Exposed to the open field of things, Crusoe manifests improvement at the "Mechanick Arts" that shows his readiness to be taught by the matter itself.

Defoe's *Essay upon Projects* proposes a "Society" which aspires "to establish Purity and Propriety of Stile, and to purge it [language] from all the Irregular Additions that Ignorance and Affectation have introduc'd." In a rare instance of agreement with his political antagonist Jonathan Swift, Defoe stipulates that "There should be room in this Society for neither *Clergyman*, *Physician*, or *Lawyer*."[22] For eighteenth-century Dissenting reformers and Tory satirists alike, the avocations of "*Clergyman*, *Physician*, or *Lawyer*" represent the abdication of reason ensured by hyper-specialized jargon. Doctrinal, medical, and legal cant sunders words from the understanding of any but narrowly learned men. Crusoe's achievement of inductive mastery therefore contributes to a projected goal of linguistic purity that entails more than, as Watt argues, the therapeutic undoing of the division of labor. Instead, Crusoe affirms the Dissenters' commitment to the anti-authoritarian remit of sensory knowledge. Far from the province of elite pedants and professionals, mechanical mastery can be replicated by any mind open to the empirical appeal of things themselves.

Robinson Crusoe also affirms the acquisitive mandate of Baconian science. Writing in *Some Considerations Touching the Usefulness of Natural Philosophy* (1663), Boyle encapsulates the new scientist's possessive stance: "in summe, the whole sublunary World is but his Magazine."[23] Crusoe likewise asserts his property in the things he saves or domesticates. Of the cave containing his "tools, nails, and iron-work," he observes that "it look'd like a general magazine of all necessary things" (56); when he encloses wild goats, he asserts that "the keeping up a breed of tame creatures thus at my hand, would be a living magazine of flesh, milk, butter, and cheese" (121). Whether a magazine of metal or flesh, Crusoe's stores reflect the definition of the possessive individual formulated by Locke in his account of natural and civil society, *Two Treatises of Government* (1690): by mingling the labor of his hand with external bodies, Crusoe establishes his right of possession. (I return below to the tame creatures – including human creatures – whose proprietorship Crusoe assumes.) But as reformist stress on the pedagogical instrumentality of things suggests, possessiveness does not exhaust Crusoe's relation to nature.

As the ideational analog of Boyle's worldly magazine, Locke designates human "*Memory* … the Store-house of our *Ideas*."[24] Memory's stock of perceived ideas ratifies the relation between human understanding and the natural world. The amassed wisdom of any receptive mind, memory's storehouse reflects the influence of the anti-scholastic medical and chemical reformers Paracelsus and Joan Baptista Van Helmont. Walter Pagel glosses Van Helmont's early seventeenth-century medical corpus to affirm the motivating self-reflection that leads the physician to experiment: "All study of nature therefore has to begin with a study of the student, the capacity and specific qualities and faculties of his mind."[25] Such study enables the "assimilation and unification of the intellect with the object" since, Pagel explains, "It is in this very act that the intellect is defined."[26] Locke's *Essay*, which transmits Van Helmont's influence, elaborates human understanding as the understanding of how worldly things are humanly apprehended.[27] By the end of *Robinson Crusoe*, Defoe's protagonist better knows his island world in the sense that he has come to better understand how he *should* know it. Crusoe's renovated self-understanding, the interiorizing directive of this inward-looking novel, hinges on his renovated capacity to understand nature – and, through nature, Defoe's God.

Between January 3 and April 14, 1660, while he builds a wall to fortify his island property, Crusoe undergoes a trial of his understanding that extends the significance of his ability to learn from things themselves. This is Crusoe's famous surprise by the crop he unwittingly sows after shaking out a "little bag, which … had been fill'd with corn for the feeding of poultry" (63) on his ship's penultimate journey from Europe. After emptying the bag of "husks and dust," Crusoe forgets "that I threw this stuff away" when, about "a month after" (63), he discovers shoots of English barley and rice growing beside the rock where he has established his fortification. Crusoe's journalistic retelling of this development magnifies its incredibility:

> It is impossible to express the astonishment and confusion of my thoughts on this occasion; I had hitherto acted upon no religious foundation at all, indeed I had very few notions of religion in my head, or had entertain'd any sense of any thing that had befallen me, otherwise than as a chance, or, as we lightly say, what pleases God; without so much as enquiring into the end of Providence in these things, or his order in governing events in the world: But after I saw barley grow there, in a climate which I knew was not proper for corn, and especially that I knew not how it came there, it startled me strangely, and I began to suggest, that God had miraculously caus'd this grain to grow without any help of seed sown, and that it was so directed purely for my sustenance on that wild miserable place. (63)

"[A]stonishment" that Crusoe finds "impossible" to relate mirrors the apparently impossible apparition of the corn. Oblivious to his prior emptying of the sack and aware that corn is not native to a southern climate, Crusoe reasons that he cannot attribute its growth to the "help of seed sown." Confused and strangely startled, he instead ascribes the crop's appearance to providential intervention. But as Crusoe affirms in advance, this explanatory leap is propelled by "no religious foundation at all": rather than evincing faith, Crusoe's conclusion that the corn is "miraculously caus'd" represents an overly hasty arrogation of divine power. Indeed, because Crusoe narrates the origin of this surmise immediately after he reports that he emptied the bag, Defoe renders the source of his protagonist's mistake transparent: Crusoe forgets what he did a month before, but his reader cannot. This scene thus illuminates the impiety of Crusoe's causal error: himself the barley's sower, Crusoe threatens to substitute God's agency for his own. This God would intercede to repair lacunae in Crusoe's plot occasioned not by miracles but by its narrator's absence of mind.

A divinity who throws stuff away portends the trivialization of providential causality entailed by Crusoe's thoughtless recourse to God. Furthermore, Crusoe's conclusion that the corn cannot possibly come from seed marks an equally grave misstep. By designating the stalks "pure productions of Providence for my support" (63), Crusoe presumes he merits supernumerary intervention that violates the laws of nature. Corn conjured from nothing enlists unnatural forces: Crusoe's belief that "such a prodigy of Nature should happen on my account" (63) reflects self-aggrandizing superstition aggravated by its proximity to the crop's real cause. When Crusoe belatedly recollects that he shook out the sack, he voices the monitory lesson of an experiment which teaches him to locate evidence of divine purpose in events that are wonderful and natural at once:

> [A]t last it occur'd to my thoughts, that I had shook a bag of chickens meat out in that place, and then the wonder began to cease; and I must confess, my religious thankfulness to God's Providence began to abate too upon the discovering that all this was nothing but what was common; tho' I ought to have been as thankful for so strange and unforeseen Providence, as if it had been miraculous; for it was really the work of Providence as to me, that should order or appoint, that 10 or 12 grains for corn should remain unspoil'd, (when the rats had destroy'd all the rest,) as if it had been dropt from Heaven; as also, that I should throw it out in that particular place, where it being in the shade of a high rock, it sprang up immediately; whereas, if I had thrown it away any where else, at that time, it had been burnt up and destroy'd. (64)

The flimsiness of religion predicated on wonder is demonstrated by Crusoe's initial denial of theological import to "what was common." As his requisite for thankfulness, Crusoe demands continual miracles, even if those miracles are spurred by amnesia. With his shift into the conditional tense "ought," however, Defoe broaches the divinity that he, and ultimately Crusoe, sanctions, a divinity that aligns providential purpose and natural causes. Crusoe proves able to identify divine favor transmitted by natural means when he redefines the corn's incredibility. First, "10 or 12 grains ... remain unspoil'd" and unconsumed by rats in a bag that traverses the ocean twice; and second, Crusoe casts the grains unawares upon the only place on the island where they may be shielded from the sun. The rationale for Crusoe's reason to remain thankful is communicated in its enhanced grammatical complexity: the corn appears "*as if* it had been miraculous"; the grains survive "*as if* ... dropped from Heaven." Defoe's "as if" extirpates omniscient agency from these empirically justifiable events, instead positing divine authorship of a world which proceeds to follow nature's laws on its own. But holding the event to a scientific standard does little to mitigate this corn's wondrousness. Because they do not rot or get eaten by rodents, because they land in partial shade – thereby sustaining some likeness to the wondrousness of Crusoe's own salvation from shipwreck – Crusoe's seeds grow. It is no violation of natural law, but a remarkable stretch of empirical probability, that compels Crusoe's continued thankfulness to God.

In *Some Considerations Touching the Usefulness of Natural Philosophy*, Boyle anticipates the revised agency of *Robinson Crusoe*'s God, which pivots on the same "as if" employed by Defoe:

> God ... having resolved, before the Creation, to make such a World as this of Ours, did divide ... that Matter which he had provided into innumerable multitude of very variously figur'd Corpuscles ... and put them into such Motions, that by the assistance of his ordinary preserving Concourse, the *Phænomena*, which he intended should appear in the Universe, must as orderly follow, and be exhibited by the Bodies necessarily acting according to those Impressions or Laws, though they understand them not at all, *as if* each of those Creatures had a Design of Self-preservation, and were furnish'd with Knowledge and Industry to prosecute it; and *as if* there were diffus'd through the Universe an intelligent Being, watchful over the publick Good of it, and careful to Administer all things wisely.[28]

He refuses three forms of agency. First, even though he promotes a theory of particulate matter or corpuscles, he repudiates the cosmogony authored by the materialist atheist philosopher Epicurus, which attributes world-creation to random atomic collision. Second, by declaring that God "put them into such Motions," Boyle denies self-moving power to particles or corpuscles although, with his alchemical colleague Isaac Newton, he does invest them with the capacity to attract and repel. Third, Boyle relieves the orderly operations of nature from supervisory regulation by a God who would continuously intrude to "Administer all things wisely." Once "figur'd" and put in motion, Boyle's matter is not propelled by God, because, Boyle writes, natural bodies are "necessarily acting." Like Crusoe's grains, they observe laws – which govern mechanical reaction, attraction, and seminal processes or *scientia* propagated by seeds – whose order may inspire some observers to credit quotidian oversight to God. But, Boyle argues, nature's "ordinary preserving Concourse" only looks "*as if* there were diffus'd through the Universe an intelligent Being." Nature's necessarily acting order precludes immediate supervision.

Confronting an awesome scene of distemper, Defoe's fictional history *A Journal of the Plague Year* (1722) nonetheless insists that London's 1665–6 visitation by the Great Plague "was really propagated by natural Means, nor is it at all the less a Judgment." As with Crusoe's corn, Defoe credits pestilence to "a divine Power [that] has form'd the whole Scheme of Nature, and maintains Nature in its Course … and he is pleased to act by those natural Causes."[29] With Boyle, Defoe delimits divine agency circumscribed by natural causes. It is this divinity, not the miraculous intercessor conjured and belatedly annulled by a forgetful narrator, that sustains Crusoe's gratitude for deliverance on and off the island.

The corn engenders perplexity because Crusoe does not espy grains among the husks and dust he discards. Although such seeds are visible, Crusoe's failure to perceive them catalyzes his recourse to providential agency that summons plants from bare soil. But because the vehicle of infection by plague really is too tiny to see, Defoe's *Journal of the Plague Year* explicitly confronts superstitious appeals to unnatural or occult causes. Defoe reclaims invisible causation as simultaneously judgment and scientific process by identifying plague as an effect of divine intention that is realized by nature: "Among these Causes and Effects this of the secret Conveyance of Infection imperceptible, and unavoidable, is more than sufficient to execute the Fierceness of divine Vengeance, without putting it upon Supernaturals and Miracle."[30] To define God's vengeance, Defoe adopts Boyle and Morton's science. Even though it is sustained by invisibly tiny particles that communicate illness, plague's "Fierceness" is no miracle. Whether the particle of matter that acts naturally is a grain among husks or a seed of disease, empirical science extends to "secret Conveyance[s]" that are corpuscles, not "Supernaturals."

Whether minuscule or perceptible, natural agents like a corpuscle or a grain of corn are secondary causes. They occur at one remove from the creative agency of "a first Cause or God," as Boyle, who paraphrases Bacon's *Advancement of Learning*, warns his reader: because "Second Causes, which are next unto the Senses, do offer themselves to the Minde of Man, and the Minde it self cleaves unto them, and dwells there, a forgetfulness of the Highest Cause may creep in."[31] With Bacon and Boyle, Locke cites nature and human art as causes that prove divine intention: "That things brought about by the ordinary course of providence & humane meanes are yet thus ascribed to the Spirit of god is very evident in the old Testament ... [T]he Spirit of god is named & yet it would be folly to ascribe the things donne to any extraordinary or supernaturall power."[32] In an argument that gainsays Crusoe's rapid recourse to miracle, Locke invokes "the ordinary course of providence" as adequately evident testimony to divinity that does not flaunt "supernaturall power." As Wolfram Schmidgen has argued, the mediation of divine will by secondary causes served historically to insulate providential theology from heavily deterministic modes of predestinarian thought.[33] Crusoe's deliverance may be providentially assisted, but no God meddles with the laws of nature to effect it.

If natural causes, Boyle writes, threaten to lull the senses into a secular focus on science, Boyle offers reassurance that anticipates Crusoe's extraction of revised theological insight from the corn scene: rightly perceiving "Persons have such piercing Eyes, that where a transient or unlearned glance scarce observes any thing, they can discern an adorable Wisdom, being able (as I may so speak) to read the Stenography of Gods omniscient hand."[34] Crusoe's "as if" proves him finally able to read "the Stenography of Gods omniscient hand": although it is a natural effect, the contingency of the corn's survival communicates divine sanction. With the uneven pretense to mastery emblematized by his pots and grain, Crusoe aligns religious observance and empirical acumen to re-enact the motivating warrant for Morton's *Compendium Physicae*: "So that you see 'tis natural Theology that men should be industrious in Natural Phylosophy."[35] On the island with things themselves, Crusoe discerns an "adorable Wisdom" that does not betray nature's order but rather weds natural philosophy – in the sense of his growing mastery of useful things – and his accession to natural theology.

The philosophical implications of the *Crusoe* story return us to Watt's claim that Crusoe's isolation on the island reflects "an ideology primarily based, not on the tradition of the past, but on the autonomy of the individual."[36] Indeed, well before composing *Crusoe*, Defoe claims himself as a metaphoric castaway when he defends his Whig journalism against the charge of mercenary self-interest: "I stand alone in the World," Defoe writes, "strip'd Naked by Publick Injustice" after having, with "no helps but my own Industry ... forc'd my way with undiscourag'd Diligence, thro' a Sea of Debt and Misfortune."[37] As Watt argues, one referent of Crusoe's isolation at sea is a deracinated economic individual, "strip'd Naked," in addition, by a hostile and competitive print public sphere. But Defoe's novel nonetheless redeems Crusoe's solitude as the positive condition for his renewed understanding of self, nature, and God. Against the backdrop of Puritan and Dissenting reformist epistemology, Crusoe affirms standing alone as a criterion not just for industry but for natural and providential knowledge.

Yet just as Defoe's claim to have single-handedly rescued himself from bankruptcy is belied by the biographical facts, so Crusoe's access to the universalizing promise of sensory knowledge does not extend to the persons on the island who labor for him.[38] Marking the deepest historical contradiction posed by Crusoe's regression to the state of a pot-botching child, the Caribbean islander whom Crusoe dubs Friday possesses feelings for his new master "like those of a child to a father" (165).[39] However, after a year's tutelage, Friday "could not tell twenty in *English*" (169). As Defoe takes pains to illustrate dialogically, after "the three last years I had this creature with me" (181), Friday counts aloud "*one, two, three canoe! one, two three!* By his way of speaking, I [Crusoe] concluded there were six" (181). Friday's sustained inability to tell six divests this child of the aptitude for mastery evinced by Crusoe. In a critical departure from the egalitarian promise of Puritan and Dissenting sense-based pedagogy, Friday's new vocation is not mechanical mastery but servitude: "in a little time *Friday* was able to do all the work for me, as well as I could do it myself" (168). Friday resembles a child not because of the readiness of his mind to engage with things themselves but because of the alacrity with which he proves "able to do all the work." Because Friday's "very affections were ty'd to me, like those of a child to his father" (165), Crusoe appropriates Friday's putative childishness not as the Puritan criterion for empirical knowledge acquisition but as the guarantor of Friday's endless obligation to serve.

Before he elaborates how willingly Friday works for him, Crusoe voices an appraisal of Friday's natural capacities that declines to cite innate inferiority as a rationale for his subjection:

> [H]owever it had pleas'd God, in his Providence ... to take from so great a part of the world of his creatures, the best uses to which their faculties, and the powers of their souls are adapted; yet ... he bestow'd upon them the same powers, the same reason, the same affections, the same sentiments of kindness and obligation, the same passions and resentments of wrongs; the same sense of gratitude, sincerity, fidelity, and all the capacities of doing good, and receiving good, that he has given to us; and ... when he pleases to offer them occasions of exerting these, they are as ready, nay, more ready to apply them to the right uses for which they were bestow'd, than we are. (165)

Unspecified here, natural philosophy and Christian theology are the "best uses" that geography denies "savages" (169). Crusoe's six-fold emphasis on powers that are the same in all persons seems to intimate that, provided occasions by men like himself, creatures like Friday will bend their powers to these same right uses. But the use to which Friday lends his faculties betrays a democratizing pedagogical agenda predicated on human sameness. Instead, Crusoe lists such capacities as "obligation," "fidelity," and "receiving good" to cement an interminable state of voluntary servitude: Friday possesses an aptitude for sentiments triggered when Crusoe rescues him from death at the hands of warring islanders, moving Friday to kneel and place Crusoe's foot on his head, thereby, in Crusoe's reading of the gesture, "swearing to be my slave for ever" (161). In so doing, Friday performs an alienation of his property in himself that exceeds Locke's liberal definition of political freedom. Locke equates voluntary slavery with the crime of suicide: "For a Man, not having the Power of his own Life, *cannot*, by Compact, or his own Consent, *enslave himself* to any one … No body can give more Power than he has himself; and he that cannot take away his own Life, cannot give another power over it."[40] As his defense of African enslavement in America confirms, Locke defines slavery not as voluntary submission but rather as "*the State of War continued, between a lawful Conquerer, and a Captive.*"[41] Rather than an abdication of political right sustained in warfare, Friday's avowal of servitude is effected by passions that redefine slavery as unforced gratitude.

In a critical slip from the political to the domestic, Friday's feeling for Crusoe dictates *how* he submits: "*Friday* not only work'd very willingly, and very hard; but did it very cheerfully" (168). By depicting Friday as a person whose gratefulness makes him work cheerfully, Defoe isolates the likeness that justifies Friday's voluntary relinquishment of his property in himself: Friday resembles not a vanquished captive taken at war but an eighteenth-century English wife. Political theorist Carole Pateman has shown the paradoxical operation of contract theory in eighteenth-century marriage, since by consenting to wed, a woman acts legally to ratify the premise that she is inferior to the man who governs her.[42] When Crusoe testifies that Friday "work'd very willingly," he recurs to the same paradoxical deployment of freedom: Friday's willing servitude denies Locke's identity of slavery and ongoing war.[43] Defoe details the sentiments that transform Friday's hard work into cheer: "never had man had a more faithful, loving, sincere servant than *Friday* was to me; without passions, sullenness, or designs, perfectly oblig'd and engag'd" (165). Like a wife, Friday is loving, a passion that, by divesting his servitude of sullenness, performatively sustains its difference from a Lockean state of slavery. Twenty years later, Samuel Richardson's novel *Pamela; or, Virtue Rewarded* (1740) depicts Pamela's performance of wifely duty in exactly the same terms. Love vindicates Friday's possession of the same faculties as other persons. But *Robinson Crusoe* recruits these faculties not to further the democratizing end of empirical pedagogy but rather to obfuscate the source of Friday's failure to contend for it.

Before he saves Friday, Crusoe experiences providential approval of his imminent action: "It came now very warmly upon my thoughts, and indeed irresistibly, that now was my time to get me a servant, and perhaps a companion or assistant" (160). Crusoe's cognition significantly undercuts the charity of his motives, but it affirms that he has internalized tokens of divine sanction in the medium of his own thoughts: as Michael McKeon argues, the felt impetuousness of Crusoe's motives signals that he has gained the "capacity to read the marks of God on his own mind."[44] Not only are Crusoe's warmly and irresistibly sensed ideas signs of providential permission; they also echo God's words in Genesis 2:18: "It is not good that the man should be alone; I will make him a helper as his partner."[45] Crusoe's desire for a servant, companion, or assistant curtails the empirical promise leveraged in Defoe's defense of women's education. Although he possesses the same capacities as persons who are not innately slaves, Friday fails to achieve mastery of every mechanic art. Defoe's betrayal of this promise deploys sameness not in the name of universal knowledge acquisition but rather in the name of voluntary servitude modeled by female helpers.

I conclude with Locke's *Essay*, which questions whether an hoary academic can rid himself of intellectual prejudice "and turn himself out stark naked, in quest a-fresh of new Notions":

> Would it not be an insufferable thing for a learned Professor ... to have his Authority of forty years standing wrought out of hard Rock Greek and Latin, with no small expence of Time and Candle, and confirmed by general Tradition, and a reverend Beard, in an instant overturned by an upstart Novelist?[46]

Surely there is no more upstart novelist than Defoe, whose *Robinson Crusoe* literalizes Locke's call for epistemological renewal as the inductive mastery realized by a stark naked castaway. But Crusoe's mastery of mechanical arts also entails his mastery of Friday. The power of empirical knowledge to overturn authority of forty years standing does not, in Defoe's novel, extend its revolutionary reach to Crusoe's slave. This intractable contradiction testifies to both the vitality and the limits of the Puritan vision of sensual pedagogy *Robinson Crusoe* reanimates.

NOTES

1 Ian Watt, *The Rise of the Novel: Studies in Defoe, Richardson, and Fielding* (Berkeley, CA: University of California Press, 1957), 71.
2 Watt citing T. H. Green in ibid., 71.
3 Ibid., 71.
4 Ibid., 71–2.
5 Daniel Defoe, *Robinson Crusoe*, ed. John Richetti (London: Penguin, 2001), 95. All further citations from this edition will be noted parenthetically in the text.
6 Jole Shackelford, "Seeds with a Mechanical Purpose: Severinus' Semina and Seventeenth-Century Matter Theory," in *Reading the Book of Nature: The*

Other Side of the Scientific Revolution, ed. Allen G. Debus and Michael T. Walton (Ann Arbor, MI: Sixteenth Century Journal Publications, 1998), 43.

7 Isaiah 64:8, *The New Oxford Annotated Bible*, ed. Bruce M. Metzger and Roland E. Murphy (New York, NY: Oxford University Press, 1991), OT 955.

8 Daniel Defoe, *An Essay upon Projects*, ed. Joyce D. Kennedy, Michael Seidel, and Maximillian E. Novak (New York, NY: AMS Press, 1999), 108. First citation in italics in original.

9 John Locke, *An Essay concerning Human Understanding*, ed. Peter H. Nidditch (Oxford: Oxford University Press, 1975), 55 (I. 2. §15).

10 John Locke, "Theologie," in *Writings on Religion*, ed. and intro. Victor Nuovo (Oxford: Clarendon Press, 2002), 5.

11 Charles Webster, *The Great Instauration: Science, Medicine and Reform, 1626–1660* (London: Duckworth, 1975).

12 Paula R. Backscheider, *Daniel Defoe: His Life* (Baltimore, MD: Johns Hopkins University Press, 1989), 15.

13 See Samuel Eliot Morison, "Biographical Sketch of Charles Morton," in *Publications of The Colonial Society of Massachusetts: Charles Morton's Compendium Physicae* (Boston, MA: Colonial Society of Massachusetts, 1940): "Defoe as late as 1704 preserved Morton's system of 'Politicks' and a 'Manuscript of Science' which can have been none other than our *Compendium Physicae*" (xvii).

14 Ibid., 5.

15 Ibid., 49–50.

16 Ibid., 50.

17 Webster, *Great Instauration*, 335.

18 Francis Bacon, *The Advancement of Learning*, ed. Stephen Jay Gould (New York, NY: Modern Library, 2001), 24–5.

19 Webster, *Great Instauration*, 189.

20 John Amos Comenius, *A Patterne of Universall Knowledge, In a plaine and true Draught*, trans. Jeremy Collier (London: T. H. and Jo. Collins, 1651), 46.

21 Both cites, ibid., 30.

22 Both cites, Defoe, *Essay upon Projects*, 91.

23 Robert Boyle, *Some Considerations Touching the Usefulness of Natural Philosophy*, Essay 2, in *The Works of Robert Boyle*, ed. Michael Hunter and Edward B. Davis, vol. 3 (London: Pickering & Chatto, 1999), 229.

24 Locke, *Essay*, 150 (II. 10. §2).

25 Walter Pagel, *Joan Baptista Van Helmont: Reformer of Science and Medicine* (Cambridge: Cambridge University Press, 1982), 22.

26 Ibid., 29.

27 On Locke's medical student notebooks at Oxford, which include transcripts from "such very recent authors as Jan Baptista van Helmont," see Robert G. Frank, *Harvey and the Oxford Physiologists: Scientific Ideas and Social Interaction* (Berkeley, CA: University of California Press, 1980), 49. On Van Helmont's pervasive influence on Boyle, another route of transmission to Boyle's student Locke, see William R. Newman and Lawrence M. Principe, *Alchemy Tried in the Fire: Starkey, Boyle, and the Fate of Helmontian Chymistry* (Chicago, IL: University of Chicago Press, 2002).

28 Boyle, *Some Considerations*, 248. Emphasis mine.

29 Daniel Defoe, *A Journal of the Plague Year*, ed. Cynthia Wall (London: Penguin, 2003), 186.

30 Defoe, *Journal of the Plague Year*, 187.

31 Boyle, *Some Considerations*, 271.

32 Locke, "Immediate Inspiration," in *Writings on Religion*, 38.

33 See Wolfram Schmidgen, *Exquisite Mixture: The Virtues of Impurity in Early Modern England* (Philadelphia, PA: University of Pennsylvania Press, 2013), 59–100.

34 Boyle, *Some Considerations*, 279.

35 Morton, *Compendium Physicae*, 4.

36 Watt, *Rise of the Novel*, 60.

37 Daniel Defoe, *A Reply to a Pamphlet Entituled The L[or]d H[aversham]'s Speech* (London, 1706), cited in Maximillian E. Novak, *Daniel Defoe: Master of Fictions* (Oxford: Oxford University Press, 2001), 285.

38 On the assistance lent Defoe during and after his bankruptcy by his mother-in-law and friends, see Novak, *Master of Fictions*, 101–19, and Backscheider, *Daniel Defoe*, 41–83.

39 For an important discussion of Friday's status as a Caribbean islander or Indian, see Roxann Wheeler, *The Complexion of Race: Categories of Difference in Eighteenth-Century British Culture* (Philadelphia, PA: University of Pennsylvania Press, 2000), 50–89.

40 John Locke, *Two Treatises of Government: The Second Treatise*, ed. Peter Laslett (Cambridge: Cambridge University Press, 1960), 284 (§23).

41 Ibid., 284 (§24). Emphasis in original. Laslett remarks: "The Instructions to Governor Nicholson of Virginia, which Locke did so much to draft in 1698 ... regard negro slaves as justifiably enslaved because they were captives taken in a just war ... Locke seems satisfied that the forays of the Royal Africa Company were just wars of this sort" (ibid., 284–5 n. to §24).

42 Carole Pateman, *The Sexual Contract* (Stanford, CA: Stanford University Press, 1988).

43 See Thomas Hobbes's *Leviathan* (1651), which suggests that the institution of marriage marks victory of all men in a war against all women.

44 Michael McKeon, *The Origins of the English Novel, 1600–1740* (Baltimore, MD: Johns Hopkins University Press, 1987), 330.

45 Genesis 2:18, *New Annotated Oxford Bible*, OT 4. I am grateful to my former student Chelsey Moler (in "New Worlds," Spring Quarter 2014) for highlighting the relation of Crusoe's thought to Genesis.

46 Both quotes, Locke, *Essay*, 714 (IV. 20. §11).

9

EVE TAVOR BANNET

Robinson Crusoe and Travel Writing: The Transatlantic World

Complaining in 1729 that "rural Esquires of good Estates ... consume two or three Tuns of French Wine yearly, yet never once look On a Book, or have any such Furniture in their Houses," the *Dublin Tribune*'s lead essay tried to shame gentlemen into reading to acquire "useful Knowledge." It did so by observing that females had the advantage of them there, since the only reading-matter currently in their households were:

> a Bible, a Prayer Book, and the Week's Preparation, which are the Property of the Lady of the House, who is generally the better Scholar, as well as the better Christian of the two. Her Woman also may happen to have a Robinson Crusoe, Gulliver's Travels and Aristotle's Masterpiece, both for her own Edification, and the Instruction of the young Ladies, as soon as they are grown up; not to mention Jack the Giant Killer, The Cobbler of Canterbury and several other notable Pieces of Literature carried about in the Baskets of Itinerant Peddlars for the Improvement of His Majesty's Liege Persons.[1]

This allusion to chapbook (eight-page) abridgments of *Robinson Crusoe*, with its suggestion that these were typically owned by female servants and read by gentlemen's daughters, is both helpful and misleading. It is helpful in confirming what reprints tell us: that the Robinson Crusoe story traveled like wild-fire up and down the social hierarchy, into the most rural regions, and across the Atlantic world, thanks to a variety of longer and shorter abridgments which made Defoe's story "more portable" and "lowered its price to the Circumstances of most People."[2] There were at least 136 abridged editions of *Robinson Crusoe* in Britain during the eighteenth century – almost three times the number of reprints of the full-length novel – plus thirty-nine abridged editions between 1774 and 1800 in America, where Defoe's complete original narrative was not reprinted at all. The "loose epitomes" or longer hundred-page abridgments, which dominated this reprint market, were reissued copiously everywhere – in London, Edinburgh, and Dublin, in Birmingham, Chester, and Philadelphia, in Boston, Worcester, and New York. Consequently, many more eighteenth-century men and women on both sides of the Atlantic knew Robinson's story from some abridged and altered version of it than from Defoe's own narrative – as indeed they still do. As the *Tribune* suggests, therefore, by producing abridgments at different lengths and prices, printers ensured that *Robinson Crusoe* was a book that even people, and classes of people, who did not have many other books and who lived in rural or out-of-the-way spots, were likely to own.

But though helpful in this regard, the *Tribune*'s allusion to *Robinson Crusoe* is misleading if we take its denigration of cheap and portable abridgments at face value. For the essayist followed his comment about *Robinson Crusoe* with an assurance that the *Tribune* would offer "Persons of Fortune" useful knowledge in abridged and easily accessible form, and with a request that "curates and other well-educated people who read … inform their neighbors that such a paper as The Tribune exists." In other words, he was using his essay to market the *Tribune* as "a cheap and easy Method of knowing the World and the different Manners and Customs, Laws and Policies of the several Nations in it," which was eminently superior to the cheap and easy method of reading chapbooks for such instruction as women and servants supposedly did. If women and servants got their knowledge of the wider world from chapbooks like *Robinson Crusoe*, men of fortune and rural esquires could demonstrate the superiority of their gender, rank, and education by getting theirs from the *Tribune*.

In comparing a paper like the *Tribune* to an abridgment of *Robinson Crusoe* as methods of acquiring information about the wider world and the various nations in it, the *Tribune*'s essayist was not comparing things which were obviously dissimilar. Eighteenth-century newspapers, which were not longer than chapbooks and often contained inaccurate, second-hand, or gossip-based information, were frequently dismissed as "romances"; while factually based travel narratives were widely considered an entertaining and accessible way for readers who eschewed serious "study" to acquire some knowledge of the terrain, climate, conditions, manners, agriculture, and commerce of other peoples and nations. Eighteenth-century abridgments of *Robinson Crusoe* had, moreover, succeeded in turning Defoe's narrative into a travel story full of information about the Atlantic world and the peoples in it.

All abridgments of *Robinson Crusoe* were variants on one or both of the two earliest loose epitomes: *The Life and Strange Surprizing Adventures of Robinson Crusoe of York, Mariner*, printed for T. Cox in 1719, the same year as Defoe's original; and *The Life and Most Surprising Adventures of Robinson Crusoe of York, Mariner*, printed for E. Midwinter in 1722. These epitomes followed the practices of travel writers in several ways. One was to give Robinson's adventures greater geographical specificity than Defoe had done, in order to turn his travels in Part 1 into a circum-Atlantic voyage. In their versions of the story, Robinson enters the ocean on a Guinea slaver at Lisbon, the last European port in the Atlantic, only to be captured by Barbary pirates near the Canary Islands just beyond the Straits of Gibraltar and to be enslaved in Morocco's Atlantic port city of Sallee. His escape with Xury in the longboat then takes them further along the same Atlantic coast to West Africa, where they encounter helpful African natives. They are close to the Cape de Verde islands and heading to Gambia when they are rescued from the longboat by a Portuguese ship which carries Crusoe across to Brazil; and when Brazilian merchants persuade Crusoe to cross back to West Africa for slaves, the storm which drives his ship off course takes him into the Caribbean, where he is shipwrecked after passing the British colony of Barbados. Upon his rescue from the island, his ship follows the tidal stream back to London by sailing along the opposite Atlantic coast, and Robinson closes his circum-Atlantic circuit by traveling back to Lisbon to settle his affairs. Giving Robinson's voyage such geographical specificity on what was British shipping's standard circum-Atlantic route to and from the Americas, enabled epitomes to make *Robinson Crusoe* a story about the perils that Robinson faced as a mariner in a dangerous multinational Atlantic world, dominated by Barbary pirates, Africans, and Caribs, as well as by the Spaniards and Portuguese. For a Protestant Englishman in this period, the natural dangers of the Atlantic Ocean (storms, shipwreck) were compounded by the fear, and real danger, of being killed, captured, or enslaved by one of the Muslim or Catholic powers, by one of the non-European peoples, and/or by vessels captained by roving and freewheeling buccaneers, pirates, or privateers. Britons who traveled as tourists for health, pleasure, or polish generally went to Paris and Italy, or during European wars, in a carriage to Scotland, rather than risk an Atlantic voyage. For even after the Peace of Utrecht in 1713, the Atlantic remained a violent, un-regulated, largely unpoliceable ocean, where the various European imperial powers were competing for mastery and outlaws of all nations abounded. As such, it constituted a major barrier to the empire-building, wealth-making, New World ambitions of a sea-going, mercantile nation like Britain.

Consequently, where nineteenth- and twentieth-century abridgments cut out most of what came before and after the island section to present *Robinson Crusoe* as the heroic story of a solitary individual's ingenuity in surviving on the island alone,[3] eighteenth-century epitomes condensed and downplayed the island section to expand on Robinson's encounters with, and survival of, the dangers presented by the larger Atlantic world. Stripping Robinson of his "Reflections, as well Religious as Moral," eighteenth-century abridgments eliminated those features of Defoe's text which have led modern critics to read Robinson's island narrative as spiritual autobiography, as an exemplum of economic individualism, or as an articulation of imperious British colonialism. Eighteenth-century epitomes excised most of Robinson's interiority and turned his attention outward to highlight the English mariner's dependence on, and often subordinate relations to, other nations in the Atlantic world. This only made more evident the fact that Defoe had drawn on an exceptionally wide range of travelers' autobiographical "Life and Sufferings" narratives to compose his text: English travelers' accounts of their own terrible Barbary captivities, mariners' accounts of frightening storms, devastating shipwrecks, and hostile peoples, buccaneer and pirate tales of mutiny on the bounty, first-hand accounts of maritime exploration, of the sugar plantations, and of the slave trade in the New World. As the putative editor in Defoe's text pointed out, "the Life of one Man" was "scarce capable of a greater Variety" than Robinson's. Eighteenth-century *Crusoe* epitomes based the strength and appeal of their versions of the story on the fact that the greatest variety of dangerous, unpleasant, and challenging things that could happen to an Englishman in the Atlantic world did happen to Robinson. Robinson conveniently encompassed in one Life, almost all the possible trials and "Sufferings" of English mariners and travelers in the Atlantic ocean, accounts of which were flooding the London book market at the turn of the eighteenth century.

Defoe's printer and publisher, William Taylor, complained somewhat bitterly of the first epitome of 1719 that "in the pretended Abridgement of this Book ... the Author's Sense throughout is wholly mistaken."[4] He was right in the sense that this and all subsequent epitomes changed the meaning/s of Defoe's book; but he was wrong in supposing that epitomizers had done this by mistake. Epitomized versions of *Robinson Crusoe* consistently "corrected" and altered Defoe's text in light of contemporary criticisms of it, while offering their own critiques of Defoe's narrative in fictional rather than expository form. Defoe summarized some contemporary criticisms of *Robinson Crusoe* in his Preface to *The Farther Adventures*, when he observed that "envious people reproach it with being a Romance" as well as with "Errors in Geography, Inconsistency in the Relation, and Contradictions in the Fact" and "pretend that the Author has supply'd the Story out of his Invention."[5] Further criticisms were published by Charles Gildon in *The Life and Strange Surprizing Adventures of Mr. D— De F—, of London, Hosier* (1719), which "outed" Defoe as *Robinson Crusoe*'s author. Gildon too characterized Defoe's narrative as a Romance – the invented tall-tale of an author who was already notable for "forging a story and imposing it upon the world as Truth."[6] This was damning because Defoe had presented his narrative without his own name, as the Life of one Robinson

Crusoe of York, Mariner, "Written by himself," thus as the true account of a real mariner's experiences, and because he had further assured readers through his putative "Editor" that this was "a just History of Fact; neither is there any Appearance of Fiction in it."

More than simple misrepresentation was involved however. To charge Defoe's narrative with being a "Romance" was to invoke a generic shift in travel writing – and in what, in travel writing, constituted "a just history of fact" – in order to indicate where contemporaries judged that Defoe's major shortcomings as a travel writer lay. There was, as Jean Vivies has put it, "a tension between the literal and the literary" in eighteenth-century travel writing.[7] Travel writing had begun in literary mode, as Epic (*The Odyssey*) or Romance. From ancient times, when they were already associated with imperial expansion, romances had offered a wonderful variety of surprising adventures – travel to new and exotic locations, battles and tempests in ships at sea, shipwrecks, abductions, pirates, gods, wonders, encounters with strange human and non-human creatures, and various forms of captivity. These plot elements had subsequently been integrated in sixteenth- and seventeenth-century Spanish chivalric romances, which had themselves been used as templates for narratives of conquistadores in the New World; and seventeenth-century French romances, which were widely read in England, integrated typical Romance plot elements, such as shipwrecks, abductions, and captivities, into their tales of separated and star-crossed lovers.[8] These plot elements had thus become the literary topoi of wonder-full fictions. But as more and more Britons embarked on New World ventures during the seventeenth and eighteenth centuries, travel to new and exotic locations, battles, tempests and shipwrecks at sea, pirates, strange peoples, captivity, and weird and wonder-full events, were also things that were actually happening to British people. They recurred in "real" stories of maritime exploration and in "true accounts" of the trials and sufferings of seventeenth- and eighteenth-century mariners and travelers in the Atlantic world. In the absence of cameras and satellites, it was essential to be able to distinguish true accounts of what travelers had actually seen and experienced from romance topoi. And in Britain, from the later seventeenth century, one important way of doing this was to use the style of writing dictated by the Royal Society's "Directions to Travellers" (1666) – which were reproduced, expanded, and reprinted throughout the eighteenth century.

The Royal Society viewed ordinary people's travels as a useful means for Britain to acquire empirical information about the geography, natural history, ethnography, agriculture, commerce, government, and military strength of other nations, and therefore asked travelers to report what they had seen and learned with a particular kind of literalness. Travelers were directed to report on their observations not on their subjective thoughts or feelings, and to provide "simple perceptible facts" without "romantic embellishment," theorization, or even commentary. As Jason Pearl points out, therefore, Romance became "a decidedly pejorative epithet used to discredit testimony deemed vain and fanciful." "Wonders," supernatural adventures, parables, and accounts of personal growth in wisdom or experience were banished from travel writing, in favor of "subordination of the great discoverer to the observed environment" and "scrupulous attention to the details of physical surfaces."[9]

Defoe had himself borrowed quite heavily from the Royal Society's literal, empirical style of reporting travel observations; indeed, this was largely responsible for those features of his writing which Ian Watt, reading back from the "great tradition" of nineteenth-century realism, called "formal" or "circumstantial realism."[10] But Defoe had tried to have it both ways – to be both literal and literary. As one of the epitomes put it, Defoe's *Robinson Crusoe* was both "Historicall" and "Allegorical";[11] or as Defoe himself admitted in his Preface to *The Farther Adventures*, it had included, alongside factual description, "a Part that may be called Invention, or Parable in the story." We, who have nothing at stake here, may view the resulting olio as rich, complex, and aesthetically pleasing; but this does not mean that Defoe's contemporaries – who were still struggling to separate fact from fiction, and truth from romance, in reports and narratives of all kinds – were wrong to condemn Defoe for using the signifiers of empirical truth to pass off an invented character as a real person, or mistaken in pointing out that, generically, the parables, allegory, wonders, and inventions made Defoe's text a Romance (or, as we might say, a novel).

Epitomes, by contrast, did all they could to ensure that their versions of *Robinson Crusoe* accorded with the norms and facts of travel writing. While sometimes warning their readers that Defoe's *Robinson Crusoe* had been described as "an inconsistent Romance" or that "the Whole was, as is suggested, a mere Fiction," all strove to "fall immediately upon Matters of Fact" by focusing and elaborating upon the "Historicall" elements in Defoe's story.[12] They eliminated from their versions whatever smacked of parable, allegory, and Romance, and adopted a style that more closely resembled that of real captivity narratives and mariners' tales, which normatively subordinated their narrators' remembered feelings and emotions to literal and dispassionate reports of the events that had befallen them and to close descriptions of the foreign cultures and environments in which these had occurred. Epitomes not only corrected and altered Defoe's geography; they also edited and corrected his "Historicall" accounts of the peoples and places that Robinson encountered on his circum-Atlantic voyage, by inserting more accurate historical, geographical, and cultural information to make the narrative a more accurate and just History of Fact. Epitomized *Crusoes* were thus among the earliest of many highly popular stories which criticized Defoe's realism by showing that the Atlantic world was not as he portrayed it;[13] but in their case, this was an ongoing process, to which a succession of printers on both sides of the Atlantic contributed throughout the century by continuing to alter, adjust, and correct the already epitomized texts. For instance, knowing that Europeans had settled on supposedly "un-inhabited" Caribbean islands, which Caribs on neighboring islands had used for agriculture as well as for religious ceremonies, some American-printed abridgments show Robinson finding traces of native agriculture on "his" island in the form of stalks of cotton or rice, as well as watching the cannibal feast. One Boston chapbook has Crusoe finding "the Catava Root, which the Indians make Bread of; also Plants of Aloes and Sugar Canes."[14] The more "just" cultural and geographical information a travel narrative included, the more "instructive" as well as "entertaining" it would be.

Successive editions could keep changing Defoe's text in large and small ways because, during this period, epitome or abridgment (the two terms were synonymous) was a well-established method of writing with its own, now unfamiliar, rules. As we might expect, epitomes were supposed to strip the text of superfluous or inessential matter in order to more clearly exhibit the substance of their author's argument by reproducing its main "heads" – or in the case of a narrative, its principal events. But eight-eenth-century epitomizers were not bound to use the same words that their author had used, and generally rewrote. More surprisingly perhaps, they were also free to alter and add to what an author had written – to correct him where they thought him mistaken, to update him when new informa-tion had emerged, to add, change, or omit scenes, and to introduce their own ideas and reflections in place of his. *Crusoe* epitomes made it clear that this is what they had done. The Preface to the "faithful" three volume abridgment of 1722 assured readers that in this version of *Robinson Crusoe* "there are not only many Errors corrected, but several palpable and gross Contradictions rectified and emended."[15] The preface to *The Wonderful Life and Most Surprizing Adventures of Robinson Crusoe* of 1737 went further to "acquaint the reader" that "in this new Epitome of *The Life and Surprizing Adventures of Robinson Crusoe* … all possible care has been taken to pre-serve the history entire, to correct some mistakes in former impressions, and to add a considerable number of acts and material observations that have lately occurred, and were never published but in this edition."[16]

In reworking Defoe's text, epitomizers corrected it in light of contem-porary criticisms, changing Defoe's words and sentiments as they went.

Here is one of many possible examples. Defoe's "relation" of Crusoe Senior's reactions to Robinson's choice of a seafaring life was "inconsistent in the relation" in the sense that Defoe had described his reactions in the course of three pages in several potentially incompatible ways. Of these, the position which predominates is that Robinson's father tries to prevent him from going to sea by telling him that, being middle class, he "was under no Necessity of seeking his Bread" on the ocean, much less of being "sold to the Life of Slavery for daily Bread"; that papa Crusoe "would do well for" his son if Robinson "would stay and settle at Home as he directed"; that as a father, he was "discharging his Duty by warning [Robinson] against Measures which he knew would be to [his] Hurt," and that "if [Robinson] did take this foolish Step [of going to sea], God would not bless [him]." But epitomizers generally agreed with Charles Gildon that showing Robinson's father trying to "dissuade and deter" him from going to sea was contrary to the public good when "our Navigation produces both our Safety and our Riches."[17] British trade, wealth, wars, and hopes of imperial expansion all depended on young men going to sea. Britain's merchant ships and ships of war were perpetually short of sailors and reliant on Press Gangs to force men onto their vessels, because a mariner's life was generally poorly paid, and often nasty, short, and brutal besides. It was therefore unhelpful, even unpatriotic, to curse young men for going to sea, never mind to teach them that they would be punished by God with tempests, captivities, and shipwrecks for doing what was only an Englishman's duty. After the first abridgment of 1719, which remained closest to Defoe's original, epitomized *Crusoes* therefore progressively changed Defoe's language and rewrote the scene to excise Crusoe Senior's arguments for staying at home and to eliminate the issue of filial disobedience. *The Life and Most Surprizing Adventures of Robinson Crusoe* printed for E. Midwinter in 1722 had Robinson's father address his son's choice of a seafaring life in the following terms:

> "I entreat you, nay I command you to desist from these Inclinations: Consider your eldest Brother who laid down his Life for his Honour, or rather lost it for his Disobedience to my Will. If you will go, added he, my Prayers shall however be offered for your Preservation; but a Time may come, when, desolate, opprest or forsaken, you may wish you had taken your poor despised Father's Counsel!" – He pronounc'd these Words with such a moving and paternal Eloquence, while Floods of Tears ran down his aged Cheeks, that seem'd to stem the Torrent of my Resolutions. (2)

This version of the narrative deflected the brunt of filial disobedience from Robinson onto his eldest brother; it converted patriarchal prerogative and command into paternalistic counsel and benevolent concern; and it had

Crusoe Senior praying for his son's safety, and weeping at the hazards he would have to face, not cursing him and predicting his destruction. *The Wonderful and Most Surprising Adventures of Robinson Crusoe*, printed for A. Bettesworth and C. Hitch in 1737, further neutralized Robinson's father:

> My father intended me for the law ... but all the pains and expence were to no purpose; my inclinations were bent another way, and nothing would serve my turn, but at all hazards I must go to sea. My father and mother were both violently against it, and used a thousand arguments to dissuade me; but it was all to no purpose; my resolutions were so firmly settled, that neither the Entreaties of the most tender father, nor the vows and tears of a most dear and affectionate mother, could make any Impressions on me. (8)

Here Crusoe Senior's objections are alluded to rather than represented. His specific arguments, together with all question of commands issued and disobeyed, have been eliminated, as has the vivid and emotive rhetoric. We are merely informed that Robinson could not be persuaded to go against his inclination to go to sea for all his parents' tears and entreaties. He was being stubborn, no doubt; but he also recognized the "hazards" that his "resolution" to go to sea entailed, and was willing to face them; and there was something quite brave and admirable about that. *The Wonderful Life and surprising Adventures of that renowned hero Robinson Crusoe*, printed in New York by Hugh Gaine in 1774, dealt with this scene differently again:

> My heart began to be very early filled with rambling thoughts, and though, when I grew up, my father often persuaded me to settle to some business, and my mother used the tenderest intreaties, yet nothing could prevail upon me to lay aside my desire of going to sea; and I at length resolv'd to gratify my roving disposition, notwithstanding the extreme uneasiness my father and my mother always showed, at the thoughts, of my leaving them. (5–6)

This Robinson is just a restless young man who is not ready to settle down. He has "rambling thoughts" and a "roving disposition" which make him long to go to sea. His parents are upset by the thought that he will leave them and that they may never see him again, but this is an expression of their affection and concern not a matter of parental authority.

These various rewritings of this scene show how different abridgers and/or reprinters of Robinson's story stripped Defoe's narrative of Defoe's "Reflections, both moral and Religious," and replaced them with fairly diverse "Reflections" of their own, thus further changing the meaning/s of Robinson's story. As epitomes made their way from printer to printer around the Atlantic world, printers acting as their own editors or epitomizers simply continued to add and change the epitomes they were using in light of their own geographical and cultural information or ideological preferences. The two earliest epitomes of *Robinson Crusoe* which everyone subsequently used as basic copy texts were already significantly different from one another; and in reprinting one of them or some combination of the two, printers on both sides of the Atlantic introduced further factual and ideological alterations of their own. We tend to assume that everyone in England, in Ireland, in Scotland, and in the diverse colonies and early Republican States were united by reading the same popular novels and stories; but as this example shows, readers in different places, or in the same place, were not necessarily reading the same text and sentiments even under the same title.

By and large, however, whether British or American, epitomes and chapbooks all moved Robinson's Life in the same general direction. To accord with their focus on the harsh realities of the Atlantic world, and on showing how Robinson managed to survive them, *Crusoe* epitomes replaced Defoe's well-educated, literate, middle-class hero with "Robinson Crusoe of York, mariner" – an ordinary seaman with a roving disposition, who risked suffering, capture, and death in the Atlantic ocean for a livelihood, to see the world, or in quest of land to work and settle in the New World. They made an ordinary, provincial English mariner heroic by showing that –with the timely assistance other equally lowly and subaltern individuals among the Portuguese, Africans, and Caribs – he found a way of surviving all the hardships and sufferings which travel in the Atlantic might entail, and succeeded in making his fortune in the Atlantic world against all odds. This Robinson triumphed over adversity thanks to his flexibility, ingenuity, and ruthless opportunism, as well as through his willingness to make temporary alliances with people of other nations. Rather than bemoaning his sufferings and waiting to be ransomed or rescued, this Robinson escaped captivity on his own, managed to profit even from the most unfavorable circumstances, and showed his can-do kind of flexibility by assuming whatever fluid and temporary character circumstances required – acting alternately or concurrently, in different parts of the Atlantic, as mariner, fisherman, tobacco planter, hunter, farmer, slave-merchant, and slave.

There was more than a little cheering and emboldening propaganda about this. For during the 1720s and 1730s, Britons could not yet claim, as the Scottish poet, James Thomson, later would, that "Britannia rules the waves" and "Britons never, never shall be slaves." Britain had been a latecomer to empire-building in the New World compared to the Portuguese, Dutch, Spanish, and French, and was as yet so far from being master of the seas that white slavery on the North African coast and in the Spanish galleys was still a fact of life. Abridgments used Robinson's story to show readers that Britons could and would prevail against all impediments and get the better of other nations, if young men who went to sea followed this Robinson's doughty example.[18] Something similar can be said of America after Independence. The doughty, flexible, resourceful qualities highlighted in epitomized *Crusoes* were also required of American sailors once the new Republic had lost the protection of the Royal Navy, and still lacked a fighting navy of its own. Reprints of epitomized *Crusoes* began to proliferate on America's eastern seaboard as American merchant ships in the Atlantic repeatedly fell victim to the depredations of Barbary pirates, to the attacks of greedy privateers, and to the assaults of the major European powers. Here, once again, what was needed was a cheering and emboldening story that modeled, and satisfactorily lionized, the conduct of the son who courageously went out to make his independent fortune in the Atlantic despite all odds – not the story which punished the son with North African slavery, tempests, and a shipwreck for daring to rebel against a controlling and authoritarian parent, and which attributed his sufferings and misadventures to his determination to do something on his own.

If that was fantasy or wish-fulfillment in the short term, in the long run, it proved as "prophetic" historically, as Defoe's paternal curse proved "prophetic" of the unfolding of Defoe's fictional plot. Britons and Americans each ultimately prevailed. Indeed, this may be one reason why the eighteenth-century's *Crusoe* epitomes could be forgotten and replaced, during the nineteenth century in the English-speaking world, by abridgments of *Robinson Crusoe* with an entirely different focus: the singular, deserted individual cast onto his own isolated island and forced to struggle for economic survival alone.

Eighteenth-century abridgments of *Robinson Crusoe* were not single or solitary even in their authorship – in part because eighteenth-century copyright law, which held principally in London, did not apply to epitomes at all. This meant that London printers could use abridgments to minimize their own financial risk by partaking in the success of some other printer's copyrighted book, and supplying the market with cheaper and more accessible versions of it. It also meant that London writers – who got a lump sum for each manuscript they produced and had no share in the printer's long-term sales (royalties) – could use abridging as a quick way of making money. The London book trade therefore often fielded more than one abridgment of particularly useful or popular works; and many authors throughout the century (including Dr. Johnson in the case of his *Dictionary* of 1755) made their own abridgments of their own longer and more expensive texts. The claim of some contemporaries that Defoe had written the first epitome of 1719 himself would thus have seemed quite feasible at the time, especially since this epitome remained closest in its stated goals and outlook to Defoe's original.[19]

But the freedom of printers around Britain and the United States to constantly alter and "improve" epitomized texts as they reprinted them, or to create new abridgments of their own, made the authorship of any particular epitome marginal to this, or any epitomized story's fate. As we saw, epitomizing progressively transformed Defoe's story – eliminating its "Romance" elements, turning it into a travel story which instructed readers about the peoples and the dangers of the Atlantic world, showing them how an ordinary mariner might survive his misadventures and encounters with other, hostile nations. In choosing to reprint the abridgments and constantly altering them as they went, successive British and American printers were not only confirming contemporary doubts about the realism of Defoe's representations of the Atlantic world; each was also creating and publishing a version of the story which accorded more closely with the Atlantic world he knew. In this process, epitomized *Crusoes* became collectively authored texts – texts written at once by Defoe and by diverse combinations of epitomizers and of British and American printers.[20] This is also to say that *Robinson Crusoe* was a transatlantic travel story in a further sense. It not only told a story of transatlantic travels and (mis)adventures, which proved hugely popular among readers in both Britain and America; it was a story which traveled from printer to printer across the Atlantic, changing as it went. Robinson Crusoe gained a whole new strange, surprising life as a traveling, transatlantically authored tale of adventure and survival in the Atlantic world.

NOTES

1 *The Tribune*, no. 11 (1729): 73.
2 Daniel Defoe, *The Life and Strange Surprizing Adventures of Robinson Crusoe of York, Mariner* (London: Printed for T. Cox, 1719): Preface.
3 For nineteenth-century abridgments, see Martin Green, *Seven Types of Adventure Tale* (University Park, PA: Penn State University Press, 1991) and Richard Phillips, *Mapping Men and Empire* (London: Routledge, 1997).
4 Note to "Just Published, 4th edition" in Daniel Defoe, *The Farther Adventures of Robinson Crusoe* (London: printed for W. Taylor, 1719), 4.
5 Ibid., 2, 4. For Defoe's contradictions and historical, as well as geographical, errors, see Dennis Todd, *Defoe's America* (Cambridge: Cambridge University Press, 2010).
6 *Read's Weekly Journal or British Gazetteer*, November 1, 1718: 1191; quoted in Kate Lovejoy, *Reading Fictions, 1660–1740: Deception in English Literary and Political Culture* (Aldershot: Ashgate, 2008), 139.
7 Jean Vivies, *English Travel Narratives in the Eighteenth Century* (Aldershot: Ashgate, 2002), 29. See also Percy G. Adams, *Travelers and Travel Liars* (Berkeley, CA: University of California Press, 1962); Marcus Rediker, *Between the Devil and the Deep Blue Sea* (Cambridge: Cambridge University Press,

1987); Philip Edwards, *The Story of the Voyage: Sea Narratives in Eighteenth-Century England* (Cambridge: Cambridge University Press, 1994); Peter Hulme and Tim Youngs, eds., *The Cambridge Companion to Travel Writing* (Cambridge: Cambridge University Press, 2002); Nigel Leask, *Curiosity and the Aesthetics of Travel Writing* (Oxford: Oxford University Press, 2002); Julia Kuatin and Paul Smithurst, eds., *Travel Writing, Form and Empire* (New York, NY: Routledge, 2009); and Margaret Cohen, *The Novel and the Sea* (Princeton, NJ: Princeton University Press, 2010).

8 David Quint, *Epic and Empire: Politics and Generic Form from Virgil to Milton* (Princeton, NJ: Princeton University Press, 1993): Roland Greene, *Unrequited Conquests: Love and Empire in the Colonial Americas* (Chicago, IL: University of Chicago Press, 1999); Diana de Armas Wilson, *Cervantes, the Novel and the New World* (Oxford: Oxford University Press, 2000); and Barbara Fuchs, *Romance* (New York, NY: Routledge, 2004).

9 Jason H. Pearl, "Geography and Authority in the Royal Society's Instructions to Travellers," in Judy A. Hayden, ed., *Travel Narratives, the New Science and Literary Discourse, 1569–1750* (Aldershot: Ashgate, 2012), 73. See also essays by Daniel Carey and Judy Hayden in the same volume; Barbara Shapiro, *A Culture of Fact: England 1550–1720* (Ithaca, NY: Cornell University Press, 2000) and Steven Shapiro, *A Social History of Truth* (Chicago, IL: University of Chicago Press, 1994).

10 Michel Barido, "Le Style de Defoe et L'Epistemologie de la New Science," *Trema* 9 (1984): 119–32; Ian Watt, *The Rise of the Novel* (London: Chatto & Windus, 1957).

11 Defoe, *The Life and most Surprizing Adventures* (London: printed for E. Midwinter, 1722), Preface, 1.

12 Ibid.; *The Wonderful and most Surprizing Adventures of Robinson Crusoe... Faithfully Epitomized* (London: printed for A. Bettesworth and C. Hitch, 1737), Preface; *The Life and Strange Surprizing Adventures* (printed for T. Cox, 1719), Preface.

13 Eve Tavor Bannet, *Transatlantic Stories and the History of Reading: 1720–1810* (Cambridge: Cambridge University Press, 2011). For some of Defoe's erroneous representations of the New World, see Dennis Todd, *Defoe's America* (Cambridge: Cambridge University Press, 2010).

14 *The Life of Robinson Crusoe, Mariner* (Boston, MA, 1757), 9.

15 *The Life and Most Surprizing Adventures* (printed for E. Midwinter, 1722), Preface, 2.

16 *The Wonderful Life and Most Surprizing Adventures of Robinson Crusoe, of York, Mariner* (printed for A. Bettesworth et al, 1737), Preface.

17 Charles Gildon, *The Life and Strange Surprizing Adventures of Mr. D— De F—, of London, Hosier* (London, 2nd edn, 1719), 3. For Gildon see Paul Dottin, "Introduction," in *Robinson Crusoe Examin'd and Criticiz'd* (London: J. M. Dent, 1923) and J. Paul Hunter, *The Reluctant Pilgrim* (Baltimore, MD: Johns Hopkins University Press, 1966), chap. 3.

18 Richard Frohock, *Heroes of Empire: The British Imperial Protagonist in America 1596–1764* (New York, NY: Routledge, 1992).

19 For this claim and the controversy surrounding *Robinson Crusoe* and its epitomes, Henry Clinton Hutchins, *Robinson Crusoe and its Printing, 1719–31* (New York, NY: Columbia University Press, 1925).

20 Two abridgers produced the two earliest long epitomes; but several more again abridged these longer epitomes to produce a variety of chapbook versions.

10

DENNIS TODD

Robinson Crusoe and Colonialism

On his first day as a castaway, Crusoe "travell'd for discovery up to the top of [a] hill" and there he saw "to my great affliction ... that I was on an island environ'd every way with the sea." The more he looks, the worse it seems:

> I found ... that the island I was in was barren, and, as I saw good reason to believe, un-inhabited, except for wild beasts, of whom however I saw none, yet I saw abundance of fowls ... I shot at a great bird which I saw sitting upon a tree on the side of a great wood, I believe that it was the first gun that had been fir'd there since the creation of the world; I had no sooner fir'd, but from all the parts of the wood there arose an innumerable number of fowls of many sorts, making a confus'd screaming, and crying every one according to his usual note; but not one of them of any kind that I knew: As for the creature I kill'd, I took it to be a kind of a hawk, its colour and beak resembling it, but had no talons or claws more than common, its flesh was carrion, and fit for nothing.
>
> Contented with this discovery ... [1]

This is one of the few moments of intentional humor in *Robinson Crusoe*. That imponderable contradiction of "innumerable number" alerts us to other incoherencies. Although Crusoe believes the island is uninhabited "except for wild beasts," he admits that he "saw none." When he fires his gun, he hears the birds "crying every one according to his usual note," though he cannot possibly know what their "usual" notes are since he has been on the island only one day. The bird he kills he takes to be "a kind of hawk," but because it "had no talons or claws," the distinguishing characteristic of a hawk, it must be another kind of bird.

And yet, in spite of the fact that he thinks he is alone on a barren island with food "fit for nothing," Crusoe feels "contented" – contented because he believes that he has learned something about the island that will allow him to begin to exercise control over it. That's why this passage is constructed around two common tropes in the literature of colonialism, the surveying of territory from a high vantage point and the firing of the gun, tropes which signify the colonist's assessing, taking possession of, and asserting mastery over the land. Crusoe's feeling of mastery here, however, is delusional. He has imposed a subjective order on the island instead of seeing it accurately. The New World is, after all, a new world, and Defoe's point is that to survive in it, Crusoe will have to look at it more closely and with new eyes.

Defoe dramatizes this point again and again. When Crusoe swims out to the ship, he sees "nothing within my reach to lay hold of," but when he rounds her "the second time" he sees "a small piece of a rope, which I wondered I did not see at first" (40). After five or six more trips, he thinks he has "nothing more to expect from the ship that was worth my meddling with," and yet he finds a hogshead of bread, three casks of rum, a box of sugar, and a barrel of flour. "This was surprising to me, because I had given over expecting any more provisions" (46). On his twelfth trip, even though he "thought I had rumag'd the cabin so effectually, as that nothing more could be found," he does find something more: razors, scissors, a dozen knives and forks, and money to the value of thirty-six pounds (47).

Throughout his twenty-eight years on the island, Crusoe repeatedly has to abandon attitudes and assumptions he brought with him and see the world anew: the rhythm of the seasons, the flux of the currents, the relative value of money and things of use, the importance of human bonds, and most of his religious views. The challenge of the New World is symbolized by that enigmatic footprint, a sign with an ambiguous referent – it may be a cannibal's, the Devil's, his own – a sign that does not yield up its meaning readily but which must be looked at more than once and reflected upon. It is an indication of his success that after many years Crusoe can finally say, "I entertain'd different notions of things" (102).

That Defoe looks skeptically on Crusoe's imposing order on his island may seem counter-intuitive. For surely one of our first responses to *Robinson Crusoe* – and especially *Robinson Crusoe* considered as a colonial novel, one "designed to serve an imperial idea"[2] – is that it celebrates precisely such an imposition. Crusoe's imposing order is the act of a prototypical colonist, the very embodiment of the masculine, imperial impulse to go out into the world and dominate it. Implicitly and explicitly, the novel seems to endorse Britain's overseas ambitions, imaginatively envisioning new lands as places to be claimed, colonized, and made over in its own image. Crusoe's progress on the island reads like a prospectus for British colonial activity and expansion: he settles, builds, plants crops, and herds livestock; he faces down a hostile indigenous population; when the island is peopled, he replicates the orderly, hierarchical society of home. Like the New World for the British colonists, the island for Crusoe is not only his for the taking but a blank slate on which he can recreate the world he had come from. "I was king and lord of all this country indefeasibly, and had a right of possession" (80), he says, and he proceeds to turn everything into his possession: "my island," "my castle," "my country house."

And, of course, "my savage." Crusoe has no doubts about his right to subjugate Friday, imposing on him English values, culture, language, and religion. For in British eyes, savages were inferior culturally, technologically, morally, and religiously, and neither Crusoe nor Defoe seems to be particularly concerned about or even aware of the enormous costs that Britain's imperial ambitions imposed on the New World natives, an indifference captured in that chilling image in J. M. Coetzee's postcolonial retelling of the Crusoe story in his novel, *Foe*: Friday's tongue has been cut out, robbing him of the capacity to tell his own story, to articulate his own identity, or to vindicate his own culture.

Defoe was enthusiastic about Britain's commercial expansion and colonization, applauding both in his economic and journalistic works, writing optimistically about colonial matters not only in *The Life and Strange Surprizing Adventures of Robinson Crusoe* but also in its two sequels, *Farther Adventures* and *Serious Reflections*, and in four later novels, *Captain Singleton*, *Colonel Jack*, *Moll Flanders*, and *New Voyage round the World*. He had good reason to be enthusiastic. In his formative years, England busily added new colonial possessions in North America and the Caribbean, laying the foundation of its first empire, and greatly expanded its trade to the African coast, the Levant, Russia, and the Indian Ocean. Spices, textiles, and tea from the East India Company's trade in Asia, slaves from Africa, sugar from the Caribbean, tobacco, hides, furs, and dyestuffs from North America: the Navigation Acts funneled all this commerce through Britain, and its economy grew vigorously. By the 1750s, nearly all of the increase of Britain's exports came from exports to the colonies, and re-exports of colonial goods made up almost half of total British exports to foreign ports. London became the center of world trade.

And yet, in spite of Defoe's enthusiasm and in spite of the fact that the novel frequently seems to parrot uncritically British imperial ideology and practice, it is often difficult to see how exactly *Robinson Crusoe* offers a straightforward and unalloyed defense of his country's colonial ventures. After all, Crusoe's island is not really a colony ("I never so much as pretended to plant in the Name of any Government or Nation … or to call my People Subjects to any one Nation more than another," he confesses in *Farther Adventures*; "nay, I never so much as gave the Place a Name; but left it as I found it belonging to no Body"), and it ends as an utter failure: the last we hear of it is in a letter sent by the colonists begging Crusoe "to fetch them away, that they might see their own Country again before they dy'd."[3]

And although the novel often is interpreted as justifying Europeans' right to appropriate native lands on the principle that land rightfully becomes the property of those who cultivate it, Defoe himself declared that he did not "think any Body has the Right to dispossess the Natives of a Country."[4]

Even more disconcerting is the fact that Defoe does not address in *Robinson Crusoe* matters he thought central to the very purpose of colonization: commerce and trade. Coming late to the New World, the British had lost out in the race to find lands rich in silver and gold, but "by the meer Force of indefatigable Application, [they] planted, inhabited, cultivated ... inhospitable Climates" and "brought them to be the richest, most improved, and most flourishing Colonies in all that Part of the World." Britain had *settled* the New World, not exploited its resources like Spain had, and by settling they had "raise[d] new Worlds of Commerce." For settling new lands, Defoe argued, generated wealth by expanding population, production, and demand; expanding population, production, and demand expanded trade; and expanding trade created the conditions that continued the virtuous cycle, further "encreas[ing] the Wealth, Strength and Prosperity of England."[5]

"Without Commerce, of what use is a Colony?" Defoe concluded.[6] And yet there is no commerce or trade on Crusoe's island, and so we need to ask, what kind of colonial novel is Defoe writing if he writes a novel that conspicuously ignores what he himself considered the essential justification of British colonialism? Unless he bungled *Robinson Crusoe* terribly, we can only assume that he had no intention of grappling with these central issues of British imperialism in the novel and that his focus is elsewhere – and probably more limited.

J. A. Downie has observed that "the character of Defoe's imperialist vision is mundane rather than ideological."[7] Rather than setting out to legitimize in grandiose ideological terms Britain's imperial ambitions, his novels typically focus on specific policies or problems of the empire. Of course, *Robinson Crusoe* is deeply informed by colonial ideology – at the core of the book, Peter Hulme points out, is a "paradigmatic fable" about "the primary stuff of colonial ideology," the "encounter between civilization and savagery"[8] – but what is noticeable is how Defoe blurs this foundational binary of British imperial thought so that he can focus on more "mundane" matters of colonial reality and practice and, by doing so, ask his readers to reconsider long-standing assumptions and prejudices. Thus the importance of the motif of Crusoe's having to look twice, rethink his presuppositions, and entertain "different notions of things." By dramatizing Crusoe's ruminations at great length, Defoe prods his readers to rethink alongside Crusoe some fundamental beliefs and attitudes about Britain's colonial ventures.

Some of the longest sequences in the novel are devoted to Crusoe obsessively rethinking cannibalism. Initially, he considers the cannibals to be savages who have degenerated to "brutality itself" (156), but over an extended period of time – covering several years of his life and a great many pages of the novel – he reconsiders what cannibals are and how he should respond to them: that in their own eyes their cannibalism is no crime; that even if cannibalism were a crime, it is no business of his; that to slaughter them would be imprudent and immoral. When Friday comes to the island, Crusoe's attitudes undergo an even more radical transformation. For Friday seems hardly savage at all but kind and loyal, a good son (unlike Crusoe himself), and "the aptest scholar that ever was" (166). The line between civilized and savage, colonizer and Other, increasingly becomes less and less definite. Cannibals, Crusoe comes to understand, are not the monsters he originally thought. They possess "the same powers, the same reason, the same affections, the same sentiments of kindness and obligation ... the same sense of gratitude, sincerity, fidelity, and all the capacities of doing good" that civilized Englishmen possess (165). In the beginning, Crusoe's impulse was to put "twenty or thirty of them to the sword" (134); in the end, his desire is to civilize and Christianize Friday.

Defoe highlights the long process of Crusoe's reassessment of the cannibals because in the three decades preceding the publication of *Robinson Crusoe* Anglo-Indian relations in the colonies had so deteriorated that the British empire in the Americas was in danger. Like Crusoe, thoughtful observers of colonial matters found themselves having to urgently rethink their relationship with the savages.

In the very early years of colonization, many English justified their ventures by promising to civilize and Christianize the savages and to treat them humanely by pursuing "a gentle course without crueltie and tyrannie."[9] After all, since the natives were created by the same God who created the Europeans, they had "reasonable souls and intellectual faculties" and consequently were "ready ... to learn of [the English] the right worship of the true God" and be "brought to ... Civilitie ... in a short time."[10] But such sentiments were not universal, and they did not survive the first years of colonization. After the bloodbath of 1622, when the Powhatans massacred nearly a quarter of the English population of Jamestown, the Virginia Company urged the colonists to "roote out from being any longer a people, so cursed a nation ... and uncapable of goodnesse ... [L]et them have perpetuall Warr without peace or truce and ... without mercie too."[11] In New England, after some sporadic gestures at proselytization during the first years of contact, relations between the Indians and the English deteriorated steadily, and in the calamitous aftermath of the Indian uprising led by the Wampanoag chief Metacom (King Philip's War, 1675–8) and the descent into almost continual warfare with other hostile tribes after 1689, most colonists felt that the Indians should be exterminated, not converted. The ferocity of the Caribbean natives and their putative cannibalism quickly blighted any wish to civilize and Christianize them. By the end of the seventeenth century, the large-minded sympathies and evangelizing ambitions that initially had justified colonization had almost entirely disappeared. Indians had become irredeemable and savage Others, "Atheistical, proud, wild, cruel, barbarous, brutish, (in a word) diabolical Creatures."[12]

The consequences of the failure of Anglo-Indian relations were brought home in the late seventeenth and early eighteenth centuries by an almost unbroken succession of four wars that pitted the British against the French and the Indians. In King William's and Queen Anne's Wars (the Wars of the League of Augsburg, 1689–97, and of the Spanish Succession, 1702–13), the fighting between Britain and France on the European continent spilled over into the Americas. To the terror of the British colonists, the French enlisted the aid of the Indians of the Wabanaki Confederacy to conduct bloody raids on the New York and New England frontiers. Queen Anne's War had not formally drawn to an end when two pan-Indian conflicts exploded in the southern mainland colonies: the Tuscarora War (1711–15), an Indian uprising led by Chief Hancock which ravaged the frontier of North Carolina, and the even more devastating Yamasee War (1715–17), in which over a dozen tribes allied with each other to attack English settlements and nearly succeeded in annihilating the South Carolina colony.

France had been rapidly expanding from Canada into the interior of the North American continent with the intention, it was thought, of encircling the British colonies and destroying them. The French did not have sufficient forces to successfully attack the British themselves, but they could easily use the natives as cats' paws to further their own imperial designs, "stirring up the *Indians*," Defoe warned, "to make Depredations" on the colonies.[13] When the Tuscarora and Yamasee Wars broke out, colonists and colonial administrators panicked, fearing that the French at last had fomented a truly pan-Indian confederacy that would involve all the British colonies, "and ye whole English Empire, Religion and Name be extirpated in America."[14]

The Victorian historian J. R. Seeley's notorious claim that the British empire was patched together "in a fit of absence of mind"[15] is an obvious overstatement, but it does point to an essential truth. The first British empire grew haphazardly and by piecemeal, and except for elite planters and colonial merchants and administrators, most people in power, particularly in the metropole, were indifferent to and ignorant of colonial matters. But as a consequence of these four wars, more and more authorities in England became aware that there *was* an empire, that the colonies were part of a global network of interests which was of increasing importance, and that they were under imminent threat from its major commercial rival, France. By 1717, the Board of Trade, alarmed at the sorry state of Anglo-Indian relations and acutely aware that the "Indians ... are capable ... of turning the European interest in those parts to which side soever they incline,"[16] began to put together a coherent imperial policy. With a surprising degree of unanimity, authorities both in the colonies and in London acknowledged that the British had nobody to blame but themselves. They had stolen the Indians' lands, broken treaties, warred with them continually, and systematically cheated them in their trade dealings. To defend their commercial and colonial interests, the Board concluded that they must lose no time in repairing their relations with the natives by dealing with them humanely and justly.

Defoe perceived the French threat earlier than most of his countrymen, and he consistently linked the success of Britain's imperial future with the strength of its relations with the Indians:

> What have the People of *England* more to do, but ... to civilize and instruct the Savages and Natives of those Countries, wherever they plant, so as to bring them by the softest and gentlest Methods to fall into the Customs and Usage of their own Country, and incorporate among our People as one Nation.[17]

"Incorporate among our People as one Nation": Defoe's advocating here of the assimilation of the natives into the British polity constitutes a call to seriously rethink British conduct to the New World natives. For most of the previous century, the practice that held sway was one of hostility, exclusion, and segregation, and it had led to nothing but mutual hatred and bloodshed. Echoing the sentiments and rhetoric of the original colonial promoters, Defoe observed that "the Natural dispositions of all the Savage Nations" was to "be very faithful" if they were "used with Humanity and Courtesy," and he thought that Britain could win back the good will of the Indians by a policy that was founded on "just and generous Behavior to the Natives."[18] This is the policy he models in *Robinson Crusoe*. Crusoe gently weans Friday from his savage ways, instructing him in the civilized arts of herding and agriculture and thus converting him from a marauding to a settled life – in English eyes, making the essential transition from being a savage to being a civilized human being – and inviting him to dwell within the boundaries of the fort. He civilizes and Christianizes Friday, as later in *Farther Adventures* he will civilize other cannibals "by kind Usage and affectionate Arguings."[19] Once Friday is fully acculturated, he is absorbed into Crusoe's domestic economy and eagerly defends civilization from the unredeemed savages, fighting shoulder to shoulder with Crusoe when the cannibals descend on the island.[20]

The blurring of the civilized–savage binary in Friday – he is "a cannibal in his nature" and yet a "faithful, loving, [and] sincere servant" (164–5) – is a contradiction that may owe something to the dichotomy between the gentle Arawak and the aggressive Carib that had possessed the European imagination ever since Columbus's first voyage to the Caribbean, but the image of the good savage, friend to the whites, is pervasive in colonial history, later mythologized by James Fenimore Cooper in his tales of Natty Bumppo and Chingachgook, but made legend much earlier by the colonists themselves in the stories they told of such figures as Cortez's La Malinche, John Smith's Pocahontas, and in New England, Squanto, Hobbomock, and Uncas. These "special friends," as the New England colonists called them, played such prominent roles in the early colonial accounts because the good Indian was a desperately needed figure – needed by the colonists to help them as go-betweens, negotiators, and comrades-in-arms against natives who refused the gifts of civilization and true religion. When literature portrays colonial experience differently from what history tells us was true, much postcolonial criticism assumes that the author is consciously or unconsciously engaged in a kind of cover-up. But in drawing such a positive picture of the relationship between Crusoe and Friday, Defoe is far from justifying the sordid history of colonization. Instead, he is reaching back to a strain of earlier, almost moribund colonial discourse about the "kind Usage" of natives and their capacity to become civilized Christians to ask the British to reconsider – as he portrays Crusoe himself reconsidering – a morally sounder and more pragmatic policy of dealing with them. For in 1719, the British greatly needed "special friends."

The Tuscarora and Yamasee Wars had many causes, but two were foremost. The first was abuse by British traders, who cheated the Indians, stole their skins and furs, molested their wives, and murdered their braves. The traders stood to make big money in the skin and fur trade, but the biggest money – and this was the second major cause of the two wars – was in the trade in Indian slaves, a trade promoted and administered by the British. From 1670 to 1717, between 30,000 and 50,000 American Indians were captured as slaves by the British or their allies, so many that the number of Indian slaves exported out of South Carolina exceeded the number of African slaves imported into the colony. Like the British traders, Crusoe is driven by greed and sells Xury into slavery. But on his island, after rethinking both his own past behavior and the way he should deal with the savages, Crusoe treats Friday, Xury's double, quite differently. Friday puts his head under Crusoe's foot, "it seems" says Crusoe, "in token of swearing to be my slave for ever" (161), but Crusoe himself never calls Friday a slave, referring to him instead as a "servant," "companion," "assistant," and "grateful friend" (160, 177), and although he treats him as his subordinate, he never treats him as chattel.

Robinson Crusoe is not an anti-slavery tract. Although Defoe was appalled by the cruelty of slave masters and by their reluctance to Christianize their slaves, he never publicly questioned the legitimacy of the institution itself, and if he harbored any doubts, he realized that slavery (at least African slavery) had become so entwined in the British economy that to abolish it would result in "the General Ruin of our Trade."[21] Still, the trajectory of Crusoe's maturation from his mercenary treatment of Xury to his more generous behavior toward Friday suggests that on the "mundane" level of policy Defoe thought that the way the British dealt with the indigenous peoples with whom they shared colonial territory needed to be rethought. Intentionally or not, *Robinson Crusoe* is a version of the story of Inkle and Yarico in which an English trader, Inkle, is shipwrecked in the West Indies and survives with the help of an Indian maiden, Yarico, who falls in love with him. But when he finds a ship to take him back to England, he sells her into slavery. That monitory tale was repeated in numerous essays, poems, and plays throughout the eighteenth century, dramatizing the mistreatment and enslavement of New World natives (and later, Africans) by avaricious British colonists and merchants.

The second "mundane" matter Defoe addresses in *Robinson Crusoe* is immigration to the colonies, and here too the blurring of the line between the civilized and savage plays an instrumental role. By blurring this line Defoe complicates the readers' perception not only of Friday, but also of Crusoe himself. Crusoe's great failing is his "wandering inclination" (5), and given the colonial context of the novel, choosing this as Crusoe's fault can hardly have been accidental on Defoe's part. For in British imperial thought, wandering was the very hallmark of savagery. Civilized people settled, building permanent dwellings, cultivating crops, and domesticating animals; savage people like the Indians were savage precisely because, as hunters and nomads, they were a "wandering People" who did but "run over the grass as do also the foxes and wild beasts."[22] If the blurring of the civilized–savage binary implies that savages like Friday have the capacity to become civilized, then it also suggests that putatively civilized people like Crusoe can be savage. True, Crusoe eventually builds permanent dwellings, plants crops, and domesticates animals, but these are things he achieves only after struggling against his own savage energies: his impulsiveness, his egocentric self-assertion and will to power, and his refusal to acquiesce to the collective wisdom of his society, to his father, to his own reason, or to his God.

Crusoe civilizes himself by looking more closely at the patterns of his life, rethinking the role his irrational self-assertion and impulsiveness have played in his being cast away, and asking himself what he must do with himself now that he understands that by acquiescing to his savage energies he has become "the wilful agent of all my own miseries" (32). And just as his reassessment of the cannibals models for the reader a reconsideration of Anglo-Indian relations, so his continual ruminations about his fate and prospects in the New World allow Defoe to guide the reader through a re-examination of immigration and of the value of the colonial experience.

Policy issues of immigration, like the pressing matter of Anglo-Indian relations, had come to the fore in the years immediately preceding the publication of *Robinson Crusoe*. In 1718, Parliament put into effect the Transportation Act. Under its provisions, criminals convicted of certain non-capital offences were punished by being sent to the colonies as indentured servants. These convicts joined the even larger ranks of those who immigrated as indentured servants voluntarily, binding themselves to labor in the fields in return for the price of their passage to the New World. Between 1700 and 1780, over half of the 270,000 British immigrants to the North American colonies went as indentured servants; between 1718 and 1775, as many as 49,000 convicts were transported.

Defoe was fascinated with transportation and indentured servitude. Three years after *Robinson Crusoe*, he wrote *Colonel Jack*, whose protagonist is an indentured servant in Maryland, and *Moll Flanders*, whose heroine is a transported felon to Virginia. Transportation and servitude play a significant, though submerged, role in *Robinson Crusoe* too. For on a figurative level, the pattern of Crusoe's life is that of a transported criminal's. He believes he has been cast away into the wilderness of the New World for his crime – not a civil crime, of course, but a moral and spiritual crime of rebelliousness, for which he has been punished as a "judgment from Heaven" (72). Transportation was a punishment but, because it was granted as a pardon for a capital sentence, it was also seen as a merciful reprieve. Crusoe comes to understand his life on the island similarly: he believes he has been cast away as a "punishment of my sins," but it is a punishment that is also a "reprieve," a "mercy," for he has been "*singled out ... to be spared from death*" and given a chance to reform (105, 38, 106, 54). And so, though he begins his life on the island in "bondage" like an indentured servant, toiling "by the labour of [his] hands" (81, 30), after several years, like Defoe's other colonial settlers and servants, Moll and Jack, Crusoe finds that in the Americas he can "begin the World on a New Foundation,"[23] building a life in which he is economically successful and morally and religiously rehabilitated.

Defoe was a strong proponent of immigration to the colonies. He thought that it offered real opportunities for the poor and a second chance for criminals. "They go there poor, and come back rich," he said; "there they plant, trade, thrive, and increase; even your transported Felons ... have, by turning their Hands to Industry and Improvement, become rich substantial Planters and Merchants" (*Plan of English Commerce*, 318). But the colonies were not popular with those who might most profit from going to them. Opportunities had begun to dry up as early as the 1680s. Much of the best land had been engrossed by the wealthy, a long-term depression in the tobacco market lessened prospects for many newcomers, and the explosive growth of African slavery depressed demand for white indentured servants, particularly for those who were unskilled. Stories of the brutal hardships of the living and working conditions in colonies were rife. Those who did immigrate were often pushed, not pulled.

Defoe knew that those who would benefit most from immigration greatly resisted it. Moll's husband, Jemy, "thought he could much easier submit to be Hang'd" than to be transported, and Colonel Jack recalls his own "wretched" servitude in the colonies as all "Labour and ... Hardship and Suffering."[24] But rather than papering over these adversities, Defoe underscores them. In fact, many of the hardships Crusoe faces are based, not on accounts of the experiences of solitary castaways, but on the typical conditions immigrants faced in the colonies. Many colonists lived lives as primitive as Crusoe did. The houses of even successful planters in the Chesapeake, for instance, consisted of a single room with an earthen floor, a table, and perhaps a few chests for storage. Unlike Crusoe, they did not even have the luxury of a chair. The less well off – the indentured servants and small planters and farmers who made up most of the colonial population – ate poorly and were clothed badly. Like Crusoe, they labored at heavy and tedious work in the field. Everyday goods and conveniences that were ready to hand in England were so scarce in the New World that colonists were compelled, like Crusoe, to develop their ingenuity and become self-reliant jacks-of-all-trades. Even as late as the 1750s, Samuel Johnson could remark "how many trades every man [in the colonies] ... is compelled to exercise, with how much labour the products of nature must be accommodated to human use, how long the loss or defect of any common utensil must be endured, or to what aukward expedients it must be supplied."[25] Above all, colonists were lonely. Outside densely populated Barbados and a handful of the larger towns of New England, there were few sizable settlements in the New World. Most colonists were isolated, living at some distance from their nearest neighbors, "so lonely," they complained, they felt like "poor hermit[s]," "buryed alive" in "this silent country."[26] Their loneliness was

more profound than the feeling of being deprived of human companionship. When William Bradford and his shipmates on the *Mayflower* landed
on Cape Cod, this was their first reaction: "What could they see but a hideous and desolate wilderness, full of wild beasts and wild men – and what
multitudes there might be of them they knew not ... If they looked behind
them, there was the mighty ocean which ... was now as a main bar and gulf
to separate them from all the civil parts of the world."[27] "Bar and gulf" –
Crusoe uses both words to describe his island condition, and the sense of
loneliness they conjure up is less a feeling of being without comrades than a
feeling of being existentially abandoned, irrevocably cut off from all that is
known, and left entirely to one's own devices.

Although he was sympathetic to those who had been pressed by poverty
and adversity, Defoe also thought that they were at least partially responsible for shaping their own lives, and he portrays colonial conditions so
starkly because he believed that the very harshness of colonial life schooled
the destitute and the lawbreaker, forcing them to take their lives in hand by
making them conscious of how their own failings have kept them in poverty
or driven them to criminality and by teaching them the demanding lesson
of self-discipline. Crusoe and Defoe's two other fictional colonists, Moll and
Jack, are all driven by irrational passions – ambition, avarice, egocentricity –
and because they are unable to discipline these energies, they impose themselves on the world, demanding it yield to their desires. As a consequence,
they become willful agents of their own miseries – and one of those miseries
is their exile to the New World. There, the long tutorial of colonial experience teaches all three that true mastery comes only with self-mastery.

But if the colonial experience teaches Crusoe to restrain himself from
imposing his will on the world, it certainly doesn't teach him to be passive
before its forces. *Robinson Crusoe*, like colonialism itself, is above all a story
of mastery, and the difference between mastering the world and imposing
oneself on it can be elucidated by one last example of Crusoe's having to
look twice and entertain different notions of things. When he decides to cir-
cumnavigate his island in his newly built canoe, Crusoe "climb[s] up upon
a hill" to study the currents (110). Though he looks at them carefully, he
misinterprets what he sees and is almost swept out to sea to his death. Years
later, after a ship has wrecked off the point of the island, he again climbs the
hill to look at the currents a second time. He sees that he had not taken into
account the effect of the tides, rethinks his original calculations, and this
time successfully navigates the currents.

While Crusoe does not impose his will on the currents to get to where
he wants to go, neither does he yield himself up to them to take him where
they will. Instead, he adapts his desires to the powers that be, getting what

he wants, as John Richetti has said, by watching the "flow of events for an opening" and then "co-operating with events at the moment when they will serve."[28] Though Crusoe's willfulness has led to his being cast away, not only does he remain willful to the end, but he survives because of his will. The difference is this: as a young man, he imposed his will on the world, trying to make it bend to his desires; as an older man, chastened by colonial experience, he has learned to govern his desires, not extirpating them, but channeling and shaping them to answer to the demands of a world he has closely observed. The imperial impulse that Crusoe comes to embody, then, is indeed a peculiarly masculine impulse, but masculine as defined in the early eighteenth century: rational and self-restrained. And when Defoe addresses colonial matters in *Robinson Crusoe*, it is rationality and self-restraint that he focuses on: celebrating them as the empowering virtues that immigrants will be taught in the colonies, recommending them as the principles that should guide the British in their rethinking of their policy to the "savage" Others.

NOTES

1 *Robinson Crusoe*, ed. John Richetti (London: Penguin, 2001), 43–4. All further page references in the text are to this edition.

2 John McVeagh, "Defoe and Far Travel," in *All before Them: Attitudes toward Abroad in English Literature, 1660–1780*, ed. John McVeagh (Atlantic Highlands, NJ: Ashfield, 1989), 124.

3 *The Farther Adventures of Robinson Crusoe*, ed. W. R. Owens, vol. 2 of *The Novels of Daniel Defoe*, ed. W. R. Owen and P. N. Furbank (London: Pickering & Chatto, 2008–9), 125–6.

4 *A General History of Discoveries and Improvements*, ed. P. N. Furbank, vol. 4 of *Writings on Travel, Discovery and History by Daniel Defoe*, ed. W. R. Owen and P. N. Furbank (London: Pickering & Chatto, 2001), 217.

5 *A Plan of the English Commerce*, ed. John McVeagh, vol. 7 of *Political and Economic Writing of Daniel Defoe*, ed. W. R. Owens and P. N. Furbank (London: Pickering & Chatto, 2000), 285, 122, 319.

6 *General History of Discoveries*, 214.

7 J. A. Downie, "Defoe, Imperialism, and Travel Books Reconsidered," in *Critical Essays on Daniel Defoe*, ed. Roger D. Lund (New York, NY: G. K. Hall, 1997), 85.

8 Peter Hulme, *Colonial Encounters: Europe and the Native Caribbean, 1492–1797* (London: Methuen, 1986), 186–7. Although the indigenous peoples Defoe writes about Britain encountering were dark-skinned, race was at best an emerging concept at this time and doesn't appear to play a significant role in *Robinson Crusoe*. Roxann Wheeler has shown that the primary categories of difference by which England declared its superiority and on which they based many of their policies were civility and Christianity versus savagery and paganism: *The Complexion of Race: Categories of Difference in Eighteenth-Century British Culture* (Philadelphia, PA: University of Pennsylvania Press, 2000).

9   Richard Hakluyt, Pamphlet for the Virginia Enterprise (1585), in *The Original Writings and Correspondence of the Two Richard Hakluyts*, ed. E. G. R. Taylor, 2 vols. (London: Hakluyt Society, 1935), 2:334.

10 Alexander Whitaker, *Good News from Virginia* (London, 1613), 24; Robert Johnson, *Nova Britannia* (London, 1609), sig. D3v.

11 Treasurer and Council for Virginia to Governor and Council in Virginia, August 1, 1622, vol. 3 of *The Records of the Virginia Company of London*, ed. Susan M. Kingbury (Washington, DC: Government Printing Office, 1933), 668.

12 Increase Mather?, "Preface" to Mary Rowlandson, *The Sovereignty and Goodness of God*, in *American Captivity Narratives*, ed. Gordon M. Sayre (New York, NY: Houghton Mifflin, 2000), 136.

13 *A Review of the Affairs of France*, ed. John McVeagh, 9 vols. (London: Pickering & Chatto, 2003–11), 1:197.

14 Abel Kettleby and other planters to the Council of Trade and Plantations, July 18, 1715, *Calendar of State Papers, Colonial Series, America and West Indies*, ed. W. N. Sainsbury and others, 44 vols. (London: HM Stationery Office, 1860–1969), 28:236.

15 J. R. Seeley, *The Expansion of England* (London, 1883), 8.

16 Council of Trade and Plantations to Secretary Stanhope, November 18, 1715, *Calendar of State Papers*, 28:345.

17 *Plan of the English Commerce*, 305.

18 *A New Voyage round the World*, ed. John McVeagh, vol. 10 of *Novels of Defoe*, 145; *Serious Reflections during the Life and Surprising Adventures of Robinson Crusoe*, ed. G. A. Starr, vol. 3 of *Novels of Defoe*, 217.

19 *Farther Adventures*, 44.

20 In spite of his resolution not to use violence against them, Crusoe does kill cannibals in two assaults, and these instances are often interpreted as Defoe's sanctioning a generalized stance of violence against the Indians. But they can more plausibly be interpreted as defining the exceptional conditions under which the policy of a "just and generous Behavior to the Natives" does not apply. The first time Crusoe attacks the cannibals he does so because he is "call'd plainly by Providence" to save Friday (160), and the second time he acts to save the life of a European Christian.

21 *Review* 9:172.

22 John Lawson, *A New Voyage to Carolina*, ed. Hugh Talmage Lefler (Chapel Hill, NC: University of North Carolina Press, 1984), 175; Robert Cushman, *Reasons and Considerations Touching the Lawfulness of Removing out of England*, in *Chronicles of the Pilgrim Fathers, from 1602 to 1625*, ed. Alexander Young (Boston, MA, 1884), 243.

23 *The Fortunes and Misfortunes of the Famous Moll Flanders*, ed. Liz Bellamy, vol. 6 of *Novels of Defoe*, 246.

24 *Moll Flanders*, 244. *The History and Remarkable Life of the Truly Honourable Col. Jacque*, ed. Maurice Hindle, vol. 8 of *Novels of Defoe*, 121, 149.

25 Samuel Johnson, *The Adventurer*, #67, in *The Idler and the Adventurer*, ed. W. J. Bate, John M. Bullitt, and L. F. Powell, vol. 2 of *The Yale Edition of the Works of Samuel Johnson* (New Haven, CT: Yale University Press, 1963), 387.

26 William Byrd to John Boyle, July 28, 1730 and February 12, 1727/8, and to Charles Boyle, Earl of Orrery, July 5, 1726, in *The Correspondence of the*

Three William Byrds of Westover, ed. Marion Tinling, 2 vols. (Charlottesville, VA: University of Virginia Press, 1977), 1:432, 372, 355.

27 William Bradford, *Of Plymouth Plantation, 1620–1647* (New York, NY: Random House, 1981), 70.

28 John Richetti, *Defoe's Narratives: Situations and Structures* (Oxford: Clarendon Press, 1975), 45, 53.

PART III

Robinson Crusoe over Three Hundred Years

II

DAVID BLEWETT

The Iconic Crusoe: Illustrations and Images of *Robinson Crusoe*

Illustration is interpretation. Of the many hundreds of illustrations of *Robinson Crusoe* – and *Crusoe* is one of the most frequently illustrated books of all time – inevitably some are commonplace and uninspired, adding little to what we already know about Crusoe and his remarkable experience, but others see Crusoe in ways we may never have imagined, opening our eyes to aspects of the story and ways of seeing its hero that is the gift of the inspired illustrator.

The accumulation over time of illustrated editions of a book such as *Robinson Crusoe* enriches the story much in the way that a play or an opera is amplified by its many performances, even when, as is sometimes the case, an interpretation does not merely add to the experience of the work but may even distort or travesty it. *Robinson Crusoe* has appeared in illustrated editions for nearly three hundred years (its tercentenary is 2019) and the illustrations reflect the many ways in which different artists and different periods have envisioned Crusoe's life, variously emphasizing, among other aspects of his tale, his terror and despair, his fortitude and survival, his religious awakening and conversion, his heroic achievement and ultimate triumph. One of the most remarkable developments over this long period of time is the divergence between the English and the French illustrated editions, which present startlingly different images of Crusoe.[1]

From the start, *The Life and Strange Surprizing Adventures of Robinson Crusoe* (1719) appeared with an illustration[2] – albeit only a single one on the frontispiece (Figure 11.1), an etching by Clark and John Pine after an unknown artist.[3] We know little about Clark, though he worked with Pine on other etchings and engravings, including the folding map of Crusoe's island, the frontispiece to the *Serious Reflections of Robinson Crusoe* (1720). John Pine (1690–1756), however, was to become a distinguished engraver and had been the pupil of Bernard Picart, who engraved the frontispiece to the first French edition of the first volume of *Robinson Crusoe* (1720). Clark and Pine's haunting portrait of Crusoe – continually reprinted for over sixty

Figure 11.1 Unknown Artist (1719). Frontispiece. Etching by Clark and John Pine. *The Life and Strange Surprizing Adventures of Robinson Crusoe Vol. 1* (London: W. Taylor, 1719). © British Library Board, shelfmark C.30.f.6.

years and a powerful influence on Crusoe portraiture ever since[4] – is in many ways puzzling. Why is Crusoe facing inland and ignoring the ship? What ship is it? And why does Crusoe seem so unmoved by it? Has he even noticed it? What does he appear to be thinking about?

As the ship is sailing past the island and appears headed out to sea, it cannot be either the shipwreck, of which Crusoe was the only survivor, nor the Spanish ship, wrecked off the coast many years later, from which Crusoe managed to salvage clothes, tools, and money and to rescue a dog. The only other ship to come to the island was the English ship, on which Crusoe eventually departs after rescuing the captain from the mutineers. But it was anchored over four miles off-shore. As we can surmise from Crusoe's downcast – somewhat vacant – expression, and his facing inland, the ship in the background is not actually there. Rather he *imagines* it, both remembering the ship that brought him to the island and longing for one that will come to take him away. His thoughts are on his lonely plight and his desperate situation. Curiously, the apparent anomaly of the original frontispiece was noticed and it was altered in the sixth edition[5] (1722) – the sea was made much rougher and the sky dark with storm clouds. The ship is no longer an image in Crusoe's mind expressing his dream of deliverance; it is a real ship about to go down and it signifies his terrible fear of being isolated forever. But the attempt to make the scene realistic destroys the poignant atmosphere of the original and makes Crusoe's unperturbed posture and meditative expression inexplicable. The compelling power of Clark and Pine's drawing owes much to the fact that we see Crusoe, not in real time but rather as a timeless figure – the castaway – strangely dressed and thinking about his fate and his deliverance, symbolized by the background ship.

Robinson Crusoe was quickly translated into French and published, the first two volumes in 1720 and the third, *Réflexions sérieuses et importantes de Robinson Crusoe*, in 1721, in a unified edition, all illustrated. The frontispiece (Figure 11.2) to the first volume is signed by Picart, who both designed and etched the portrait of Crusoe. Bernard Picart (1673–1733) was a distinguished engraver[6] working in Amsterdam, where the French edition was published. He was clearly familiar with the English etching and would certainly have been interested in the work of Pine. Picart had the advantage of familiarity with the text[7] and his portrait of Crusoe follows the "sketch of my figure" that Crusoe provides, including the "great clumsy ugly goat-skin umbrella."[8] Other details confirm Picart's careful attention to Crusoe's account: his stockade is indicated not by a flimsy picket fence but is shown with the stakes that have sprouted into trees and the ladder that can be pulled up for security. Picart's design eschews a moody evocation of Crusoe's predicament. Consequently, the phantom ship has been eliminated (replaced by a large rock indicating the treacherous waters). Moreover, while the English frontispiece shows a fearful Crusoe armed to the teeth, the French frontispiece, which depicts Crusoe carrying a saw and a wicker basket for gathering food, gives us a Crusoe already adjusted to life on the island and making a go of it.[9] It was the image of Robinson as *Homo faber*[10] that appealed to the Enlightenment and especially to Rousseau. But for all the differences between the two designs, they created a lasting visual image of the extraordinary man who was to become one of our great iconic figures.

ROBINSON CRUSOE.

Figure 11.2 Bernard Picart (1720). Frontispiece. *La vie et les aventures surprenantes de Robinson Crusoe Vol. I* (Amsterdam: L'Honoré & Chatelain, 1720). Etching.
© British Library Board, shelfmark 12611.df.6.

Retaining its popular appeal, *Robinson Crusoe* was continually reprinted throughout the eighteenth century, both in the full two-volume edition[11] and in chapbook versions designed for children. But for a long time it failed to attract the interest of publishers prepared to commission new illustrations and to produce a more expensive edition designed for a gentleman's library.[12] In 1762 Rousseau published *Émile, ou de l'éducation* in which he praised *Robinson Crusoe* as the best treatise on natural (that is, not bookish) education and declared that it would be Emile's first and for a long time his only book.[13] It was Rousseau's testimony that made *Robinson Crusoe* a world classic, widely used as an educational handbook. As early as 1783 Dr James Beattie said that he agreed "with Rousseau, that this is one of the best books that can be put into the hands of children."[14] The Preface to an edition published in two volumes in London by Cadell and Davies in 1820 extolled *Robinson Crusoe* for its morally elevating qualities: "Next to the

Holy Scriptures, it may safely be asserted that this delightful romance has, ever since it was written, exerted the first and most powerful influence upon the juvenile mind of England – nor has its popularity been much less among any of the other nations of Christendom.'

Rousseau's admiration of *Robinson Crusoe* extended only to the central section of the first volume; he dismissed the pre- and post-island sections as a hotch-potch. The young Emile would identify himself with Crusoe and acquire an education by living close to nature and discovering for himself all that is worth knowing in science and morality. Rousseau's emphasis on the island section of the story – on Crusoe's heroic survival and triumphant achievement – was the impetus in French illustration for the gradual transformation of Crusoe into a man of stupendous accomplishments. By cutting out Crusoe's initial disobedience, thus downplaying the religious theme, Rousseau effectively secularized the novel. During the French Revolution, Crusoe's resolution and courage made the story more popular than ever and the commendation of Rousseau made it a work eminently suited to the new republican ethos. In the Year III (1794–5) a rewritten version of *Robinson Crusoe* was published – *L'Histoire corrigée de Robinson Crusoe ... sur l'avis et le plan de Jean-Jacques Rousseau* – in which Friday refuses to accompany Crusoe to England because love of his country is greater than gratitude to his master.

In 1787 Charles Garnier published all three volumes of *Robinson Crusoe* as the first three volumes of a thirty-six volume collection of imaginary voyages.[15] The illustrations were by Clement-Pierre Marillier (1740–1808), one of the foremost book illustrators in France. Marillier provided two splendid drawings for the first volume, both set on the island and portraying a man of unusual self-possession: the young Crusoe's gratitude at his miraculous escape from the shipwreck and many years later his rescue of Friday (Figure 11.3). Crusoe's command of the situation is indicated by his powerful stance. Behind him the pine tree extends his height and emphasizes his dominant position. An ungainly Friday makes his submission, while in the background a group of savages is reduced to insignificance. Marillier's design reveals an important difference between the French and English perceptions of Defoe's hero. In English illustration Robinson Crusoe remained for the most part an Everyman figure, admired for his survival and his capacity for recreating a domestic life for himself on the island. Marillier inaugurated the tendency in French illustration to elevate Crusoe into heroic stature, and later French illustration would develop Marillier's vision by picturing Crusoe as a superman, larger than life, or approaching god-like stature.

At the end of the eighteenth century a pair of pictures was painted by Antoine-Pierre Mongin (1761–1827), a well-known landscapist, and engraved

Figure 11.3 Clément Pierre Marillier (1786). Il prend un de mes pieds et le pose sur sa tête, pour me faire comprende sans doute qu'il me juroit fidélité. Engraving by Remi Henri Joseph Delvaux. *Voyages imaginaires, songes, visions, et romans cabalistique* (Amsterdam: Charles Garnier, 1787), facing p. 376. Edition and image is author's own.

by Simon-Charles Miger (1736–1828), one of the most distinguished men in his field. Only one of these appears to have survived, Crusoe's discovery of the footprint in the sand (Figure 11.4),[16] one of the earliest depictions of this scene, and one which was to become for later readers a predominant image

Figure 11.4 Antoine-Pierre Mongin (1799). *Footprint*. Engraving by Simon-Charles Miger.

in Crusoe iconography. Larger than any book illustration, these free-standing etchings were meant to be framed and hung on a wall. Like the subjects from classical mythology that Miger engraved, Robinson Crusoe had by now acquired such fame that he could be depicted in splendid drawings for the well-to-do to decorate their houses. Accompanied by an appropriate quotation in French as well as in the original English, these pictures indicate the extraordinary position Robinson Crusoe had gained in France. Eighty years after its first publication *Robinson Crusoe* had acquired the enduring status of myth.

In 1779 in England the enterprising publisher James Harrison began his reprint series, *The Novelist's Magazine*. The appearance in 1781 of *Robinson Crusoe* in Volume IV, illustrated with seven drawings by Thomas Stothard (1755–1834) for the two volumes of the novel, helped to stimulate a revival of interest in *Robinson Crusoe* and in Defoe. Stothard's imaginative designs – a major advance upon the simple, often rather crudely drawn, illustrations of the 1722 edition – highlight a few of the more poignant and pathetic moments in Crusoe's story. In 1785 George Chalmers brought out his *Life of Defoe*, a significant early re-assessment of Defoe's achievement, and in the same year John Walter published an edition of *Robinson Crusoe* with two illustrations by Mather Brown (1791–1831), engraved by Robert Pollard (c.1755–1818). Five years later this edition was republished (with additional plates[17] in both volumes) and two fine new editions were published, one by William Lane and the other by John Stockdale. Of these three editions, the most sumptuous was Stockdale's.[18] Stothard was again asked to provide the illustrations; his fourteen designs gave a visual summary of the main lines of the story, very much in the tradition of eighteenth-century narrative painting in the manner of Hogarth's well-known "progresses."

Mather Brown's depiction of the rescue of Friday, the sole illustration in the first volume of *Robinson Crusoe* (1785) and reproduced in the three-volume edition of 1790, may be usefully compared with the same scene, depicted in the two other editions of 1790. Brown, an American, who studied in London in the studio of his countryman, Benjamin West, and at the Royal Academy Schools, makes use of a formal device borrowed from Renaissance religious painting, the triangle formed by Crusoe and the two Indians (Figure 11.5). Appearing miraculously out of nowhere, Crusoe has just rescued Friday by slaying his enemies invisibly. In the background can be seen a ring of dancing cannibals and on the other side Crusoe's stockade, the two poles between which Friday is moving. Crusoe appears as a figure of authority, an all-powerful father or even a god, as Brown subtly indicates by employing the pictorial convention of hair streaming in the wind to denote such a powerful figure.[19]

In Stothard's design (Figure 11.6)[20] Friday is presented, not as he was in Stothard's earlier pictures as a figure of pathos or comedy, but as the Noble Savage, the idealized primitive man of uncorrupted virtue so much discussed at the time. Friday's nobility is indicated by the muscular torso, based on antique statues, and the "noble" face identified by the long hair, straight nose, and small mouth. Crusoe had pointed out the noble (that is, classical) features of Friday. "He was a comely handsome fellow, perfectly well made ... His hair was long and black, not curl'd like wool; his forehead very high, and large ... his nose small, not flat like the Negroes, a very good mouth, thin lips, and his teeth well set, and white as ivory" (162). Stothard, who learned to draw not from life studies, but from copying antique sculptures and the works of Raphael, interprets his features in the light of classical ideals.[21] The Friday we see here appears to possess those innately good traits that are the marks of Rousseau's vision of what man would be if not corrupted by society. Crusoe is a civilized European who has been forced to return to a state of nature where he encounters an uncivilized, but noble, savage whom he introduces to the benefits of clothing, civilization, and Christianity. This

Figure 11.5 Mather Brown (1785). Rescue of Friday. Engraving by Robert Pollard. *The Life and Adventures of Robinson Crusoe, Vol. 1* (London: John Walter, 1790), facing p. 323. © British Library Board, shelfmark 88.d1,2.

Figure 11.6 Richard Stothard (1790). Robinson Crusoe first sees and rescues his man
Friday. Engraving by Thomas Medland. *The Life And Strange Surprizing Adventures of
Robinson Crusoe, Vol. 1* (London: John Stockdale, 1790), facing p. 256.
Edition and image is author's own.

icon presents the two men, Crusoe and Friday, moving in opposite directions,
at the point at which they meet.

The romanticizing of Friday in the late eighteenth century is carried a step
further in Charles Ansell's design (Figure 11.7)[22] for William Lane (1790),
in which Crusoe, who has set aside his rifles, offers grapes and bread to
Friday, who approaches the benevolent figure of Crusoe, not crouching but
standing. A jug of water stands at Crusoe's feet and light breaks through
the trees to create a nimbus around his head. It is a sacramental scene in
which Crusoe, as the caption – *Robinson Crusoe Rescuing & Protecting
Friday* – makes clear, appears as Friday's saviour. The idealization of Friday,
which we can see in all three of these engravings, turns Friday from an

Figure 11.7 Charles Ansell (1790). Robinson Crusoe Rescuing & Protecting Friday.
Engraving by Inigo Barlow. *The Life and Adventures of Robinson Crusoe, Vol. 1*
(London: William Lane, 1790), facing p. 194. Edition and image is author's own.

ordinary Caribbean Indian into a prince. In an edition printed in Dublin in 1820, Crusoe's description of Friday was altered to include the sentence, "I had saved the life of an Indian prince, no less graceful and accomplished than the great Oroonoko."[23] For well over a century, since the time Aphra Behn first used the name for her hero,[24] Oroonoko had been a type of the admirable, but oppressed, primitive nobleman. His association with Friday underscores the transformation that Crusoe's companion underwent in the Romantic period.

The Romantic critics, notably Walter Scott, Samuel Taylor Coleridge, and Charles Lamb, recognized Defoe as a major novelist and *Robinson Crusoe* as his most important work.[25] In 1830 Walter Wilson brought out his *Memoirs of the Life and Times of Daniel De Foe* in three volumes. In the following year three new illustrated editions of *Robinson Crusoe* appeared, of which the edition published by John Major, illustrated by George Cruikshank (1792–1878),[26] is of exceptional interest. Not only was Cruikshank a highly accomplished artist, he also represents a different tradition in book illustration. The development by Thomas Bewick of a new technique for making wood engravings meant that, as they could be set up – unlike copper engravings – with the letterpress, illustrated books could be printed more cheaply. The result was the proliferation of vignettes throughout the text and a closer interplay between picture and text. Cruikshank's training as a political cartoonist and graphic satirist played into his lively and often witty vignettes, such as the scene of Crusoe dining alone in his cave (Figure 11.8).[27] No caption is required as the text supplies the context. The confined atmosphere of the crowded scene, reinforced by the heavy frame of beams enclosing Crusoe and his "little family," is relieved by the happy play of emotions between Crusoe and the animals. Realism and delight lie within the picture, which is made witty by the accompanying text. Crusoe is aware of the irony of his dining alone, like royalty, but on a desert island. The reader, like the stoic, will smile at the scene. Cruikshank was the first illustrator to be aware of the comic element in Defoe, the smile of comic self-awareness that is occasionally on Crusoe's lips.

During the course of the nineteenth century, Robinson Crusoe was often the subject of paintings exhibited at the Royal Academy or at the British Institution.[28] In 1835, five years after Wilson's biography, which had acclaimed *Robinson Crusoe* for its uplifting "moral and religious tendency,"[29] Alexander Fraser (1786–1865) exhibited *Robinson Crusoe Reading the Bible to his Man Friday* (Figure 11.9)[30] at the Royal Academy. Crusoe explains the biblical text, Friday – set one step below Crusoe – kneels to listen, while the hour-glass on the table measures the time devoted to the study. The image here – the Englishman coping admirably under difficult

Figure 11.8 George Cruickshank (1831). Crusoe in his cave. Engraving by John Jackson. *The Life and Surprising Adventures of Robinson Crusoe… illustrated with numerous engravings from drawings by George Cruikshank Vol. 1* (London: John Major, 1831), 210. Edition and image is author's own.

circumstances, attended by his faithful servant of a different colour, and spreading the Christian gospel into foreign parts – was to become a central icon in the Victorian self-image.

The companionable relationship of Crusoe and Friday in Fraser's picture is typical of English illustration. In France, by contrast, Crusoe was frequently depicted, not as an ordinary man in an extraordinary situation, but as an heroic survivor, as we see in the monumental frontispiece (Figure 11.10)[31] to an edition published in Paris and London in 1840,[32] illustrated by Grandville (Jean-Ignace-Isidore Gérard, 1803–47), and frequently reprinted throughout the century. Surrounded by the familiar attributes of parrot, dog, basket, hatchet, and rifle, a gigantic Crusoe sits on a plinth decorated with

Figure 11.9 Alexander Fraser (1835). *Robinson Crusoe Reading the Bible to his Man Friday*.
Engraving by Charles G. Lewis (1836) (London: Henry Graves, 1836).
Edition and image is author's own.

rams' heads and a cameo head of Friday. Below a group of parents and children have come to admire Crusoe and honour his stupendous achievement. Tiny human figures emphasize the vast size of a monument, which rises to the height of the palm trees. Grandville's imposing frontispiece affirms the pre-eminence which Crusoe has attained after more than a century of pictorial interpretation. His twenty-eight years on the island are seen not as a just punishment for his sins and an opportunity for conversion, but as a triumphant accomplishment that elevates him into a larger-than-life-size symbol of survival, endurance, and authority.

Friday too changed in Grandville's illustrations. No longer the Noble Savage that Stothard and others had depicted or even Crusoe's agreeable companion and helpmeet, Friday is an ex-cannibal, rescued, converted, and submissive. Grandville's vision of *Robinson Crusoe* in the first part of the story is in some ways an escapist fantasy, a celebration of solitary innocence and the pleasures – as well as the trials – of the simple tasks of life in a wonderfully lush and remote tropical setting, a romantic vision of life partly

Figure 11.10 Grandville (Jean-Ignace-Isidore Gérard) and François-Louis Français (1840).
Frontispiece. Engraving by Louis Henri Brévière. *The Adventures of Robinson Crusoe*
(Paris: H. Fournier Aîné; London: William Strange, and Robert Tyas, 1840).
Edition and image is author's own.

influenced by Rousseau, but given Grandville's own mark by his fascination
with animals and his love of nature. When he discovers the footprint in
the sand the reverie ends. Crusoe reacts not just with fear but also with
dismay and horror. When Crusoe rescues Friday – whose face and posture,
in Grandville's picture, register fear and subservience – the relationship that
develops between them is that of master and servant, rather than that of
father and son.

In the middle years of the century new illustrated editions of *Robinson
Crusoe* in English appeared at a rate of about one a year,[33] clear indication

of the popularity and market value of Defoe's by now famous work. The publishers often engaged promising or well-known artists and engravers, such as H. Knight Browne ("Phiz," 1813–82), John Gilbert (1817–97), and J. D. Watson (1832–92). We need not pause long over these illustrators. Browne's designs are decidedly quirky; there are, for instance, no illustrations of Crusoe alone. It seems likely that he was working not from the text but from Cruikshank's superior illustrations, selected for their appeal to Browne's penchant for the comic and bizarre elements in the story. J. D. Watson's designs, although realistic and frequently charming, may be said to be lacking in fire, though the engraving by the Brothers Dalziel[34] is always very fine. The designs of Ernest Griset (1844–1907) are of rather greater interest. They appeared[35] in 1869 – the 150th anniversary of the first edition – with an introduction by William Lee, whose three-volume *Defoe: His Life and Recently Discovered Writings* came out the same year. Griset's one hundred illustrations, rather than depicting the idealized, sometimes even idyllic, life of successful problem-solving that is part of an earlier emphasis on the practical rather than the emotional side of Crusoe's experience, are in the Anglo-French tradition of graphic satire, so well exemplified by Grandville and Browne. Indeed, Griset shared with Grandville a fascination with anthropomorphism and with Browne with the grotesque and he employed the dark plate technique, used by Browne for the later, darker novels of Dickens, to convey the eeriness of landscapes and the often rather sinister atmosphere of Crusoe's island. Griset provides several full-page illustrations of the remains of the cannibal feast and of their feasting and celebrating, a reflection of his interest in the grisly and grotesque. In a striking vignette, Crusoe is shown walking through a dark and threatening forest with climbers and curious plants, not unlike epiphyte bromelia, hanging like huge spiders above the diminutive figures of Crusoe and his dog, both on the alert to possible danger (Figure 11.11). Unlike illustrators who depicted Crusoe at one with nature, happily re-creating a life for himself on his island, Griset is aware of the psychological element in Crusoe's eerie existence, totally alone, puny, vulnerable, and overwhelmed by the natural world around him.

Griset's was the last English illustrated edition for some time to show much insight into the darker aspects of Crusoe's experience on the Island of Despair. Book illustration in England in general passed into a period of relative decline until the efflorescence of illustration in the 1890s. *Robinson Crusoe* was increasingly seen as a book for boys, especially after Leslie Stephens' essay in the *Cornhill Magazine*[36] in 1868 declared that it "falls short of any high intellectual interest" and hence was "a book for boys rather than men." Nineteenth-century English illustration created a variety of Crusoes – the romantic solitary, the practical manager, the empire-builder – but

88 *ADVENTURES OF*

I spent all that Evening there, and went not back to my Habitation, which by the Way was the first Night, as I might say, I had lain from Home. In the Night I took my first Contrivance, and got up into a Tree, where I slept well, and the next Morning proceeded upon my Discovery, travelling near four Miles, as I might judge by the Length of the Valley, keeping still due North, with a Ridge of Hills on the South and North side of me.

At the End of this March I came to an Opening, where the Country seemed to descend to the West, and a little Spring of fresh Water, which issued out of the Side of the Hill by me, run the other Way, that is due East; and the Country appear'd so fresh, so green, so flourishing, everything being in a constant Verdure, or Flourish of *Spring*, that it looked like a planted Garden.

I descended a little on the Side of that delicious Vale, surveying it with a secret Kind of Pleasure, (though mixed with my other afflicting Thoughts) to think that this was all my own, that I was King and Lord of all this Country indefeasibly, and had a Right of Possession; and if I could convey it, I might have it in Inheritance, as completely as any Lord of a Manor in *England*. I saw here Abundance of Cocoa Trees, Orange, and Lemon, and Citron Trees; but all wild and very few bearing any Fruit, at least not then:

Figure 11.11 Ernest Griset (1869). Crusoe in a forest. *The Life and Adventures of Robinson Crusoe, Vol. 1* (London: John Camden Hotten, 1869), 61. Steel engraving. © British Library Board, shelfmark 12613.gg.9.

in all cases, a resourceful fellow whose ordinariness is one that the reader can share.

Again, it was another story in France. As early as Marillier's designs French illustration had created a tradition of Crusoe as a superman, a powerful figure dominating both his physical environment and Friday, the heroic survivor worthy of an enormous statue in Grandville's vision of the story. Jules Fesquet's frontispiece portrait (Figure 11.12)[37] for an edition published in Paris by Jules Bonnassies in 1877 – the most remarkable of all portraits of Crusoe – shows Crusoe with the attributes of Hercules, consisting of a lion's skin head-dress, the paws knotted in front, and a club or, in this case,

Figure 11.12 Jules Fesquet (1877). Frontispiece, steel engraving by Gabriel Hubert
Alexandre Légenisel. *Etranges aventures de Robinson Crusoe*
(Paris: Jules Bonnassies, 1877), facing p. xx.
© British Library Board, shelfmark 12612.ff.1.

a sword. Also traditional in the iconography of Hercules, the prototype of
masculine strength, are the nude muscular body, short hair, and beard.[38]
To this powerful image Fesquet has added an orb, the ancient symbol of
the cosmos, derived from the Romans, by whom it was associated with
Jupiter and with the emperor, his earthly representative. Both a hero and a
god, Hercules – "the very incarnation of human suffering, endurance and

triumph"[39] – was by far the greatest of Greek heroes. In Fesquet's engraving Crusoe achieves the highest level of heroic virtue

But who is the Indian, lying under Crusoe's foot? While he may be Friday, he is probably one of his pursuers.[40] For one thing, he is not prostrate but supine. For another, he has his hand on a tomahawk. The portrait of Crusoe as Hercules, moreover, is an anomaly, a flamboyant rhetorical statement about Crusoe's power and, by extension, about the power of Defoe's story.[41] It is also a powerful icon of the European conquest and domination of America. Like Grandville, Fesquet depicts an apotheosis. The image of Crusoe, placed at a key position at the beginning of the story, represents a figure more than human[42] – a man several times larger than life in Grandville's version or, here, one who has become a god.[43]

The 1890s, a golden decade in English book illustration, saw the appearance of several important illustrated editions of *Robinson Crusoe*. Late Victorian Britain had embarked upon a sustained period of empire-building, acquiring along the way a fascination with big-game hunting. Children's literature – notably the more than one hundred historical adventure stories by G. A. Henty[44] – reflected the widespread interest in warfare and adventure abroad and *Robinson Crusoe*, seen as a book for boys, became an expression of imperial nationalism.[45] In its imperial propaganda,[46] its social and spatial mobility, and its violent adventures, *Robinson Crusoe* has clear affinities with the sort of stories that appeared in the late Victorian boys' weekly papers. Stanley Berkeley (1840–1909), known for his animal illustrations and for his popular depiction of dramatic episodes in the Boer War, illustrated both volumes of *Robinson Crusoe* in 1890,[47] beginning with an impressive frontispiece picture of Crusoe shooting a lion[48] off the coast of Africa. His design for the rescue of Friday (Figure 11.13) is a far cry from earlier illustrations that showed Crusoe in a sentimental or semi-religious role as the savior of Friday. In Berkeley's drawing it is not Friday we notice but the cannibal who leaps up in the throes of death, shot by Crusoe, whose back is turned to us. The Introduction to this edition, by Thomas Archer, praises the realism and the sincerity of the narrative and predictably pronounces it "the most famous book for boys ever" published.

Berkeley's illustrations, full of violent action or the expectation of it, were followed a year later by Walter Paget's 120 illustrations for an edition of volumes I and II published by Cassell & Co. The sheer number of Paget's illustrations afforded him the opportunity to bring out Crusoe's ingenuity in making a life for himself on the island, though the emphasis is always upon practical activity rather than upon introspective reflection. Scenes of Crusoe's illness, his terrible dream warning, even his reading the Bible, are not depicted. Like Berkeley, he set the tone for his illustrations in the frontispiece

Crusoe's first attack on the Cannibals, when he saves Friday.

Figure 11.13 Stanley Berkeley (1890). Crusoe's first attack on the Cannibals when he saves Friday. *The life and surprising adventures of Robinson Crusoe of York, mariner, Vol. 1* (London and Sydney: Griffith, Farran, Okeden & Welsh, 1890), 171. Photogravure. © British Library Board, shelfmark 012611.g.11.

(Figure 11.14) – the killing of a lion on the African shore – but it is not the ferocity of the beast or the terror of Crusoe and Xury that matters. The sport is what counts, as the quotation from the text – "This Was Game Indeed" – indicates. The disappearance of the spiritual element in Paget's illustrations and the ascendency of national pride, militarism, and commercial exploitation in the period generally point to a widespread attitude that saw *Robinson Crusoe* as a didactic and inspirational work for boys.[49]

"THIS WAS GAME INDEED."

(See p. 22.)

Figure 11.14 Walter Paget (1891). This Was Game Indeed. Frontispiece. *The Life and Strange Surprising Adventures of Robinson Crusoe of York Mariner as related by himself* (London, Paris, and Melbourne: Cassell & Company, Ltd., 1891). Wood engraving. Edition and image is author's own.

In 1898 Service and Paton brought out an edition[50] of *Robinson Crusoe* with illustrations by Charles Edmund Brock (1870–1938). Brock was a popular book illustrator of the day, one of a pair of brothers known for their attachment to the fiction of the eighteenth century. Brock's illustrations are not devoid of violent scenes, but he is at his most characteristic when expressing personality, as in the companionable picture showing a delighted Friday and a benevolent and rather curious Crusoe (Figure 11.15). Brock was a fine figure draughtsman and his imaginative pen has caught and

Figure 11.15 Charles Edmund Brock (1898). This Friday admired very much. *The life and adventures of Robinson Crusoe, Vol. 1* (London: Service and Paton, 1898), facing p. 168. Edition and image is author's own.

developed the play of emotions of which there is only the slightest hint in Defoe's account. While Brock attempts to give expression to the inner human qualities, like Paget and other late Victorian and early twentieth-century illustrators, he ignores the spiritual theme in the novel that in Defoe's account alone makes sense of the extraordinary story of Crusoe's afflictions. In many ways Brock's pictorial interpretation is very much of its time. Crusoe's story is still primarily a tale of action and adventure, much of it clearly meant to appear rather enjoyable.

The sixteen illustrations in colour, supplemented by forty-five black and white vignettes, of J. Ayton Symington (fl. 1890–1908), for an edition published by J. M. Dent in 1905, are representative of the mood of most *Crusoe* illustrations in the period leading up to World War I, although they are on the whole superior to rival editions. Once again emphasizing such themes as resourcefulness, violence, conquest, survival, and ultimate triumph, *Robinson Crusoe* is presented as an adventure story for boys. There is no doubt in Symington's pictures that right (that is, authority) will win out over unlawfulness. Cannibals are shot, victims rescued, and mutineers captured, their leader executed. Intermingled with such scenes of danger and excitement, however, are quieter scenes, including the colored cover of the book, showing Crusoe at moments of solid satisfaction or in contented repose. In the cover illustration, framed by palm branches and the ship's tackle, Crusoe sits on a rock on the shore, dressed in his famous goat-skins with a rifle in his hands but contemplatively smoking a pipe. He is not gazing out to sea but musing to himself, rather more contented than either lonely or disturbed. In this, and the picture entitled "I was King and Lord of all this country" (Figure 11.16), something of the attitude of the colonial administrator in Africa or India can perhaps be felt. Here, *mutatis mutandis*, is the English colonial administrator in some far-flung corner of the empire, pausing for a moment when his duties have been done, in charge of his patch of the earth's surface and reasonably contented with his lot.

In virtually all the pre-World War I British illustrated editions, little or no attention is paid to the spiritual dimensions of the story or of Crusoe's inner life, the agony of his despair, given such poignant expression by Defoe. On the other side of the Atlantic, however, American illustrators, free of the imperialist rhetoric of their British counterparts, gave greater expression to the psychological dimension of the story, to Crusoe's loneliness, his despair, and his communion with nature.

The edition illustrated by Elenore Plaisted Abbott (1875–1935)[51] for G. W. Jacob and Co. (Philadelphia) in 1913, printed in large type and divided into chapters, resembles the typical editions for children published in England at the time. But its frontispiece and six full-page color drawings are quite unlike contemporary English illustration. Except of course for Friday, no cannibal makes an appearance, and even Friday shows up in only one picture, an untypical one at that, in which he is shown bringing Crusoe the bird he has shot. Moreover, most of the big scenes – the shipwreck, the footprint in the sand, the rescue of Friday, for instance – are not included, though there is an illustration of Crusoe rescuing his goods (but without the wreck in the background) and one of his leaving home. Even in such scenes, however, Abbott's vision of Crusoe's experience is unusual. In the picture of his leaving home (Figure 11.17), for example, rather than his father (or both his parents), it is his mother – an attractive, exceptionally well-dressed, *young*

"I WAS KING AND LORD OF ALL THIS COUNTRY"

Figure 11.16. J. Ayton Symington (1905). I was King and Lord of all this country. *The Life Adventures of Robinson Crusoe of York, Mariner, Vol. 1* (London: J. M. Dent & Co., 1905), facing p. 72. Watercolour reproduced in colour.
© British Library Board, shelfmark 012612.ee.9.

woman[52] – whom Crusoe disobeys. The subsequent illustrations do not suggest that either punishment or very much hardship followed. Abbott's is essentially a secular interpretation. In this respect at least she does not differ from other contemporary illustration. Crusoe's dream is not included, nor do we see him reading the Bible or praying. The grace of affliction is not felt or interpreted. Instead, in a series of close-up pictures of the gradually aging Crusoe, surrounded by the dense, at times almost oppressive, vegetation of the island, we are brought face to face with the remoteness and silence of Crusoe's existence. Her dark colours, predominantly strong blues and

SHE WOULD HAVE NO HAND IN MY DESTRUCTION   18

Figure 11.17 Elenore Plaisted Abbott (1913). She would have no hand in my destruction.
Robinson Crusoe (Philadelphia: G. W. Jacob and Co., 1913), facing p. 18.
Reproduction in colour.
© British Library Board, shelfmark 12800.aa.20.

greens, and her close-up technique, focusing our attention on Crusoe himself, create an atmosphere that is intense and introspective. She suggests the
claustrophobia of enforced isolation, while at the same time her impression-
istic designs anticipate the later abstract illustration of McKight Kauffer.
In these dark interiorized pictures, the great sweep of the seashore and the
endless sunshine of other illustrators of the pre-war years disappear, to be
replaced by a psychological portrait of a man who has to learn to live not

only by himself but with himself. Abbott's pictures are an early instance in twentieth-century illustration of an increasing fascination with the psychological dimensions of the novel.

In 1920 the Cosmopolitan Book Corporation of New York published a fine bicentenary edition of *Robinson Crusoe* with illustrations by the famous mural painter and book illustrator, Newell Conners Wyeth (1882–1945).[53] Wyeth included an "Illustrator's Preface," in which he expressed his enthusiasm at finally having the opportunity of illustrating *Robinson Crusoe*, which, he tells us, he had "anticipated for years." For Wyeth, *Robinson Crusoe* is essentially a romance, whose appeal "to me personally" lies in "the remarkably sustained sensation one enjoys of Crusoe's contact with the elements – the sea and the sun, the night and the storm, the sand, rocks, vegetation and animal life." Wyeth's magnificent panoramas, a celebration of the elements as much as "a lone man's conquest over what seems to be inexorable Fate," were intended to aid "in the clearer visualization" of the story. In technicolor splendor they do just that, though of course the vision is more Wyeth's than Defoe's. Wyeth's rapturous paintings (Figure 11.18) of the wonders of the universe in which his Crusoe lives is an extension of his own romantic vision of the beauty and awesomeness of the elements expressed in his murals and his other illustrated books, such as the designs for Jules Verne's *The Mysterious Island* (1919).[54] Like all romantic artists, Wyeth identifies with his subject, delighting in his capacity to "live and move with his hero so intensely." For Crusoe, as for Defoe, the elements were more to be endured than admired.

After Wyeth the illustration of *Robinson Crusoe* continued as vigorously as ever, both in the conventional mode of realistic illustration designed for children's books and, increasingly, as an art book in expensive editions intended for the collector. The restoration of *Robinson Crusoe* as a book for adults was confirmed in the decade that followed when limited editions were published in both French and English. In 1926 in Paris a de luxe edition in three volumes (that is, Parts I and II), illustrated by Pierre Falké (1884–1947), was published in an edition of only 151 copies. In 1930 the Limited Editions Club in New York published a handsome edition of volume I, illustrated by Edward A. Wilson and with an introduction by Ford Madox Ford. In 1929, the year before Wilson's edition, a de luxe edition of the novel was published in London by Frederick Etchells and Hugh Macdonald with designs by E. McKnight Kauffer (1891–1954). McKnight Kauffer's illustrations are significant since, by attempting not merely to depict the scenes already described in words but to project the unspoken thoughts (as the artist envisages them) of Defoe's hero, they attempt to communicate the psychological journey into the human mind as it undergoes the

© C. B. C.

" All this while I sat upon the ground, very much terrified and dejected "

Figure 11.18 Newell Conners Wyeth (1920). All this while I sat upon the ground, very much terrified and dejected. *Robinson Crusoe* (New York, NY: Cosmopolitan Book Corporation; London: Harrods Ltd., 1920), facing p. 106. Watercolour reproduced in colour.
© British Library Board, shelfmark 012802.d.2.

unimaginable experience of a quarter century of absolute isolation. The most exciting twentieth-century illustration would move beyond the book itself and attempt to capture the vison of the human mind behind it. In the illustrations of McKnight Kauffer and later of Edward Gordon Craig, *Robinson Crusoe* lent itself admirably to this striking new type of book illustration.

Of the modern illustrators of *Robinson Crusoe* the most famous, and the strangest, is Edward Gordon Craig (1872–1966). In the edition, published in several versions[55] in 1979 by the Basilisk Press, Craig's lifetime obsession with *Robinson Crusoe* found posthumous expression. Craig suffered from severe and prolonged periods of depression, lasting many months and occasionally years. At such times he would retreat into Crusoe's silent world, which allowed him to live "a kind of make-believe" life, a "world of his own imagining." Craig thought and wrote extensively about Crusoe, leaving his ideas in unfinished manuscript notes filled with fantasizing about Robinson Crusoe "as though he had known him and his contemporaries personally."[56]

What appealed to Craig about the Crusoe story was his empathy with Crusoe's isolation. The very element of Crusoe's experience most terrifying to Defoe and to readers was, for Craig, the attraction of this book: "Is it not our desire to be alone – to be rid of all dear friends, the only less dear enemies – the babble of things and of people – to be alone at last? And we experience all that through him – for we become Robinson." Craig's deeply-felt identification with Crusoe, his insight that "we secretly enjoy loneliness through him,"[57] reveals yet another dimension of Defoe's profound and enduring tale.

NOTES

1 This chapter, amended and brought up to date, is based upon my study of the illustrated editions of *Robinson Crusoe*, published as *The Illustration of "Robinson Crusoe" 1719–1920* (Gerrards Cross: Colin Smythe, 1995; New York, NY: Oxford University Press, 1996).

2 Tim Clayton has pointed out that "it was unusual for first editions of new works to be embellished. Important exceptions include the first edition of *Robinson Crusoe* in 1719 with a frontispiece engraved by John Pine." See his "Book Illustration and the World of Prints," in *The Cambridge History of the Book in Britain*, vol. 5 (1695–1830), ed. Michael F. Suarez, SJ and Michael L. Turner (Cambridge: Cambridge University Press, 2009), 231.

3 While it is entirely possible (even probable) that Pine designed the portrait, his name appears along with that of Clark only as one of the engravers: "*Clark & Pine Sc.*" (for *sculpserunt*).

4 In the Introduction to H. C. Hutchins, *"Robinson Crusoe" and Its Printing: 1719–1731: A Bibliographical Study* (New York, NY: Columbia University Press, 1925), A. Edward Newton pointed out that "This illustration has outlasted several centuries of criticism. We always look for it and are disappointed when we do not find it ... It has come to be the accepted portrait; no legend is required: one knows that he is looking at Robinson Crusoe" (xvii).

5 Six illustrations were added in the sixth edition (1722), one of which is signed "*Clark &c Sc*". It is likely that Clark altered the background in the frontispiece reprinted in the sixth edition. Pat Rogers provides a succinct account of the early editions in his *Robinson Crusoe* (London: George Allen & Unwin, 1979), 6 and 7.

6 He has been called "the most famous engraver of the eighteenth century after Hogarth." See Lynn Hunt, Margaret C. Jacob, and Wijnand Mijnhardt, *The Book that Changed Europe: Picart & Bernard's Religious Ceremonies of the World* (Cambridge, MA and London: Belknap Press, 2010), 1.

7　The artist and the engravers of the English portrait may well not have been able to read the manuscript, which would have been in the hands of the compositor.

8　*Robinson Crusoe*, ed. John Richetti (London: Penguin Books, 2001), 118–19. Further references are provided in the text.

9　Lise Andries, "Les images and les choses dans *Robinson* et les robinsonnades," *études françaises* 35: 1 (Printemps, 1999), 95–122 of a special number entitled "Robinson, la robinsonnade et le monde des choses." See 103.

10　Monique Brosse, *Le mythe de Robinson* (Paris: Lettres Moderne, 1993). See chap. IV, esp. 72–3. In France and other Continental countries Crusoe is always called Robinson.

11　Until well into the nineteenth century, editions of *Robinson Crusoe* included the sequel, *The Farther Adventures of Robinson Crusoe*, though rarely the third volume, the *Serious Reflections … of Robinson Crusoe*.

12　Owing in large measure to perpetual copyright, which was not broken until 1774. On the breaking of perpetual copyright, see Richard D. Altick, *The English Common Reader* (Chicago, IL and London: University of Chicago Press, 1957), 53–4.

13　Martin Green points out that *Emile* "was one of the most powerful of all editings, and reshapings, of a myth." See his *The Robinson Crusoe Story* (University Park, PA and London: Pennsylvania State University Press, 1990), 39.

14　*Dissertations Moral and Critical* (Edinburgh, 1783), "On the Fable and Romance," 567.

15　*Voyages imaginaires, songes, visions, et romans cabalistique* (Amsterdam, 1787). The first plate was engraved by Louis Berthet; the second by Remi-Henri-Joseph Delvaux (1748–1823). There were also two plates in the second volume, engraved by Jean-Louis Delignon (1755–1804) and Gérard-René Le Villain (1740–1836).

16　Picture and text measure 45cm x 38cm.

17　Engraved by C. Metz – either Conrad Martin Metz (1719–1827) or Caroline Metz – and by Robert Pollard.

18　It included Chalmers' *Life of Defoe*, first published by Stockdale in 1785, considerably enlarged and revised. Defoe was now placed "in the foremost rank" (II, 436) of novelists.

19　The convention descended from Michelangelo, who represented God the Father with hair streaming in the wind. Blake similarly depicted Urizen in the frontispiece to *Europe* (1794).

20　Engraved by Thomas Medland (d. 1833).

21　See Mrs. Bray, *Life of Thomas Stothard, R. S.* (London: John Murray, 1851), 77–8.

22　Charles Ansell (b. 1752?), engraved by Inigo Barlow.

23　*The Life and most surprising Adventures of Robinson Crusoe of York, Mariner*, 2nd ed. (Dublin: John Jones [1820]), 122–3.

24　*Oroonoko: or the royal slave*, 1688. Thomas Southerne's tragedy, *Oroonoko*, was first performed at Drury Lane in 1695. See Edward D. Seeber, "Oroonoko and Crusoe's Man Friday," *Modern Language Quarterly* 12 (1951): 286–91.

25　See Pat Rogers, ed., *Defoe: The Critical Heritage* (London: Routledge & Kegan Paul 1972), 16–18.

26　Cruikshank's association with *Robinson Crusoe* extended over many years. Albert M. Cohn, *George Cruikshank, A Catalogue Raisonée* (London: The Office of "The Bookman's Journal," 1924), lists editions illustrated by Cruikshank in 1819 (227, 228). A Banbury chapbook of seven wood cuts, "engraved by Dranston," has been attributed to Cruikshank (*c.*1840).

27 Engraved by John Jackson (1801–48).

28 See Richard D. Altick, *Paintings from Books: Art and Literature in Britain, 1760–1900* (Columbus, OH: Ohio State University Press, 1985), *s.v.* Defoe, 380–1: "Some twenty-five pictures [of Robinson Crusoe] in all are recorded." Founded in 1805, the British Institution for Promoting the Fine Arts in the United Kingdom was disbanded 1867.

29 Rogers, *Defoe: The Critical Heritage*, 92. Quotation from Wilson, *Memoirs of the Life and Times of Daniel De Foe* (1830), III, 444.

30 Mezzotint and engraving made in the following year by Charles G. Lewis (1808–80) and published in London by Henry Graves, October 15, 1836. 52cm x 64cm.

31 Engraved by Louis-Henri Brévière. François-Louis Français (1814–97), whose name as artist appears with Grandville's on the frontispiece, was responsible for the background in this and other illustrations.

32 Published in Paris by H. Fournier Aîné and in London by William Strange and by Robert Tyas.

33 The most complete list is Robert W. Lovett, *Robinson Crusoe: A Bibliographical Checklist of English Language Editions (1719–1979)* (New York, NY, Westport, CT, and London: Greenwood Press, 1991), which records an average of over six editions (including reprints) for each of the years between 1831 (Cruikshank) and 1869 (Griset). Most of these are illustrated, though the artists and engravers are not always identified on the title-page or elsewhere. An online list (to 1850) may be found at http://robinsoncrusoe.jamesmckane.com.

34 The distinguished firm of George (1815–1902) and Edward (1817–1905) Dalziel, founded in 1839.

35 Published in London by Frederick Warne and by John Camden Hotten and several times reprinted in the 1870s, including in New York by Scribner, Welford and Armstrong.

36 Vol. 17, no. 99 (March): 293–316, and reprinted in his *Hours in a Library* (London: Smith, Elder & Co., 1874), 56. Quotations are from Rogers, *Defoe: The Critical Heritage*, 174.

37 Jules Fesquet (1836–90), engraved by Gabriel-Hubert-Alexandre Légenisel (fl. 1860–75).

38 *Enciclopedia Dell'Arte Antica: Classica e Orientale* (Rome: Istituto della Enciclopedia Italiana, 1960), III, 378.

39 Anthony Grafton, Glenn W. Most, and Salvatore Setis, eds., *The Classical Tradition* (Cambridge, MA: Belknap Press, 2010), *s.v.* Hercules.

40 In a discussion of this image in *The Illustration of Robinson Crusoe*, I suggested that "He may be one of Friday's pursuers, whom Crusoe was forced to kill, or, more likely I think, he is Friday himself" (128). I did so then largely because Fesquet seemed to be invoking the rescue of Friday scene, memorably illustrated by both Marillier and Grandville. This chapter provides a welcome opportunity to correct that interpretation. The design does not so much depict the rescue and submission of Friday – which Fesquet provides in a conventional, far less dramatic scene facing p. 266 – as it makes a statement about the European subjection of America.

41 Fesquet's depiction of Crusoe as Hercules may have been, to some degree at least, intended ironically.

42 The difference between earlier English representation of Crusoe as an all-powerful god-like figure (as in the Brown-Pollard frontispiece of 1785 and the Ansell-Barlow etching of 1790) and Fesquet's depiction here is that in the English illustrations Crusoe appears as a god only to Friday; in the French picture Crusoe appears as a god to us.

43 Fesquet may have been influenced by the opinion of Friday's father, much later on in the story, that the Savages would no longer visit the island since "they believ'd whoever went to that enchanted island would be destroy'd with fire from the gods" (191).

44 Robert A. Huttenback, "G. A. Henty and the Imperial Stereotype," *Huntington Library Quarterly* 29 (1965): 63–75. See also John M. MacKenzie, *Propaganda and Empire: The Manipulation of British Public Opinion. 1880–1960* (Manchester: Manchester University Press, 1984), 6.

45 In his study of the literature of imperialism, *Dreams of Adventure, Deeds of Empire* (London: Routledge & Kegan Paul, 1980), Martin Green calls Defoe "my candidate for the prototype of literary imperialism" (5).

46 See J. A. Downie, "Defoe, Imperialism, and the Travel Books Reconsidered," *The Yearbook of English Studies* 13 (1983): 74, 76. See Green, *Dreams of Adventure*, 75–83.

47 London and Sydney: Griffith, Farran, Okeden & Welsh, 1890.

48 The lion was seen as "the most fearsome foe," a "dragon substitute" for the modern St. George to kill, "a national and imperial symbol ... the epitome of empire itself." See John M. MacKenzie, *The Empire of Nature: Hunting, Conservation and British Imperialism* (Manchester: Manchester University Press, 1988), 27, 47.

49 Louis James in "Tom Brown's Imperialist Sons," *Victorian Studies* 17 (1973) observes that after *Tom Brown's Schooldays*, the "next most common influence" on the vogue of the schoolboy story was probably *Robinson Crusoe* (97). The Introduction to an edition of *Robinson Crusoe* by J. Howard B. Masterman published by Cambridge University Press in 1900, stating what must then have seemed unexceptional, is breathtaking: "One great secret of the charm of *Robinson Crusoe* is that in the hero of the story we recognize those qualities of resourcefulness, activity and practical common sense that have made Great Britain the greatest colonizing power in the world. The act of 'making the best of things' was one that Englishmen had to learn when they went out to plant the flag of England in the waste places of the earth ... And so the simple story of a man who by labour and patience conquered despondency and doubt can never lose its charm for those who know that labour and patience – effort and faith – are still the forces that overcome the world."

50 Volume I and volume II (abridged).

51 Like N. C. Wyeth, E. P. Abbott was a pupil of the highly influential American book illustrator, Howard Pyle (1853–1911).

52 Crusoe's mother, the youngest of whose three sons is nineteen when the story opens, is usually depicted as a fairly elderly woman. In Stothard's design for the same scene, Mrs. Crusoe is shown holding a pair of reading glasses, while her husband, who suffers from gout, sits in an armchair, his walking stick by his side.

53 Published simultaneously in London by Harrods Ltd. The edition was of volume
    I only.
54 Verne's *L'Ile mystérieuse* (1874), as Martin Green has pointed out, is itself
    an important Robinsonnade, consciously inspired by Defoe's tale. See Green,
    Dreams of Adventure, 129. Verne's fascination with *Robinson Crusoe* found
    expression in a number of the other novels of his fifty-four volume series,
    Voyages Extraordinaires, notably in *L'École des Robinsons* (1882).
55 *The Life & Strange Surprising Adventures of Robinson Crusoe of York*
    (London: The Basilisk Press, 1979). The publication policy is explained at the
    end of the volume: 500 numbered copies for sale; 1–5 with 20 original prints;
    6–30 with 10 original prints; 31–500 with 1 original print.
56 Edward A. Craig, "Introduction" to the Basilisk Press edition, 11. Edward
    A. Craig was Edward Gordon Craig's son.
57 Ibid., 12.

12

JILL CAMPBELL

Robinsonades for Young People

A striking point of constancy in Americans' experience of growing up from the 1960s to the present adheres in a small paperback book that generations of American schoolchildren have each encountered in their turn, like waves breaking successively against a tall rock not far from shore: despite the many differences between the lives of young people now, in the 1960s, and in-between, conversation in a mixed-aged group of middle-aged adults and teenagers may turn up a common reference point in recollections of reading *Lord of the Flies*. The American school curriculum, in the midst of often rapid cultural change, has retained William Golding's *Lord of the Flies* as a fitting and important book for young readers. Another enduringly popular selection for school classes, Scott O'Dell's *Island of the Blue Dolphins* – lyrical, attuned to the natural world, centered on a single female protagonist – seems a very different kind of book. Put together, however, as a pair of books chosen by educators again and again, *Lord of the Flies* and *Island of the Blue Dolphins* demonstrate the remarkable persistence of the "Robinsonade" as a favored model of what makes a book instructive and compelling for young people, and also the wide variations among works that may be placed under that rubric.

In terms of the history of reading, literature for children and young adults is arguably the arena in which Defoe's most famous novel has had the greatest ongoing impact. Any number of writers of the nineteenth and twentieth centuries voice versions of Leslie Stephen's dictum that *Robinson Crusoe* is a proper book for children rather than adults – or more specifically, "for boys rather than men."[1] For that matter, the circulation of *Robinson Crusoe* itself, abridged or unabridged, in illustrated or unillustrated or comic-book form, represents just one aspect of the massive and complex role the novel has played in the history of children's literature: as the point of origin and eponymous prototype of a distinct genre, Defoe's novel provides the basis for innumerable new works, many of them aimed at a young readership, from the late eighteenth century to the present. The history of the Robinsonade is vast and sprawling, with sub-types branching off in many directions (tales of travelers lost in space, "last man" or post-apocalypse scenarios, retellings of the Crusoe story from a native's point of view, among others). Several works for young people of particularly extraordinary and lasting popularity form one strong and continuous strand, however, knit together in a cosmopolitan genealogy across national boundaries and languages by their many direct and indirect relations to each other. This strand originates in German with Joachim Heinrich Campe's *Robinson Der Jüngere* (1779, translated into French and then English, 1782–8); followed by Johann Wyss's *Der Schweizerische Robinson* (1812, translated into French and then English as *Swiss Family Robinson*, 1814–18); Frederick Marryat's *Masterman Ready; or, the Wreck of the Pacific* (1841); R. M. Ballantyne's *The Coral Island* (1858); and the twentieth-century curricular favorites mentioned above, the British William Golding's *Lord of the Flies* (1954) and American Scott O'Dell's *Island of the Blue Dolphins* (1960). I will be tracing this strand in what follows and will use it to puzzle over several questions: why would narratives about a person forced by catastrophe to rely solely on himself be deemed especially suitable for children and young people, unusually dependent as they are on others' care? Why would adult writers, parents, and instructors, bent as they so often are on advancing young people's "socialization," encourage them to contemplate a character shaped by long periods of unmitigated social isolation? Is Leslie Stephen right that, when read by children, *Robinson Crusoe* and its descendants are essentially books for *boys*?

One partial answer to the first two of these questions is that in the hands of early writers for children, *Robinson Crusoe* is recast from a spiritual autobiography – a tale of religious punishment, repentance, conversion, and relapse – to a narrative about education and progressive developmental change. Sometimes in these narratives the Crusoe character is made more youthful than Defoe's protagonist to accommodate this recasting; sometimes he becomes "they," not a solitary castaway but a member of a marooned group. Such group-Robinsonades allow the exploration of family relations and friendship as powerful forms of human connection, apart from a larger social network. Many Robinsonades for young people also bring to the foreground castaways' relations with the animals on their island – sharing with other works of children's literature an emphasis on interesting animals, and also repeating, in the process of depicting the domestication or taming of wild animals, their general concern with human education and change. They frequently depict the violent killing of animals as well, and link their treatment of humans' relationships with animals to the seemingly adult topics of colonialism and racial difference.[2]

Lineage

Abridgments and adaptations of *Robinson Crusoe*, many of them sharply simplified, shortened, illustrated, and otherwise made more suitable for inexperienced readers, began to appear shortly after the first publication of the novel in 1719. Such adaptations of *Robinson Crusoe* were not, however, specifically targeted at an audience defined by age or "age-leveled," as Teresa Michals puts it.[3] The chapbook editions of *Robinson Crusoe* that streamed from presses throughout the British Isles and in America in the eighteenth century – outnumbering complete editions of the novel, in fact, by a ratio of three to one – were aimed at a popular audience of lower-class and other inexpert readers, undifferentiated from the children who might also delight in the books' brief texts and wood-cut illustrations.[4] As Michals explains, "It is Rousseau who begins Crusoe's life as a hero of specifically childhood reading."[5]

He did so in 1762 in *Émile, ou de l'éducation*, when he declared that he would banish all books from the early education of his pupil, with a single exception: *Robinson Crusoe*. "This book shall be the first Emilius shall read: In this, indeed, will, for a long time, consist his whole library, and it will always hold a distinguished place among others."[6] Emile's tutor makes an exception for *Robinson Crusoe* because he anticipates that it alone will sponsor rather than interfere with his pupil's learning about the "actual relations of things" through direct experience: he imagines Emile "tak[ing] on himself the character of such a solitary adventurer," "affect[ing] even his dress," judging "of every thing about him, as a man in such circumstances would, by its real utility," and thus eagerly driven forward in his inquiries by his own needs and curiosity while his tutor approvingly looks on.

In *Robinson der Jüngere*, or as it was entitled in its English translation, *The New Robinson Crusoe; An Instructive and Entertaining History, For the Use of Children of Both Sexes*, the German linguist and educator Joachim Heinrich Campe responds directly to Rousseau's polemic, quoting Rousseau on the educational value of *Robinson Crusoe* in his preface. He reduces the age of Robinson Crusoe to seventeen, shifting the emphasis of Defoe's narrative from an adult's fluctuating spiritual state to a developmental story of education and maturation through experience. His book recasts the pedagogical scenario imagined by Rousseau, however, providing a retelling of Defoe's story expressly for children within a frame narrative of an enlightened father's instruction of his boys and girls. Campe follows Rousseau in singling out *Robinson Crusoe* as a text that can, because of the necessary self-reliance of its protagonist, paradoxically contribute to a pedagogy of unmediated encounters with the natural world; but when he creates a father-instructor who absorbs the content of Defoe's book into his own voice, using its events as scaffolding for instruction of his children in everything from geography and practical skills to moral principles and the exercise of compassion, he initiates a series of reconfigurations of Rousseau's triad of book/mentor/child that will unfold in successive variations over hundreds of years.

In the decades following the publication of *Robinson der Jüngere*, as it ran through numerous editions in German, French, English, Latin, and other languages, the Swiss pastor Johann David Wyss and his four sons enacted for themselves the family scene of paternal story-telling and instruction that forms Campe's frame-narrative. The text of *Der Schweizerische Robinson* or *Swiss Family Robinson* – by some accounts one of the most popular books of all time – is based on Wyss's notes about the tales he had spun to amuse and instruct his sons, adapting episodes from *Robinson Crusoe* but replacing its lone adult protagonist with fictionalized versions of the members of his own family. In merging Campe's frame-story of inter-generational instruction with the narrative content of *Crusoe*, Wyss moves children themselves directly into the scenario of shipwreck and survival, placing child-characters at the mercy of the elements and marooning them on Crusoe's desert island for the first time, but softening that perilous position by sending them there in the company of each other and of their wise and knowledgeable father and mother, as a family group. The essential feature of Crusoe's remarkable story – his absolute solitude, his complete lack of human companionship for many years – thus disappears at this stage in its adaptation for children and does not return until O'Dell's *Island of the Blue Dolphins* in 1960.

At the same time, the tradition that the genre of Robinsonades and *Robinson Crusoe* itself are books specifically for *boys* is established in *Swiss Family Robinson* on the basis of what Wyss refers to as biographical happenstance, that he "had himself no girls."[7] While the English title of Campe's work makes explicit that it is intended for the "use of children of both sexes," the tradition that children's Robinsonades are specifically about and for boys would persist in such widely read and influential works as *The Coral Island* and, a century later, *Lord of the Flies*. An intermediary work between *Swiss Family Robinson* and *The Coral Island*, Marryat's *Masterman Ready*, varies the familial/pedagogical configuration by splitting the all-knowing father in *Swiss Family Robinson* into two complementary figures – the father of the marooned family ("a very well-informed, clever man" steeped in book-learning) and an uneducated "weather-beaten old seaman," the aptly-named "Ready" of the book's title. Marryat also includes one girl among the four children in the marooned family, but she is featured very little in the plot, which focuses heavily on the contrasting characters of her two older brothers.[8]

R. M. Ballantyne's *The Coral Island* reworks the same familiar elements of Defoe's novel as earlier adaptations – shipwreck, marooning, a hill-top survey of the island, boat-building, discovery of a cave, exotic flora and fauna (including coconuts and penguins, introduced by Campe and Wyss) – but it radically alters the book/mentor/child paradigm passed on from Rousseau by simply eliminating the father figures who instruct the children in Campe's frame-story and within the desert island narratives in Wyss and Marryat. When shipwreck threatens in *The Coral Island*, fifteen-year-old Ralph casts in his lot with two other boys and, clinging together to an oar, they are washed ashore as the wreck's sole survivors. Although the oldest of the boys provides leadership, it is as peers, "the best and staunchest friends that ever tossed together on the stormy waves," that the trio survives and indeed flourishes on the island.[9] Social solace and the practical advantages of collaboration are founded here in an ethos of friendship rather than family, and the pleasures of companionship among equals give the boys' island life an idyllic, even utopian, quality. Disharmony and danger appear on the boys' island only in the novel's second half, brought to it abruptly by the arrival of groups of alien adults: warring tribes of bloodthirsty black savages and a band of sadistic pirates. The novel is thus sharply bifurcated between an idealized view of peaceable and cooperative human relations and sensational scenes of grotesque brutality and the human will to domination and power, as unleashed by exoticized and godless Others.

Writing almost a hundred years later, William Golding felt that the mystifications wrought by this bifurcation in *The Coral Island* – the displacement of the human potential for superstition, cruelty, and violence onto groups of barbaric Others – still exerted such a hold on readers' imaginations that he set out to systematically rewrite its story, unflinchingly driving together elements from its two halves, marooning another group of British boys on a similar island and depicting those boys' own growing barbarism and their enactment of the horrors committed by black savages and pirates in Ballantyne's novel. Golding clearly signals his book's relation to *The Coral Island* within *Lord of the Flies*, as well as referring to it in interviews: he names main characters after two of Ballantyne's boys (Ralph and Jack) and provides a variation on the name of the third (Piggy for Peterkin); he constructs dialogue in which characters refer to *The Coral Island* by title both near the novel's beginning and at its end; and he models the features of the South Pacific island the boys inhabit closely on Ballantyne's.[10] Although their ages are younger than those of the castaways in *The Coral Island* and the number of them considerably larger, the children left to fend for themselves in Golding's story, like those in Ballantyne's, are *all boys*.

In an interview late in his life, Golding reports that girls have asked him, "and very reasonably, why isn't it a bunch of girls, and why did you write this about a bunch of boys?" One answer, he says, is simply that his own experience was that of a boy; but he goes on:

> Another answer is of course to say that if you, as it were, scaled down human beings, scaled down society, if you land with a group of little boys, they are more like scaled-down society than a group of little girls will be. Don't ask me why ... This has nothing to do with equality at all. I think women are foolish to pretend they are equal to men. They are far superior and always have been. But one thing you cannot do with them is take a bunch of them and boil them to home, so to speak, into a set of little girls who would then become a kind of image of civilization, of society. That's another reason why they were little boys.[11]

While innumerable study-guides reiterate the idea that the central "theme" of *Lord of the Flies* is "human nature," Golding's remarks suggest that the book's thought-experiment is about boys in particular, and about a group of boys as a microcosm of "society" or "civilization" rather than of nature.

When Scott O'Dell wrote *Island of the Blue Dolphins* several years after the publication of *Lord of the Flies*, he chose not only to center his story on a real-life "girl Robinson Crusoe," as he calls his main character, but also to accentuate her differences from the boys and men of her own people through plot events and qualities of narrative voice.[12] O'Dell's first-person narrator – loosely based on a historical individual – is herself one of those "natives" treated with such suspicion in earlier Robinsonades; she is left alone on her native island through a series of depredations by profit-seeking white men, rival native groups, and Christian missionaries, rather than marooned like Crusoe in an unknown land. The plants and wildlife of the island and its surrounding waters are known to Karana, then, through what she has been taught and what she has observed of her elders' skills; her ability to survive on the island depends on the communal knowledge that has been passed on to her orally or by practice, not through either book-learning or independent empirical inquiry. Of necessity, she learns to craft weapons and use them, despite her culture's proscription against girls and women doing so. As the years pass on her island, Karana chooses to lay these weapons by and to see the animals on the island as her companions and equals.

The Coral Island and *Lord of the Flies*: Long Pigs

The three sailor-boys who arrive in a storm on their own South Sea island in Ballantyne's *The Coral Island* bring with them no family unit; no domesticated livestock or pets; and almost no European goods. Like Campe's

Crusoe, as distinguished from Defoe's Crusoe before him and Wyss's and Marryat's marooned families after, the three boys who wash ashore in *The Coral Island* are able to salvage nothing from the ship. Even more radically, the boys have been stripped by the shipwreck of all adult companions who might advise them practically and guide their process of education in their new island home. Thrown upon their own psychic resources, absent a family structure, books, formal education, and European firearms or tools, the boys discover the strength of their mutual affection and common cause. Unlike the brothers in *Swiss Family Robinson* and *Masterman Ready*, whose struggles for pre-eminence and whose aggressive impulses often cause conflict, Ralph, Jack, and Peterkin form a fully "harmonious" trio: "There was, indeed, no note of discord whatever in the symphony we played together on that sweet Coral Island" (165).

If they ever were domesticated, the pigs on Coral Island have run wild, and the sailor boys who arrive on their island have no interest in domesticating them or any other animal, in contrast to characters in *The New Robinson Crusoe* and *Swiss Family Robinson*. Instead, the boys domesticate each other, but only in a limited and provisional way; they improvise a home together on the island that features neither hierarchy nor rivalry, nor any process of supervised, corrective education. Peterkin, the youngest of the three, resembles younger brothers in earlier Robinsonades in his recklessness, mischief, and strong appetites. Though less proficient than the other boys at most physical activities, he sharpens a stick into a primitive spear and proves the best hunter among them, so eager is he to fill his appetite for meat. That appetite seems to affiliate Peterkin with pigs even as it makes him their main human predator on the island. Unlike in *Swiss Family Robinson*, however, in the idyllic first half of *The Coral Island* a boyish enthusiasm for killing animals and for eating meat is not linked to resentful self-assertion or antagonistic rivalry with other boys: Peterkin with his sharpened stick remains loving and beloved. The possibility of conflict and violence among humans, and the attendant need for disciplinary education, appear on the island only in the novel's second half, when "wild, bloodthirsty savages" and soon thereafter a band of pirates arrive on its shores.

The savages quickly confirm the stories of cannibalistic practices that Ralph, the book's narrator, had heard before journeying to the South Seas, and the pirates are not much better. Cannibalism's function as the hallmark of savagery harks back to the Robinsonade's original, where it epitomizes the threat posed to the solitary Crusoe by the prospect of any encounter with a human "other," glimpsed first in a single human footprint found in the sand. Until the abrupt arrival of savages and pirates on their idyllic island in *The Coral Island*'s second half, the only footprints found by the boys there are those of animals, most commonly pigs. When human savages do appear, they quickly establish that their ravenous appetites encompass both the pigs that the boys themselves enthusiastically devour and what the savages term "*long pig*": human flesh, called such because of the supposedly similar appearance of "baked pigs and baked men" (286, 309–10). The metaphoric substitution in *long pig* encapsulates for the narrator the horrific barbarism of the South Sea natives: the phrase defies "civilization's" axiomatic distinction between humans and non-human animals, relied upon to preserve humans both from being subjected to arbitrary violence and from committing it. The English pirates who kidnap Ralph treat human life with roughly the same indifference, although they abstain from roasting and eating the victims of their "bloody deeds" and "frightful and wanton slaughter." They call the big brass gun on their ship "*Long Tom*" (echoing the cannibals' horrific phrase), and they relish the way it "speaks" in a loud roar as it reduces a "living mass" of men to "mutilated forms writhing in agony" on a beach of "bloody sand" (280–1). The pirates' barbarism is more technologically advanced than that of the "savages," but Ralph learns that they are no more enlightened or humane. Once Ralph has escaped from the pirates, what leads him and his friends to endanger their lives by opposing the inhumanity of the natives, rather than of the pirates, is the feminine nature of one of the savages' intended *long pigs* – a light-skinned Samoan woman whom a chief had vowed to kill and roast because of her refusal to marry as he commands (433).

With the exception of the mild mother figures in such Robinsonades as *Swiss Family Robinson* and *Masterman Ready*, whose sexual currents are safely grounded in their strict orientation toward maternal duties, children's Robinsonades rigorously suppress both sexuality and gender differentiation on their islands.[13] Gender relations are pushed beyond the horizon of these Robinsonades but, as we have seen, gender is not: the occupants of the islands are crucially characterized as men and boys. Human sexuality, or even the narrower question of biological reproduction, is largely ignored. Futurity itself is banished from the islands' bounds, as becomes explicit in J. M. Barrie's *Peter Pan*: Neverland.

Part of what makes the narrative space of the first half of *The Coral Island* feel so idyllic is the impression it gives of timelessness; at its halfway point, change, along with the forces of ambivalence, antagonism, and sexuality, arrives suddenly and from outside the island in the form of "savage" adults. Left to themselves, the boys do not evince harmful aggression or conflictual desires that threaten the equilibrium of their harmonious state or require a process of change within themselves. Adulthood is a grotesque and alien condition that Ballantyne identifies with other races, with weapons of mass destruction, and with sexual tyranny. The implausible turn of events that rescues the boys from imminent death at the hands of savages in the book's final chapters – sudden conversion of the savage chief to Christianity by missionaries – condenses the "education plot" of earlier Robinsonades for young people to a brief plot twist, sensationalized and displaced onto adults of another race. In this way, *The Coral Island* returns the focus of the *Robinson Crusoe* plot from education to Defoe's story of conversion, but the transformation wrought by conversion has been externalized there and enfolded within the drama of colonial fantasy and phobia.

"We've got to have rules and obey them. After all, we're not savages," Jack declares early in *Lord of the Flies*. "We're English, and the English are best at everything. So we've got to do the right things" (42). Nonetheless, as every reader of *Lord of the Flies* will recall in images that remain indelible after many years, unlike Jack, Ralph, and Peterkin of *The Coral Island*, Golding's Jack and his English fellows themselves become the savages who over-run the island as time passes. With painted faces that afford a "liberation into savagery," they engage in all the iconic behaviors of savages, chanting, dancing around a fire, brandishing spears, thirsting for animal blood, and even murdering in their frenzy (172). As Golding tells it, what we might understatedly term this "de-domestication" of marooned English boys unfolds along the axis of a passionate rivalry for preeminence between two of them. The activity of hunting pigs provides the main content of that rivalry, which ends in human death. The powerful claim that Jack opposes to Ralph's initial primacy is his own leadership as a hunter of pigs, and readers of Robinsonades (though not of *Robinson Crusoe*) have met these pigs before: they may be found grunting, rushing, and rapidly proliferating in the woods and underbrush in the island habitats of *Swiss Family Robinson*, *Masterman Ready*, and *The Coral Island* before *Lord of the Flies*. They are not indigenous to these islands, or simply "wild" inhabitants: sometimes explicitly, sometimes implicitly in these works, the pigs that populate the islands' woods descend from domesticated animals brought to the South Seas and elsewhere by European explorers and settlers.[14] The relations of antagonism, violence, and mental derangement that they elicit are bound up in the legacies of European colonial dominance, as well as in the war of great powers that plays out in the background of Golding's novel.

The brutal conflation of pigs and human victims encapsulated in the cannibals' lingo of *long pigs* in *The Coral Island* is what leads Jack and his followers beyond a fierce desire to kill animals and consume meat (not so different from the aggressive contests of the Swiss family boys) to "savage" and horrifying acts of ritual murder. First they play-act their conquest of a boy-as-pig in a bout of brutal "boyish" play (114–15); later they kill a boy mistaken for a beast, biting and tearing at his flesh with "teeth and claws" (152–3); finally they hunt the one hold-out from their "tribe," ready to throw their spears at him "like at a pig" (189). Golding models specific episodes in this devolution closely on elements from Ballantyne's novel, including Peterkin's killing of a tough old sow to get pig-leather for new shoes. Golding renders these episodes horrifying partly by investing them with a perverse and violent sexual force that is absent from their precedents: "the sow staggered her way ahead of them, bleeding and mad, and the hunters followed, wedded to her in lust, excited by the long chase and the dropped blood"; when Roger conclusively spears her, he forces the point of his spear "right up her ass!" (135). As critics have remarked, this is both an Oedipal and an anal sexuality which Golding associates with "the overpowering and unaccustomed emotions of sexual love experienced by the half-grown boys."[15] While Wyss and Marryat suggest that, without supervision and guidance from an adult man, boys' appetites for food and physical activity may lead to dangerous antagonisms – and Ballantyne, dispensing with the boys' need for adult supervision, brings back adults as themselves the locus of threat – Golding's blending of sexual with alimentary and aggressive drives places the older boys on his island at a threshold between childhood and something beyond, and makes violence appear elemental. Yet what turns boyish rivalries and aggressive energies murderous in *Lord of the Flies* is not the current of sexuality that flows into them but rather the human capacity for symbolic action. Jack and his followers' improvised substitution of Robert for the pig they hope to kill is a rehearsal for three acts of later violence: their cannibalistic murder of Simon in a ritual transport, their careless killing of the boy known only as "Piggy," and their rechanneling of their pig-hunting skills to pursuit of Ralph in a deadly pack.

In a more pervasive way, the literary technology of free indirect discourse, which allows the novel's focalization primarily through Ralph and at times through the epileptic Simon, associates consciousness itself with the experience of entrapment, ambush, predation, and the approach of death. Golding's Ralph inherits his central place in the focalization of an island story from Ballantyne's Ralph, who is the first-person narrator of *The Coral Island*'s story of marooned boys, promoted to that position by the absence of an adult male (such as the Swiss family's father) to report their experiences. When the technique of first-person narration falls away in Golding's re-rendering of Ballantyne's tale, so too does the retrospection with which an implicitly adult, sadder and wiser Ralph relates his boyhood adventures and loving bonds. There is no such temporal distance insuring survival nor any coloring of nostalgic recollection in *Lord of the Flies*, but only a truncated and dissociated experience – severed from past and future, as from the mainland – pressing closer and closer, closing in. From his covert, the hunted Ralph struggles to sustain human consciousness.

> If only one had time to think!...
> Think...
> Think...
> Hide, then.
> He wondered if a pig would agree ...
> (195–7)

Island of the Blue Dolphins: "a girl Robinson Crusoe"

The protagonist and first-person narrator of *The Island of the Blue Dolphins*, one of the few girl-characters in the literary lineage we have traced, is left stranded and alone in her island home because of the drive to domination of men and boys, and of non-human male animals, too. In Defoe's *Robinson Crusoe* and in such Robinsonades as *The New Robinson Crusoe* and *The Coral Island*, people native to the region where European travelers are marooned appear late in the story in pairs of conflicting tribes, battling each other and cannibalistically eating each other's remains, posing a threat to the European castaways as well through their alien brutality. This threat of warring "tribes" emerges from within the group of English boys marooned in *Lord of the Flies*. Karana, the protagonist of Scott O'Dell's *Island*, is herself native to the island on which her story takes place, and her story commences, rather than culminates, with a battle between two non-European peoples, her own San Nicoleño tribe and an intruding people, the Aleuts. The Aleuts, however, have been brought to hunt otter on the island and to contend with the island's people over its resources by a Russian sea-captain and profiteer; historically, their own territory in the Pacific Northwest had been occupied and controlled by Russians beginning in the eighteenth century. Explicitly, then, in the case of *Island of the Blue Dolphins*, native or "uncivilized" antagonisms follow from imperial enterprise.

But the men of Karana's people, including her own beloved father, step into those antagonisms with shoulders thrown back and new spears sharpened (5–6, 17). "I am the Chief of Ghalas-at," her father declares to the Russian captain and then, in asserting his authority, recklessly exposes his secret name: "My name is Chief Chowig" (5, 23). Chief Chowig's authority among his people, his firmness in bargaining, his fighting prowess, and his new spear do not prove sufficient to counter the captain's command of the Aleutian men he has hired and of mysterious weapons that operate at a distance. "A puff of white smoke came from the deck of the ship. A loud noise echoed against the cliff. Five of our warriors fell and lay quiet" (21). O'Dell sets this battle, from which few of the San Nicoleño men emerge alive, at a location on the island he calls "Coral Beach," a name that evokes not only Ballantyne's *The Coral Island* but also the coral reefs that intrigue European castaways in *Swiss Family Robinson*, *Masterman Ready*, and *Lord of the Flies*. The name promises the exotic appeal of a tropical island, as approached by an outsider and therefore seen generically – marking a point of contact between worlds. After Karana's people have lost husbands, fathers, and their way of life in the battle with the Aleuts and the "dishonest Russian" at Coral Beach, they will welcome there another ship of white men, sent by the Catholic mission to save them by taking them from their home. Were it not for Karana's brother's miniature, juvenile version of their father's urge to masculine self-assertion, her story would not have become a Robinsonade: instead she would depart from the island with the surviving members of her tribe (only to perish within thirty days on the mainland, as, historically, they all did).

It is six-year-old Ramo's attachment to his fishing spear and Karana's own attachment to him that lead Karana to jump from the departing ship and swim back to the island when she discovers that Ramo has been left behind while running to the village to retrieve his spear. Karana is marooned by the love of weapons that her younger brother shares with the European boys in *Swiss Family Robinson*, *Masterman Ready*, and *Lord of the Flies*. Like other younger brothers in children's Robinsonades, Ramo is "always into some mischief" (27). Separated from the rest of her people by her brother's impetuous decision, Karana is soon left without even Ramo's company by the consequences of his willful insistence on his masculine prowess and autonomy, despite his young age. The morning after little Ramo has proudly declared himself "the son of Chowig ... now Chief of Ghalas-at," Karana awakes to discover that he has disappeared, acting on his boast that he can put a canoe in the water alone. She finds him in the middle of a circle of wild dogs, "lying on his back," with "a deep wound in his throat" (45). The dogs who have killed Karana's brother replicate the human pattern of male conflict over dominance and territorial rights that sets the story's events in motion; we later witness a violent struggle among the dogs for standing within the pack.

Because O'Dell's story is so psychologically compelling, it is easy not to notice the insistence with which he reiterates this pattern across various registers. The effects of one episode of male conflict ripple into the next: as Karana pursues her plans to get rid of the wild dogs, she encounters two sea-elephant bulls fighting to the death for territory and mating dominance; she is so injured in her hurried retreat that she has to hide from the wild dogs for eleven "suns" while her leg heals (76–86). The pattern of violent male struggle appears even among the gods, forming and defining natural features of the island. Karana explains that trees are small and scarce on her island because the two gods who ruled at the beginning of the world quarreled, and the one who wished people to die withdrew to an underworld, "taking his belongings with him" (71). When great tidal waves threaten the island during an earthquake and a receding wave meets one coming in, Karana's description of the collision between these vast inanimate masses harks back to the originary quarrel of the gods, to the battle that destroyed her people's way of life, and to the fights between rival dogs and sea-elephants she has witnessed: the crash of giant waves created "a roar as if great spears were breaking in battle, and in the red light of the sun the spray that flew around them looked like blood" (161). The "victor" wave nearly kills Karana as well as rolling over and "vanquishing" the wave that is its predecessor. She survives by climbing up a rock-face and holding tight: when the wave recedes she discovers that she is still alive.

Moments of holding tight – unexpected acts of refraining from action in the midst of conflict and loss – constitute some of the key turning-points in Karana's story, and her most radical departures from earlier Crusoe characters. Typically, Karana narrates these climactic moments of non-action as beyond her own understanding and ability to explain. Grieving for Ramo after he is killed by the wild dogs, Karana vows revenge and works with fierce resolve to create weapons strong enough to kill the dogs, and especially their leader. To do so, she must defy her tribe's prohibition against women making weapons. Yet when Karana bravely attacks and then tracks the wounded leader to a pile of rocks and fits a newly fashioned arrow to her great bow, aiming it at his head, she "stood on the rock with the bow pulled back and my hand would not let it go." "Why I did not send the arrow I cannot say" (91). Similarly, when she sees an Aleut girl who has accompanied another group of hunters to the island, Karana refrains from throwing her spear at her, though it is near at hand: "Why I did not throw the spear, I do not know, for she was one of the Aleuts who had killed my people on the beach of Coral Cove" (131). Out of these moments in which the determined non-action of a hand overrides the mental logic of justice or revenge comes friendship for Karana and relief from Robinsonian loneliness: she and the Aleut girl enjoy a temporary but affecting friendship despite their lack of a common language, and the leader of the wild dogs becomes her closest and most lasting friend on the island, relieving her loneliness and making it a "happy" place at last (97, 100).

Like the marooned Europeans in *The New Robinson Crusoe* and *Swiss Family Robinson*, Karana relieves her human isolation on the island by domesticating a number of animals: the wild dog whom she names Rontu and later his son; a pair of birds; a red fox who was caught in a snare; and a wounded otter found in a tide-pool, whom Karana feeds and names. As in *Swiss Family Robinson*, naming allows both individuation and attachment between non-human and human animals. Karana also engages in naming the stars whose names she does not already know, finding "company" in "the natural landscape itself," as Lois Lowry puts it (x). Karana's consoling intimacy with both animals and nature does not, however, exclude elemental force or danger. The pack of wild dogs that lives on Karana's island has become especially dangerous because of the way the dogs have passed between wildness, domesticated relations with humans, and back to wildness, incorporating the violent hostilities among humans into their life as a pack and becoming "much bolder" than before (25, 87). The de-domesticated San Nicoleño dogs are joined in the pack by ones that had belonged to their enemies the Aleuts, including their leader, "a big gray dog with long curling hair and yellow eyes" who plays a key role in the killing of Ramo and who eventually becomes Karana's companion, Rontu (87, 45). This deadly "enemy," wounded and rendered vulnerable and dependent by Karana's attack on him, becomes her true "friend" in defiance of the categorical oppositions of earlier Robinsonades (103).

The staying of Karana's hand as she is poised to finish off her canine enemy, and the laborious carrying, nursing, and feeding of him that follow, entail a taming of Karana's own anger and capacity for violence – a reckoning with the necessity of emotional strife and physical aggression, and with their costs. Like *Lord of the Flies*, O'Dell's *Island of the Blue Dolphins* exposes as illusory *The Coral Island*'s projection outward of conflict and aggression onto alien peoples; but it moves away from that bifurcation in a different direction, inflecting the alternative it offers with a juxtaposition of genders. O'Dell's story depicts the activity of *play* not as a rehearsal for murderous violence, as in *Lord of the Flies*, but as a release from predatory relations, and as an aspect of human and non-human animals' capacity for aesthetic pleasure. O'Dell's "girl Robinson Crusoe" also takes pleasure in self-adornment in a way that the male protagonists of earlier Robinsonades do not, and this pleasure forms the bridge between girls of enemy tribes, Karana and the Aleut girl Tutok, that allows their unlikely friendship. Exchanging ornaments, they discover that the one word with recognizably related forms in their two languages is " *Wintscha*" (Aleut) or " *Wintai*" (San Nicoleño) – in English, "pretty" (136).

This episode reminds us that, linguistically, Karana's first-person narration is an impossibility, an imaginative construction to the very core: the historical Lone Woman of San Nicolas, on whom O'Dell's Karana is based, had not one word that could reach us, her readers, to make us companions and sharers after the fact in her solitary inner life. The fur-trapper who found hei alone on her island in 1853 and the priest who received her at the Santa Barbara Mission, where she would survive only seven weeks, agreed that "she could not speak any known language."[16] Having learned to find company in animals and in the natural world, Karana still attests to her deep longing for the sound of the human voice – "There is no sound like this in all the world" – and O'Dell's book offers us the sound of a singular voice: as longing or wish, as an aesthetic construct, as an act of play rather than fact. O'Dell asks us to imagine, through words and a literary genre that we know, an essentially different kind of heritage, a different *worlding* of a solo self.

NOTES

1 Leslie Stephen, *Hours in a Library* (New York, NY: Johnson Reprint Corp, 1968), 174; quoted in Teresa Michals, *Books for Children, Books for Adults: Age and the Novel from Defoe to James* (New York, NY: Cambridge University Press, 2010), 55. Michals provides a rich sampling of such views, including statements by Charles Lamb (54–5), two anonymous reviewers in 1856 (57–8), and Charles Dickens (141).

2 I explore one case of these linkages in "Taming Llamas: Joachim Heinrich Campe's *New Robinson Crusoe*, Political Economy, and Children's Literature," in *Story Time! Essays on the Betsy Beinecke Shirley Collection of American Children's Literature*, ed. Timothy Young (New Haven, CT: Yale University Press, 2016).

3 Michals, *Books for Children*, 13 and 25–83.

4 Andrew O'Malley, *Children's Literature, Popular Literature, and "Robinson Crusoe"* (New York, NY: St. Martin's Press/Palgrave Macmillan, 2012), 2–15.

5 Michals, *Books for Children*, 38.

6 *Emilius and Sophia: or, a New System of Education*, trans. William Kenrick (1762), excerpted in the Norton Critical Edition of *Robinson Crusoe*, 2nd edn, ed. Michael Shinagel (New York, NY: W. W. Norton & Co., 1994), 262–4.

7 Author's Preface, *Swiss Family Robinson*, ed. John Seelye, translated from the French by Mary Jane Clairmont Godwin, 1816 (New York, NY: Penguin, 2007).

8 "Captain [Frederick] Marryat," *Masterman Ready: Or, The Wreck of the Pacific. Written for Young People*, one-volume edition with ninety-three wood engravings (London: Bell & Daldy, 1867; first published 1841), 6 and 2.

9 Robert Michael Ballantyne, *The Coral Island: A Tale of the Pacific Ocean* (London: T. Nelson and Sons, 1858), 16.

10 William Golding, *Lord of the Flies*, with biographical and critical note by E. L. Epstein (New York, NY: Penguin, 2006; first published 1954), 34–35, 202.

11 Interview, William Golding, accessed on YouTube, February 8, 2015. www.youtube.com/watch?v=vYnfSV27vLY.

12 "Author's Note," *Island of the Blue Dolphins* (New York, NY: Houghton Mifflin Harcourt, 2010), 175.

13 Significantly, in his instigation for the lineage of children's Robinsonades we have traced, Rousseau anticipates that Emile will leave *Robinson Crusoe* behind as soon as his desire for the opposite sex begins to stir (263 in Norton excerpt).

14 Brett Mizelle quotes Alfred W. Crosby: "One who watched the Caribbean islands from outer space during the years from 1492 to 1550 or so might have

surmised that the object of the game going on there was to replace the people with pigs, dogs and cattle" (*Pig* [London: Reaktion Books, 2011], 41).

15 See, for example, E. L. Epstein's comments in the afterword notes to the Penguin edition, 206–7.

16 Quoted in Lois Lowry, Introduction, *Island of the Blue Dolphins*, vii and v.

13

ANN MARIE FALLON

Anti-Crusoes, Alternative Crusoes: Revisions of the Island Story in the Twentieth Century

Everyone thinks they know the plot of *Robinson Crusoe*. The story of the man who is shipwrecked on an island alone is ubiquitous and feels deeply familiar, even for those who have not read it. *Robinson Crusoe* has been plagiarized, cannibalized, and serialized almost since the moment it hit the streets of London in 1719. Here is a passage from an Argentinean novel by Victoria Slavuski published in 1993 that captures the sense of familiarity and also the distance twentieth-century readers have in their relationship to *Robinson Crusoe*: "On days like these we promised each other that at long last we would take the time to read the copy of *Robinson (Crusoe)* that each household kept alongside the Bible and *Twenty-five Ways to Prepare Lobster*, written on Juan Fernandez by Amelita Riera. Nobody got past page fifteen of *Robinson* and almost nobody opened the *Bible*."[1]

Literary critics often treat the multitude of twentieth-century versions of Crusoe as antagonistic to Defoe's character. They tend to consider contemporary novels or films or poems as entities in competition with Robinson Crusoe's fictional world. However, these modern renderings are never so neatly drawn. More often than not, writers use these alternative Crusoes to forge lines of affiliation and empathy, between the eighteenth century and our own time as well as between different regions and languages. Argentinean, Caribbean, and African Crusoes are in conversation with one another as much as they are in dialogue with the historic Defoe. Writers around the globe adapt and transform Crusoe and Defoe's novel to establish a literary web of connection that has come to define our own global moment where fiction travels beyond national and linguistic borders. In this chapter I will move through a few observations on nineteenth-century Crusoes before delving into the twentieth-century map of literary islands criss-crossing the globe.

Writers create surrogate visions of Crusoe as well as anti-Crusoes, and by making Crusoe unfamiliar, they interrupt our comfortable assumptions about *Robinson Crusoe* as well as about our own world where we find ourselves isolated on islands, circumscribed by our expectations or by our political circumstances. It becomes easy in all these revisions to start to conflate *Robinson Crusoe* the novel with Robinson Crusoe the character; conflation is often part of the point, the book and the character frequently merge through references in contemporary fiction. Part of the late twentieth-century aesthetic is to be supremely self-conscious in the way one borrows, adapts, or reworks materials. Because *Robinson Crusoe* is often considered the first English novel, retelling the novel allows writers to create alternative histories of colonialism, racism, and other forms of oppression. These retellings also bring us closer to Defoe's Crusoe and his Friday; complex stories can often create new empathetic ties to Defoe's novel and his early exploration of isolation.

In the eighteenth and nineteenth centuries, so many reiterations of *Robinson Crusoe* were published that it became a separate genre, the *Robinsonade*. Especially in France and Germany, the story of a young boy who is cast away and self-educated on an island held tremendous appeal for writers and readers. The scenario seemed to contain an ideal pedagogical model; children could be raised, like the hero of Rousseau's novel, *Émile* (1762), far from the corrupting influence of society. Even whole families could escape this corruption!

Der Schweizerische Robinson (1812, by the Swiss pastor, Johann David Wyss, translated into English in 1816 as *The Swiss Family Robinson* by William Godwin) took a whole nuclear family to an isolated island where they develop a familial self-reliance. The Robinson Crusoe figures marching through these adventure stories frequently seem to be much more confident and quickly self-sufficient than Defoe's Crusoe. They easily survey the island, build shelters, plant crops, cook, sew clothes, conquer native cannibals and pirates until they successfully escape the island to rejoin society but with a profound new sense of inner values. They are not seduced by society's corruption, and they are also usually the objects of some great material windfall. The creative time of exile on the island is rewarded spiritually and materially.

The references to *Robinson Crusoe* in these titles function as both marketing tool and touchstone. As Lucy Ford says of her 1837 novel, *Female Robinson Crusoe, A Tale of the American Wilderness*, the title was meant to generate interest in this "not uninteresting" narrative.[2] Like other female Crusoes in the nineteenth century, Ford's character deviates from the confident explorer. The Crusoe Ford paints for us is tremulous and shy. Her descent into the wilderness to escape savages finds her ill-equipped to build the most basic shelter or find any food in the forest: "I actually looked with longing eyes upon the flesh of my own hands and arms, as victuals appropriate to gorge my cannibal desires."[3] Here the cannibalism that appears first in Defoe's novel and lives through nineteenth-century Robinsonades turns inward to self-consumption.

At the turn of the twentieth century, Crusoe crosses over from realist explorer to modernist hero and that reflects a changing readership. The Crusoe Virginia Woolf draws for her readers in her 1919 essay on *Robinson Crusoe* is a far cry from the swashbuckling adventurer of earlier Robinsonades. Her Crusoe is most interested in pots: "Thus Defoe, by reiterating that nothing but a plain earthenware pot stands in the foreground, persuades us to see remote islands and the solitudes of the human soul."[4] Rather than drawing a portrait of Crusoe as a man intent on subduing the island to his will, Woolf emphasizes a Crusoe intensely focused on the problem of throwing pots, an enterprise feminine and domestic in nature. Woolf domesticates Crusoe but she also humanizes him for a new generation. Gertrude Stein picks up this thread in her very brief allusion to Crusoe at the end of her *Autobiography of Alice B. Toklas*: "About six weeks ago Gertrude Stein said, it does not look to me as if you were ever going to write that autobiography. You know what I am going to do. I am going to write it for you. I am going to write it as simply as Defoe did the autobiography of Robinson Crusoe. And she has and this is it."[5] Stein not only domesticates Crusoe, she makes him the equivalent of Alice B. Toklas. In these gestures, both Stein and Woolf bring Crusoe into greater intimacy with the twentieth-century reader.

In the second half of the twentieth century alternative and antagonistic Robinson Crusoes, and a few Fridays, abound. The versions of Robinson Crusoe who appear in these pages are often quite distinct from one another and yet they seem as often to be referring to one another as they refer to Defoe. Some writers deploy Defoe's novel as a textual referent in order to make political or aesthetic points. Robinson Crusoe appears as a significant character or the novel is cited in representative ways in the following texts: Muriel Spark's *Robinson* (1958), Nadine Gordimer's short story, "Friday's Footprint" (1960) in her collection of the same name, Michel Tournier's *Vendredi et les limbes du pacifique* [*Friday and the Limbo of the Pacific*] (1967), Sam Selvon's *Moses Ascending* (1975), Maxine Hong Kingston's *China Men* (1977), Bessie Head's "The Wind and a Boy" (1977), Derek Walcott's play *Pantomime* (1978), Elizabeth Bishop's poem, "Crusoe at Home" (1979), Julieta Campos' *El Miedo de perder a Eurídice* [*Fear of Losing Eurydice*] (1979), Jane Gardam's *Crusoe's Daughter* (1985), J. M. Coetzee's novel *Foe* (1986), Louise Erdrich's *Love Medicine* (1993, revised edition), Marianne Wiggins' *John Dollar* (1989), Victoria Slavuski's *Música para olvidar una isla* [*Music for Forgetting an Island*] (1993), Thomas King's *Green Grass, Running Water* (1993), Cormac McCarthy's *The Crossing* (1994), and Yann Martel's *The Life of*

Pi (2001). The Crusoes here range from a middle-aged English housewife to a young Indian boy marooned in a boat with a tiger.

In *Vendredi*, *Foe*, and the poem "Crusoe at Home," Tournier, Coetzee, and Bishop reimagine Defoe's story in the early eighteenth-century context and in doing so create new potential lineages for Crusoe, fictions going beyond the colonial fantasy of the nineteenth century. In Tournier's novel Crusoe's island becomes an anti-Western idyll. Crusoe learns to be appalled by European colonialism and violence, as he reverts to a kind of Edenic state of nature. He literally copulates with the island, producing flowers from his semen. Friday joins him on the island adventure but ends up running off with their would-be rescuers while Crusoe chooses this time to stay behind and reject Western civilization. Coetzee's Crusoe, written in South Africa almost twenty years later, is a bitter curmudgeon who dies in the first part of the novel after rescuing another castaway, Susan Barton. *Foe* then follows Susan Barton to London where she stays in the apartment of the elusive writer, Daniel Foe. Bishop's Crusoe is an old man reflecting nostalgically on his life on the island from the comfort of his English retirement. These very different Crusoes imagine a new story in three fairly distinct versions of both the island and London. The island story they imagine generates an alternative history. In Tournier's account, Crusoe opens himself to greater creative and personal freedom. No longer constrained by religion, he is a hero for the twentieth century. Tournier strips Crusoe of his colonial tendencies and creates a figure possessing cultural and religious tolerance. Especially in the context of the 1960s, this embrace by Tournier of a counter-cultural Crusoe transforms the story for a contemporary audience.

Coetzee's revision is more complicated and demonstrates the compromised position of any writer of fiction. Coetzee's severe and uncommunicative Crusoe, a man who refuses to plant crops or to keep the journal we have come to rely on as central to the Crusoe myth, suggests yet another pathway from the eighteenth century to our own time. Coetzee points to a violent legacy of oppression and deliberate silencing. The Friday in Coetzee's novel has had his tongue cut out of his head and it remains unclear if this is the work of Crusoe or of slave traders. When Susan Barton picks up the thread of the Crusoe story and carries it with her to London with the intention of writing and publishing her own castaway story, Coetzee puts into motion an alternate history for Crusoe not focused on the character but on the text itself. The novel, not Robinson Crusoe the character, is the entity under scrutiny. We see Coetzee take a variety of perspectives on who actually gets to be the subject (or the object) of the novel and who gets to tell the story. The letters and journals Susan compiles and leaves for Foe are presumably the "raw materials" this new fictional Defoe compiles later, offstage. Coetzee's portrait of the novelist evokes an author who edits and elides, who never appears directly on stage and yet silences dissident voices in order to create a singular authoritative voice. For a writer working at the height of apartheid in South Africa, this statement about the inherent dangers, elisions, and silences involved in the creative writing process is a powerful testament to writing under oppression. Coetzee directs our attention away from Crusoe as a hero of modern individualism and toward the otherwise invisible victims of it.

Elizabeth Bishop gives us Robinson Crusoe as an old man looking back on his island adventure and thereby offers a metaphor for the author struggling against the weight of the past. "My brain/bred islands," says this nostalgic Crusoe in describing his obsessions as well as his deep loneliness until Friday appears on the scene. The Crusoe in this poem is a stand-in for the poet who reproduces islands and tries to mark them with his/her own mark. At one point he describes trying to mark a baby goat with red for a change of scene, a move that backfires when the mother goat rejects her offspring. The most resonant metaphor in the poem becomes Crusoe's knife, another instrument he uses to try to inscribe himself on the island: "The knife there on the shelf – /It reeked of meaning, like a crucifix/ ... My eyes rest on it and pass on."[6] The knife reeks of meaning, holding all the multiple levels of meaning Bishop wants it to contain. The knife speaks to the problem of trying to distill or even control what Crusoe means in the midst of all of the reproductions that emerge even as writers try to make their individual marks with him. Like Coetzee, Bishop wants to continue to use Crusoe as a metaphor for the modern writer but also underline how problematic it has become to ask this Crusoe to stand in for just one thing, when generations of writers have reshaped what he seems to stand for.

So far I have discussed writers who rewrite Defoe's novel within an eighteenth-century context. Other writers introduce the Crusoe character into a contemporary scene. In having Crusoe walk among us they emphasize a greater intimacy with the text and its problems. They have characters play Crusoe within their texts or have characters named Crusoe or Robinson introduced into the story, usually walking around in the background, appearing at key moments. These stories might also have characters recognizable as Robinson Crusoe traveling through the text. Derek Walcott's play *Pantomime* (1978) is one of the most important examples of this type of revision. Set in Tobago, *Pantomime*'s main character is Trewe, a white innkeeper at a failing resort (aptly named The Castaway) who decides to stage a pantomime of *Robinson Crusoe*. He asks his black handyman to play Crusoe and he decides to play Friday. After some initial hesitation, Jackson the handyman agrees. Act 1 is devoted to a rehearsal, which goes seriously awry from Trewe's perspective, as Jackson improvises his new role and renames Friday, Thursday. Act II is devoted to the aftermath. Trewe argues that he meant his little play to be a light comedy, Jackson makes it very clear that reversing race relations in the Caribbean is a serious matter. The "minor" act of reversing the characters' racial identification changes the entire political spectrum. This is especially true in Tobago in 1978, fewer than twenty years after independence. Jackson asks Trewe to imagine fully the implications of his little pantomime:

> He (Crusoe) comes across this naked white cannibal called Thursday, you know. And then look at what would happen ... This cannibal, who is Christian, would have to start unlearning his Christianity. He would have to be taught ... I mean ... he'd have to be taught by this African that everything was wrong, that what he was doing, I mean for nearly two thousand years was wrong ... and what we'd have on our hands would be ... a play and not a little pantomime.[7]

Simply reversing racial roles of course has profound political implications. The Crusoe Walcott (and Jackson) consequently creates for the stage is a black man who is enlisted to save the white Christian from 2,000 years of misguided violence.

Another Trinidadian writer who reverses the Friday/Crusoe partnership during the same period is the novelist Sam Selvon in his novel *Moses Ascending* (1975). Moses is an immigrant to England from Trinidad who decides to purchase a boarding house in Shepherd's Bush, then a poor London neighborhood, and rent out rooms to other even more recent immigrants. Moses fashions himself as a Robinson Crusoe castaway in his boarding house and hires his own man Friday, a white man from the Midlands. In his journal, Moses writes of him: "He was a willing worker, eager to learn the ways of the Black man. In no time at all he learn to cook peas and rice and to make a beef stew ... I decided to teach him the Bible when I could make the time."[8] The comedy of Selvon's novel is that Moses himself is in complete denial of his own racial oppression. Members of the Black Panthers stage futile debates with him until he is finally exiled to his own basement by the end of the novel. Whereas in Walcott's play, the two main characters are able to come to a sort of rapprochement with their dual and equal roles as actors, Moses has a more fraught ending. He imagines himself as the master novelist, but he is instead a failed and unreliable narrator in a first-person novel.

The island is as much a character as Crusoe or Friday in many re-visitings of Defoe's novel. In Julieta Campos' experimental fiction, *The Fear of Losing Eurydice* (1979), a French schoolteacher, Monsieur N, sits in a café and sketches an island on his white napkin. This picture of an island opens up to a host of other related island images: "Island: The sum of all improbabilities; intoxicating improbability of fiction Island: image of desire ... All islands formulated by human beings and all islands appearing on the maps comprise a single imaginary archipelago – the archipelago of desire."[9] Monsieur N's initial plan to use a Jules Verne novel about shipwrecked schoolboys as a translation exercise for his pupils becomes an obsession to collect every reference to islands he can find and to meditate on them in a diary of his imaginary travels – his "Islandiary," or island book. This island collection is interrupted by a love story developing in the marginalia of the book's pages. The desire, for the island, for love, for freedom, manifests itself on a napkin in a Caribbean café.

The archipelago I trace in this chapter, like Monsieur N's islandiary, connects each story to the next, a chain linking all of them with familiar boundaries and characteristics. Each island remains familiar and yet, in their dissimilarity and their changing contours, they transform the literary and political geography of *Robinson Crusoe*. We recognize Crusoe in our own time but subtly changed. Like so many of the characters we've seen, Monsieur N begins to lose control over his island vision. The story printed in the margins becomes surrounded by other literary quotations and eventually overtakes Monsieur N's singular vision.

Campos' text builds around images rather than plot. She layers associations. The image of an island sketched on a white napkin becomes just as significant – if not more so – than the islands, real and imagined, that are catalogued throughout the text. The islands themselves are connected only by free association. Free association as an ordering principle creates a freedom of movement between geographic and textual spaces. In Monsieur N's islandiary, Campos creates new islands and questions the status of old literary islands. She creates a poetics of relation between the dislocated New World space the island represents in the Caribbean café and the dislocations of postcolonial and postmodern experiences we will see along the way. Like the other writers in this chapter she imagines that, as in *Foe*, "the world is full of islands."[10] This Islandiary is also a metaphor for rethinking literature through comparative reading practices. Campos is writing at the cusp between Caribbean decolonization as represented in Selvon and Walcott and the postcolonial movement that follows. A Cuban exile living in Mexico, Campos uses the metaphor of islands to examine Cuba as an isolated island. But she also wants to trace relationships between literatures. Literature and literary influence are connected like an archipelago of influence, she argues by analogy. They are not one system of call and response between British writers and the former colonies. Instead, they are equal parts on a chain of literary influence. The archipelago eliminates the image of hierarchy, meaning that writers from South Africa influence Caribbean writers as much as British ones. The chains of influence stretch in multiple directions and follow different tides.

While Campos maps our world of islands through the 1970s, we have glimpses of Crusoe wandering into other novels of the 1980s, including Jane Gardam's *Crusoe's Daughter* (1985), Louise Erdrich's *Love Medicine* (1993), Thomas King's *Green Grass, Running Water* (1993), and Cormac McCarthy's *The Crossing* (1994). These apparitions of Robinson Crusoe feel ghostlike and insubstantial. Individual characters suddenly stumble into Crusoe's ghost or into a minor silent character who admonishes the main character into remembering something shared but apparently forgotten. In Erdrich's *Love Medicine*, Robinson Crusoe is a hermit who exiles himself to an island in the middle of the reservation. He wears his clothes on backwards and shares the island with hundreds of cats. A minor character who never speaks he nonetheless acts as a link in the middle of the novel to the past, a quiet figure protected from the violence elsewhere in the novel and also part of it in the sense that he fathers children who carry the narrative but then he distances himself from these children and their community. This Crusoe is at once unreachable and patriarchal, he founds a familial line but refuses to be integrated into the community. This elegiac figure is repeated in Cormac McCarthy's bleak novel set on the Mexican–American border, *The Crossing*. Robinson Crusoe is once again a hermit in a ruin, far from civilization and, tellingly, surrounded by cats. The central protagonist of *The Crossing*, a young boy named Billy, has left his family to return a captured wolf to Mexico. He encounters the Crusoe-like hermit in the very center of the novel, which is also the very center of McCarthy's trilogy. The hermit invites the boy in for breakfast and begins to tell him about the ruined church in the middle of this ruined town and his own search for God. The old man had been a priest and he bore witness to the death of another man, a wanderer who had lost his son and gone looking for God. "In the end," he says, "we shall all of us be only what we have made of God. For nothing is real save his grace" (159). With no further explanation, at the end of this almost mystical encounter, Billy decides to return to his family. The novel though, does not end with reconciliation or renewal. His brother and father die. Coming back out of the desert the detritus of modernity greets him. He comes out of a primitive isolated and ruined landscape and eats out of sardine cans, he crosses highways and the hulks of ruined airplanes. The Crusoe of this novel is a figure at a crossroads between the pre-modern and the modern, between a reliance on God and a loss of faith. He is standing, in some sense, as we do, between a desire for some eternal meaning and our clear knowledge of the violence and destruction we live with.

Robinson Crusoe is part of a quartet of characters in Thomas King's *Green Grass, Running Water*. These four characters, Hawkeye, the Lone Ranger, Robinson Crusoe, and Ishmael, are four Native American elders who have escaped from a mental institution. Each of them also represents an ancient Native American mythic woman and they take turns telling creation stories in short vignettes interspersed between chapters. The novel jumps from these creation stories back to multiple plot lines involving family members in and around the Blackfoot reservation near the Canadian/US border. The plot culminates in the final destruction of a dam running in the middle of the reservation and the return of the river to its native course, a return that also results in one of the central character's homes being swept away. The Crusoe that ultimately emerges from this narrative is a Native American elder. Crusoe here is a mythic holder of ancient wisdom as well as one who foretells major catastrophes. Unlike Coetzee's stoic and even cruel Crusoe or Walcott's changeling representation, this Crusoe reinterprets and channels Native American identity.

The haunting quality of these Crusoe figures is brought home in a slightly different way in Jane Gardam's *Crusoe's Daughter*. Polly Flint, daughter of a sea captain, is orphaned and left to live in her aunt's house, where she discovers the book, *Robinson Crusoe*. Polly carries the book with her over the course of the twentieth century as she survives wars and depressions. In the final chapter Crusoe himself appears to her and they hold a debate about the merits of Defoe's novel and Crusoe's legacy. This version of Crusoe is probably the most akin to Defoe's Crusoe, if only in the sense that Gardam's character seems to mimic Defoe's language and speech, although its framing of Crusoe attempts to establish a matrilineal succession for Defoe's novel. Polly Flint is Crusoe's daughter, his literary successor. The text of Defoe's *Robinson Crusoe* shapes and directs Gardam's work. Polly is constantly compared to Crusoe; she uses his story to help navigate the moral thickets of the Holocaust and nuclear disarmament. Crusoe's moral clarity, with his lists of good and evil, becomes a basis for judging her own actions. Gardam, however, begins the novel with a quote not from Defoe's *Robinson Crusoe* but with an excerpt from Virginia Woolf's essay on Crusoe, "The pressure of life when one is fending for oneself alone on a desert island is really no laughing matter. It is no crying one either."[11] Beginning with Woolf's interpretation of Crusoe rather than Defoe's text suggests once again the creation of a divergent legacy for *Robinson Crusoe*. Rather than seeing him through the lens of early eighteenth-century colonialism or New World conquest, here he is diverted again to a legacy beginning with British women writers from the turn of the twentieth century.

Perhaps the most obvious versions of Robinson Crusoe in twentieth- and twenty-first-century fictions and films are the castaways. In the film *Cast Away* as well as Yann Martel's *The Life of Pi*, the screenwriter and the novelist respectively recreate a Robinson Crusoe-like story in the modern world. Rather than being images of Robinson Crusoe walking through the modern city, these characters experience instead the island castaway narrative. There are many versions of this particular fantasy, from *Gilligan's Island* to *Crusoe on Mars*. Some of these versions are discussed in Chapter 14 in this volume. I focus on *Cast Away* and *The Life of Pi* because they pose the problem of what it means to be isolated individuals in our own global moment; a moment quite similar to Defoe's experience if only in terms of the rapidly changing sense of the expanding world in the early eighteenth century as the British first established the nation of "Great Britain" and began to found overseas colonies in competition with the Spaniards in the Americas.

The contradiction of being alone in the midst of crowds was as familiar to Defoe as it is to us. London in the early eighteenth century was a city teeming with new urban-dwellers and Defoe wrote his story of isolation in the midst of this unwieldy and heterogeneous population. Cynthia Wall has argued that the deserted island, counter-intuitively perhaps, is yet another representation of London in that time, a place where one struggled to feel at home in the midst of its rapidly changing contours.[12] In the film *Cast Away* a FedEx agent, Chuck Noland, played by Tom Hanks, is the only survivor of a plane crash who washes ashore on a deserted island. Since he has drifted far from the wreckage, rescuers give up their search and he is left on the island for four years. Noland manages to survive using the detritus washed up from the airplane, packages with all the random stuff of consumer culture in the twenty-first century. He even imagines that a volleyball is his Man Friday. Eventually he is able to rescue himself by using the tin of a port-a-potty that floats ashore. He had been unable to build a raft with enough weight and momentum to propel him beyond the surf. The tin becomes a sail and finally gets him beyond the white water. This Crusoe doesn't critique but rather is dramatized by the film as adapting with contemporary materials to Defoe's original creation. He seems in many ways one of the truest reincarnations of Defoe's Crusoe, transported to a modern setting. Like Crusoe, efficient from the outset of the film, Noland tracks time and goods precisely. By reinventing Crusoe as an American executive, director Robert Zemeckis and writer William Broyle recreate the Crusoe story in terms of contemporary capitalism. Rather than founding a colony, or finding salvation in God, this new global American version of the castaway employs the detritus of consumer goods to make his escape. Unlike the other Crusoes we have looked at so far who seek to found alternative legacies for

Defoe's hero, this film translates the story into a contemporary setting and in doing so re-establishes its relevance. Crusoe/Noland is deeply sympathetic, translated to our own time, his basic values and perspectives intact.

The Life of Pi is the story of a young Indian boy who is shipwrecked in a boat accompanied by a tiger. Our young friend is a contemporary Crusoe figure as well, but rather than being a replica, he embodies an apparently new kind of globalized self. Setting sail from India with his family, en route to Canada when the ship sinks, Pi ends up drifting around the globe in a narrative that also drifts from magical realism to ordinary realism. Like Noland, Pi represents a modern re-inscription of the castaway story. To be cast away today, these narratives suggest, is not qualitatively different from what it was to be cast away in the early eighteenth century. One is simultaneously intensely isolated and struggling to survive and yet at the same time constantly reminded of connection. Placing the island on a boat emphasizes the sense of globalized motion inherent in the modern experience. While Defoe's Crusoe moved restlessly across the globe in the early part of his book, he is stuck in one place waiting twenty-eight years for someone to find him. But Pi is stuck in motion, drifting the globe and yet somehow always out of touch with any other ship or continent. He is reduced to basic bodily survival in a lifeboat with a tiger that may or may not turn out to be real. Pi is a mathematical constant, the ratio of the circle's circumference to its diameter, which is also an irrational number. To see Pi the boy as both irrational and constant, a reinvention of Crusoe who is also a constant and irrational figure in the global literary stage, is once again to emphasize Crusoe's legacy as a modern myth in transit.

Alternative and anti-Crusoes abound, but they are character re-enactments rather than rejections. This textual legacy of *Robinson Crusoe* becomes a much stronger theme in the work of Marianne Wiggins, Victoria Slavuski, and Julieta Campos. These three writers have bits and pieces of Crusoe-like characters drifting through their narratives, but much more prevalent is an abiding interest in Defoe's book. Characters experience the shock of recognition when they experience a Crusoe-type moment, and they then stand in for the readers who also stumble upon passages that are deeply familiar but made unfamiliar by the context. Wiggins very nicely encapsulates this problem of recognition in her novel, *John Dollar*. Wiggins not only cannibalizes the story of Crusoe; she literally has her horrifying schoolgirls eat her central character, John Dollar, a Crusoe stand-in. The real problem in Wiggins' novel, however, is that everyone is already immersed in the *Robinson Crusoe* narrative:

> Everyone who stepped ashore that day (except the bearers) had either read or
> heard the story of *The Life and Adventures of Robinson Crusoe*, so there was

> that, that sense of exhilaration which comes when one's life bears a likeness
> to the fictions that one's dreamed plus there was the weighty thrill of bringing
> light, the torch of history, into one more far-flung "reach of darkness."[13]

British colonialism is being satirized in this passage. Wiggins' schoolgirls attempt to understand their lives through the legacies of British fiction. Stepping ashore is participating in fiction, living in it. Wiggins' re-enactment of this colonial scene reconnects the reader to the history of British colonizing; everyone (including readers) experiences the thrill of recognition in fiction. The overwhelming desire "for the fictions one's dreamed" threatens the development of female characters throughout *John Dollar*. When the young schoolgirls eventually resort to cannibalism, the act is a horrific literalizing of the colonial project of consumption of natural resources.

While everyone on Marianne Wiggins' island has heard and read the story of *Robinson Crusoe*, no one in Victoria Slavuski's Argentinean novel, *Música para olvidar una isla* [*Music for Forgetting an Island*; translation mine] (1993), has actually read the novel. This failure, something alluded to at the beginning of this chapter, emphasizes the problems of differentiating truth and fiction as well as memory, especially under political oppression. These characters are like many contemporary readers in their failure to read at all, let alone read carefully. Slavuski's characters live or spend their vacation on Alexander Selkirk's "real island" off the coast of Chile and are familiar enough with the history of the novel to debate among themselves the details of Defoe's account versus histories of Alexander Selkirk's abandonment on this particular island. The novel follows a US anthropology student finishing writing her dissertation about Selkirk's island. She makes friends with another woman who is producing a documentary about the island. They in turn become connected to various inhabitants, some of whom are political dissidents. The characters engage in long debates about the relationship between Selkirk and Defoe/Crusoe. Finally, they stumble into magical grottoes, which reveal different aspects of the island's past to different observers. Slavuski's narrative techniques and her title emphasize the problem of memory and truth in the face of political oppression.

Translation in Slavuski is an act whereby a text is possessed, moving it from one language and one cultural context to another. Translation in this sense becomes not just a linguistic act of transference; it is a metaphor of crossing, a linguistic act of creating new narrative territories. One character claims the name Robinson Crusoe is just the English translation of Selkirk.[14] Translation becomes a political act of appropriation. Slavuski returns often to the idea of an authentic castaway, whose history has been undermined by Defoe/Crusoe. Several characters spin conspiracy theories about the ways that Defoe stole and translated Selkirk's work. Characters in the novel constantly revise the various histories of the island for themselves as a way of resisting censorship and military oppression. These multiple stories add to an increasing sense of claustrophobia on the island. No one can invent an original story just as no one can escape from their political fate as the military approaches the island and prepares its invasion.

Crusoe's island is translated by Slavuski into a modern-day temporary refuge from political, spiritual, and romantic difficulties. The military ultimately orders everyone off the island just as Defoe says he has "done with" the island. In the end, the layers of narrative history and loss are overwhelming. All the main characters walk around lamenting their fate and quoting Alexander Selkirk, "Beloved island, I never should have abandoned you." Slavuski recognizes both the futility of the island and the impossibility of letting it go.

As with the other modern versions of Defoe's novel, *Robinson Crusoe* operates as the central textual touchstone – every household keeps a copy of the novel alongside their family Bible. In Slavuski's novel, the irony is that all the central characters are obsessed with the history of *Robinson Crusoe*, even as they are unwilling to read the actual text. Like the Bible, *Robinson Crusoe* is ubiquitous. Furthermore, the book by the only native islander, *Twenty-Five Ways to Prepare Lobster,* also referred to in this passage, seems like an oblique commentary on revision itself, twenty-five different versions of the same lobster. Slavuski's narrative enacts the increasingly thick layers of cultural and literary meaning that have piled up over Crusoe's island. The novel acts out in miniature the premise of this essay: multiple stories, including postcolonial, postmodern, and feminist ones, have transformed the boundaries of Defoe's original island. Placing *Robinson Crusoe* and the Bible together on the bookshelf, alongside a recipe book for lobsters, establishes a small canon of island reading. *Robinson Crusoe* is both global and local.

"Where are you Robin Crusoe? Where are you? Where have you been?"[15] Six years into his twenty-eight-year island habitation, Robinson Crusoe wakes up to a disembodied voice asking for his whereabouts. The voice turns out to be his trained parrot. The question itself haunts twentieth- and twenty-first-century literature as novelists, playwrights, poets, and filmmakers from around the globe call back to Defoe's novel, echoing the mimicry of Crusoe's Poll the parrot. Much of the criticism of revisions of *Robinson Crusoe* frames the relationship between the eighteenth-century novel and its successors as adversarial, the new and improved revisions pitted against the original text, colonialism versus postcolonialism, slavery versus freedom, realism against abstraction. Yet the proliferation of Crusoes, and indeed the search for that nebulous island, goes on, suggesting that what we have before us is not a struggle between two potential alternative readings of Crusoe but really an altogether new way of mapping how we understand and read literature in motion across the globe. We are still searching for Robin Crusoe not because we know what he means or what he stood for in the early eighteenth century but because with each revision he has come to mean something new again. We recognize the island everywhere and nowhere as each new generation of writers renders the familiarity of Crusoe unfamiliar again.

NOTES

1 "En días como ése todos nos prometíamos que por fin íbamos a aprovechar para leer el Robinson que junta polvo en cada casa de la isla junto a la Biblia y al Veinticinco maneras de prepara una langosta escrito en Juan Fernández por Amelita Riera. Nadie pasaba de la página quince de Robinson, casi nadie abría la Biblia." Victoria Slavuski, *Música para olvidar una isla* (Buenos Aires: Planeta, 1993), 12.

2 Lucy Ford, *Female Robinson Crusoe, A Tale of the American Wilderness* (New York, NY: New York, 1837), 1.

3 Ibid., 22.

4 Virginia Woolf, "Robinson Crusoe," reprinted in *Robinson Crusoe: An Authoritative Text, Context and Commentary* (New York, NY: W. W. Norton, 1994), 287.

5 Gertrude Stein, *The Autobiography of Alice B. Toklas* (New York, NY: Vintage Books, 1990), 237.

6 Elizabeth Bishop, "Crusoe at Home," in *Geography III* (New York, NY: Farrar, Straus, and Giroux, 1998), 17.

7 Derek Walcott, "Pantomime," in *Remembrance and Pantomime: Two Plays* (New York, NY: Farrar, Straus, and Giroux, 1980), 126.

8 Sam Selvon, *Moses Ascending* (Oxford: Heinemann, 1984), 4.

9 Julieta Campos, *The Fear of Losing Eurydice*, trans. Leland Chambers (Champaign, IL: Dalkey Archive Press, 1994), 102.

10 J. M. Coetzee, *Foe* (London: Penguin Books), 71.

11 Jane Gardam, *Crusoe's Daughter* (New York, NY: Europa Editions, 1985), 8.

12 Cynthia Wall, *The Literary and Cultural Spaces of Restoration London* (Cambridge: Cambridge University Press, 1998), 195.

13 Marianne Wiggins, *John Dollar* (New York, NY: Harper & Row, 1989), 69.

14 Slavuski, *Música para olvidar una isla*, 347.

15 Daniel Defoe, *Robinson Crusoe*, ed. John Richetti (London: Penguin, 2003), 113.

14

ROBERT MAYER

Robinson Crusoe in the Screen Age

The history of the adaptation of Defoe's most famous narrative for the screen goes back as far as the history of the screen arts themselves. The earliest important film narratives appear in the first decade of the twentieth century as does the first cinematic treatment of *Robinson Crusoe*.[1] Shortly after Georges Méliès' *A Trip to the Moon* (1902) and in the same year as Edwin S. Porter's *The Great Train Robbery* (1903), Méliès himself produced a *Robinson Crusoe* and Siegmund Lubin, a key early American film producer, released *Swiss Family Robinson*. After that, films based on *Crusoe* served as vehicles for such stars as Douglas Fairbanks, Dick Van Dyke, Peter O'Toole, Tom Hanks, and Pierce Brosnan; works that appropriated Defoe's novel were presented to film and television audiences, as cartoons, in serial form, and in both lavish and low-budget feature-length film productions.[2] Thus, anyone considering the history of *Robinson Crusoe* on screen finds, if not exactly an embarrassment of riches, then at least a diverse array of refashionings of the book. This chapter examines that body of visual texts, first surveying the many screen versions that have appeared since 1903, and then focusing mainly on movies and television programs made after 1950, especially on two works based on *Crusoe* produced in 1964: Byron Haskins' cult classic, *Robinson Crusoe on Mars*, and a thirteen-part serial made on the Continent but shown on the BBC in 1965.[3] If one considers the potential audiences for the many screen productions of the Crusoe narrative from 1903 to 1953, a period when, in the middle of the twentieth century, more than a hundred million people regularly went to the cinema in the United States and Europe *every week*, and then, after 1960, at least a hundred million households in Europe and North America had television sets, it seems likely that since the advent of motion pictures in 1895, more people have encountered Defoe's narrative, however transformed, through screen adaptations than have actually read either the novel itself or the many responses to the Crusoe story that make up the tradition of the Robinsonade.[4] In short, if one wants to specify the crucial elements of what has been called the Crusoe myth as it endures in popular culture in our own day, one needs to look to works for the screen.[5] That is the purpose of this chapter. Treating the two 1964 *Crusoe*s, along with other important versions released after World War II, I will argue that in such works the Crusoe story is a secular vision of man, isolated and in extremis, that focuses on the issue of man's mastery, over nature as well as himself, and, although in an increasingly problematic way, over an ethnic or racial or even interspecies Other. The screen contributions to the Crusoe myth entail, that is, both the recapitulation of important elements of Defoe's narrative and notable revisions of the original.

First, a bit of history. There were a host of silent Crusoe films, made in Denmark, Italy, the United Kingdom, France, and the United States, including three American versions in 1916 and 1917, one of them produced by the Edison Studio near the end of its existence. The most notable and ample silent retellings of Defoe's narrative were an eighteen-part serial produced by Universal in 1922 and a British version made by the actor-director-producer M. A. Wetherell and released in 1927. The Wetherell film is, for its length (forty-six minutes), a relatively full retelling of the castaway's island experience, with a thin framing narrative about a woman, Sophie (Fay Compton), who waits for Crusoe while he is on his island and joyously greets him upon his return to England. Like the Edison production in crediting "Daniel Defoe's famous old book," Wetherell's film represents the protagonist's sense of isolation as a "living death"; shows his efforts to make bread, clothes, and other necessities; and highlights his finding of a footprint and effortlessly exerting control over Friday.[6]

In the early sound era, with the notable exception of the farcical and fairly racist *Mr. Robinson Crusoe* (1932), Defoe's novel was the inspiration of mainly cartoons or serials for Saturday-afternoon matinees, which is to say it was largely relegated to entertainments for children.[7] After World War II, however, *Robinson Crusoe* is generally transformed by filmmakers into more adult fare.[8] The key work signaling this change is the motion picture that is often thought of as the best screen adaptation of the novel, certainly the only version by a certified film auteur, Luis Buñuel, whose *Adventures of Robinson Crusoe* appeared in 1954. Subsequent major features making use of Defoe's narrative included *Lt. Robin Crusoe* (1966; with Van Dyke); *Man Friday* (1975; with O'Toole); *Crusoe* (1988; with Aidan Quinn); and, finally, *Cast Away* (2000; with Hanks).[9] At the same time, television – especially American television – repeatedly appropriated the Crusoe story for comedy (*Gilligan's Island* [1964–7]), science fiction (*Lost in Space* [1965–8] and *Lost* [2004–10]), seemingly straightforward adaptations of the novel (*Crusoe* [2008–9]), and even reality television (*Survivor* [2000–13]).[10] As

I show elsewhere, Defoe's works have been used by screen artists much more than those of any other eighteenth-century writer, and *Robinson Crusoe* has been, by far, the most popular of Defoe's narratives.[11]

The two screen versions of *Robinson Crusoe* produced or acquired by major Anglo-American media organizations in 1964 – *Crusoe on Mars*, by Haskins (who also made popular versions of *Treasure Island* and *War of the Worlds* in the 1950s), and the serialized *Crusoe* directed by the little-known French filmmaker Jean Sacha and starring the equally obscure Austrian actor Robert Hoffmann – suggest the power and significance of the Crusoe story in Anglo-American culture during the last half-century and more.[12] Although these works for the screen may not have been noticed upon their release by Defoe scholars who were transforming the treatment of *Robinson Crusoe* in academic discourse around the same time, internet sources demonstrate that the 1964 versions were memorable events for the people who saw them when they appeared.[13] In one of the many enthusiastic "user reviews" of Haskins' film at IMDB.com, the writer declares that he "loved this movie as a child"; a more professional assessment comes from David Filipi's comment in a list of his top ten favorite films in the Criterion Collection. Filipi asserts that his inclusion of the Haskins film is "for nostalgic reasons, plain and simple," but he also reports: "I've seen it a couple of times as an adult, and thankfully it stands up very nicely."[14] Similarly, original viewers of the BBC *Robinson Crusoe* recall their love for the series when they saw it on BBC2 during the summer school holiday. A substantial number of former viewers commented on the serial as the thirteen episodes were posted on YouTube between July 2011 and October 2013; one individual, for example, writes that the postings "Bring ... back such great memories of my childhood. These [episodes] are so good and remind me just what a fantastic production this was." These online comments also highlight a point made earlier: that in the twentieth century more people encountered Defoe's most famous narrative in screen versions than read the novel. The individual who posted the whole of the BBC series on YouTube reports as he begins uploading the serial: "I loved this series so much that now this is my favorite book," but his is one of the few remarks that invokes Defoe's text and even he seems to acknowledge that he knew the Crusoe story from television before he read the book. Another such comment is made by a contributor to the online discussion of the series, describing Defoe's original ("First – it's a work of fiction") and then scolding other contributors: "Read the book," implying of course that almost no one who waxes nostalgic about the BBC series actually knows Defoe's work.[15] All of which serves to emphasize the fact that the Crusoe story remains a *popular* narrative in the late twentieth and early twenty-first centuries to an important degree because of its varied career on screen.

What do the various screen *Robinson Crusoe*s tell us about the continuing life of Defoe's narrative in Western culture? Both 1964 versions make it clear that for screen artists appropriating Defoe's novel, only the hero's experience as a castaway really matters.[16] The BBC *Adventures of Robinson Crusoe* opens with the hero crawling out of the sea and ends, except for a momentary glimpse of Crusoe back in England (with Friday as his amanuensis), with Crusoe's somewhat regretful departure from his island. Similarly, *Robinson Crusoe on Mars* begins with a brief sequence on the command module of a NASA mission to Mars before the astronauts (only one of whom will survive) and a monkey that accompanies them are forced down to the surface of the planet; the film ends when a second American space vehicle arrives to rescue the castaways. While the thirteen-episode BBC version does flashback to Crusoe's experiences before his shipwreck – conflict with his father, his experience of slavery and life in Brazil – that material serves mainly to show how Crusoe came to his island and how he responds to his new life.

Both 1964 versions highlight the Crusoe figure's undertaking, as the novel puts it, "a more particular survey of the island it self" (79) and, principally, acquiring the skills necessary for survival.[17] In the Haskins film there is no animal husbandry or agriculture because Mars is depicted as essentially a dead planet and there are no animals aside from Mona, the monkey. But the surviving astronaut, Kit Draper (Paul Mantee), does find water and a food source, and he makes a calendar, a sand clock, cloth from a plant he discovers growing in the water on Mars, and clothing. The BBC serial's Crusoe acquires a much more extensive set of skills, one that approximates the accomplishments of the novel's protagonist; he records hard-won successes in "housekeeping," cooking, hunting, fishing, pottery (a "new trade"), basketry, farming, and cheese-making, and ends by declaring "I'll become a jack of all trades" (Episodes 5, 8), seemingly echoing the moment in Defoe's text when the hero judges he can eventually become the "master of every mechanick art" (55). In addition, *Cast Away*, in a very dramatic cut (leaping over four years on the island), from a clearly middle-aged and quite heavy to a comparatively slight and much younger-looking Tom Hanks, effortlessly shows how the Crusoe figure in that film – a FedEx systems engineer, Chuck Noland – becomes not just an expert at spearfishing but also someone who is at least physically equal to the challenges of life on his island.[18] These matters take us to the very heart of Defoe's book for a good deal of its historical audience; one can cite not only Jean-Jacques Rousseau's famous characterization of the novel as a representation of an individual "destitute of human assistance, and of mechanical implements, providing, neverthe-less, for his subsistence, for self-preservation, and even procuring for himself a kind of competency" but also Virginia Woolf's description of the book as more than anything else a text that shows how "serious" and "beautiful" it is "[t]o dig, to bake, to plant, to build."[19] Seemingly in agreement with these readings of the novel from the eighteenth to the twentieth century, most of the screen adaptations of *Robinson Crusoe* concentrate on how the hero by "experiment" becomes the "master of my business" (84).

In addition to exploring the hero's successes, however, the screen versions of Defoe's novel also consider the dire psychic consequences of his solitude. In *Crusoe on Mars*, Draper, keeping the twentieth-century equivalent of a journal on a recording device, observes that the planners of his mission did not anticipate the "hairiest problem of all: isolation ... the problem of being alone forever." Similarly, the Crusoe of the 1964 BBC serial first acknowledges that his island seems not to contain "wild animals or poi-sonous snakes" but does present "another, more serious danger: solitude," and he later laments that his loneliness "has become too heavy to bear. I feel I am about to lose my sanity" (Episodes 3, 6). Madness and suicide, indeed, are more-or-less constant features of recent Crusoe screen versions. Buñuel's film features a mad scene, and *Man Friday* ends with a desperate Crusoe alone on a beach; in the original version of the latter film, shown at the Cannes Film Festival, Crusoe is preparing to commit suicide.[20] And Noland, in *Cast Away*, has tried and failed to hang himself. Isolation, then, is the occasion in recent screen *Crusoe*s not only for the protagonist's acquisition of life-saving technique but also for his psychological disintegration. While Defoe's narrative represents Crusoe's desolation – as he begins his journal he describes his "unfortunate island" as "*The Island of Despair*" (57) – the Crusoe of the novel, unlike the screen castaways after 1950, masters himself as well as his physical environment.[21]

A key difference between Defoe's original and recent screen appropriations of it that helps to explain the darker psychological cast of the latter is the view of religion embodied in the various versions of the castaway narrative. In the novel, a few months after he describes his desperation, the ill Crusoe has the "terrible dream" that marks the beginning of a religious awakening that concludes with his praying with "a true Scripture view of hope" (70, 77). That his piety helps him avoid the worst psychic consequences of his isolation is suggested by the balance sheet he draws up containing "the description of good and evil" arising from his condition. Crusoe declares "*I am divided from mankind, a solitaire, one banished from human society,*" but he also, after lamenting in the last "EVIL" on his sheet that he has "*no soul to speak to, or relieve me,*" notes a compensating sense of God's providential care for him: "*God wonderfully sent the ship in near enough to the shore that* [it] *… will either supply my wants, or enable me to supply my self even as long as I live.*" Thus, in the novel, Crusoe's faith is "something *positive* to be thankful for" that balances out the "*negative*" of his solitary state (54).[22]

Screen versions of Defoe's narrative, by contrast, have for the most part pointedly rejected this feature of the novel. There is attention to religion in *Robinson Crusoe on Mars*, but only late in the film, after Friday has appeared. Draper, the Crusoe figure, becomes ill and when he wakes after a long sleep he has a vision of his lost fellow astronaut (Adam West) and cries out to him, "Mac … Aren't you ever going to talk to me?" It is at this point that Draper reflects on the agony of loneliness, but his forlorn state does not lead him to reflect on God or divine mercy. Later in the film, after Friday has learned some English, Draper, having discovered a new source of water when the two men sorely need it, exclaims "Thank God," and Friday (Victor Lundin) queries: "God?" Draper explains: "Yeah. Supreme Being. Uh, father of the universe. Big father," and Friday responds "Kaihechipek … Order … God … Good." Draper agrees: "Yeah, that's right. Divine order … Good." This conversation seems to refer to the discussion in the novel of "old *Benamuckee*, that liv'd beyond all" (170), but as virtually the only reference to religion in the film, particularly given the far too easy reconciliation of two different belief systems with the facile assertion "Divine order … Good," it is hard not to see this brief moment as a mere bow toward religion in a film (and a culture at large) that seems disinclined to take such matters seriously. This view is borne out by a consideration of how the BBC's *Crusoe* serial treats religion. That longer rendering of the novel includes more references to Crusoe's religious feelings.[23] Most notably, in Episode 9, the hero reflects on his first three years on the island: "Remember the long, difficult road along which Almighty God has made you walk – to test your obedience, and also your strength … And to see if you shall remain faithful." Crusoe celebrates his anniversary on the island with a party at which he reads to his "guests" – his dog, parrot, and goat – from the Bible. This scene, however, has a clear comic aspect, and what is more notable about the treatment of religion is that in this version (and in *Crusoe on Mars*) there is neither any "first prayer" (73) nor any sense of the castaway being "born again." In the 1964 screen appropriations of Defoe's novel, the hero has faith but it is notional and unconvincing.

In other screen versions of *Crusoe* since 1950, furthermore, the attitude toward religion is much more clearly negative. In the Buñuel film, the protagonist reports in a moment of desperation: "the scriptures came meaningless to my eyes," and in *Man Friday*, Crusoe's religion is represented as a disease. We see him engaged in self-flagellation, and Friday decries the fact that Crusoe is full of "guilt, and fear of a cruel god." In *Cast Away*, as Noland is burying one of his fellow FedEx employees, he evidently considers the possibility of offering a prayer for the dead man but dismisses the idea with a shrug that suggests Noland's sense of the pointlessness of such a gesture.[24] Screen versions of *Robinson Crusoe* since 1950, then, either turn the powerful religious feelings of Defoe's protagonist into an attenuated and seemingly pro forma piety or assertively reject that element of the original narrative.

The other major issue presented by Defoe's text that virtually all of the screen versions of Crusoe confront is the relationship between Friday and his Western "master." Wetherell's 1927 film (like other silent and early sound versions) essentially adopts the book's representation of Crusoe with his "savage companion," but films made after 1950 approach the Friday–Crusoe relationship with more care. Buñuel's *Robinson Crusoe* represents Friday's subordinate relationship to Crusoe in a relatively untroubled way but it also at times takes a critical view of the Englishman.[25] The 1964 screen versions are also of two minds about the relationship between Crusoe and Friday. In the BBC's *Robinson Crusoe*, the protagonist repeatedly asserts the superiority of "civilized" Englishmen over "savages." On his first morning on the island, he awakes and immediately performs his morning ablutions, commenting: "No matter what the circumstances, an Englishman must wash every morning. Our customs of decency and cleanliness distinguish us from other people." Later, in a flashback, Crusoe and his friends in Brazil justify his undertaking a voyage to Africa to obtain new slaves for all of them; "those poor creatures will be infinitely better treated here than where they're living," comments one of Crusoe's associates (Episodes 1, 7). Such assertions prepare the ground for the development of the relationship between Crusoe and Friday, which commences with Friday's "token," as the novel puts it, "of swearing to be my slave for ever" (161). Early in their time together, the BBC Crusoe decides to teach Friday "how to behave at table" after observing, "his manners are revolting," and he also introduces Friday to Western clothes because "Civilization begins with trousers" (Episodes 10, 11). But the television serial also undermines Crusoe's assertion of Western superiority to some extent by at times viewing it ironically. Crusoe and Friday, for example, discuss the relative utility of the bow and the rifle, with Crusoe describing the former as "savage" and the latter as "civilized." And when Friday learns to shoot, he runs around wildly firing the rifle and exulting: "Me very civilized" (Episode 11). Similarly, earlier in the same episode a self-satisfied Crusoe declares of Friday, who is learning to do all their chores, "I must admit he's profiting from my lessons," as the camera shows the Englishman lazing in a hammock while Friday fans him. More important, Crusoe has second thoughts about his assertions of ethnic superiority; when the two men quarrel about Friday's failure to do some of his work, the latter runs away, and after Crusoe has been alone again for some time, the Englishman has an illumination:

> I thought I was superior to him, and I wasn't … I had considered Friday my slave, and he couldn't bear that. Now that I understand, he's come back. If he hadn't acted that way, our relationship would have grown more distant with each day. Basically, he was right.

This insight leads to Crusoe's declaring that Friday "is almost always right" and remarking: "Time goes by – more pleasantly now that Friday and I are real friends" (Episode 12). As I have indicated, the serial ends with a reminder that Crusoe is still the master and Friday still the servant, but it also features a major qualification of the hero's assertion of his natural superiority.

Much the same is true of *Robinson Crusoe on Mars*, which seems imbued with early 1960s (Kennedy and Johnson) liberalism.[26] The Friday in the Haskins film is a human-like alien brought to Mars as a slave in other (unseen) aliens' mining operations, and Draper, after rescuing him, establishes his dominance in the relationship. The astronaut informs Friday: "Me. I'm the boss, and remember that," but this American Crusoe is clearly uneasy with his role as the "civilized" man dominating a "savage" Other. Draper is at one point seen by Friday as having chased away his former captors, who torment him by means of some transmission to black bracelets that he wears, and the alien bows down to the American, a gesture that clearly evokes Friday's submission to Crusoe in the novel. As this Friday pays obeisance, however, Draper first turns away the suggestion that he has come to Friday's rescue ("Oh, I got rid of them, huh? I've got the power, is that it?"), and then is clearly abashed by Friday's behavior: "Okay, okay, that's enough! I'm not supernatural." Subsequently, we see Friday working while Draper looks on, but there is far less of the assertion of superiority by this Crusoe than we find in either the 1964 BBC serial or earlier screen versions. And this American Crusoe also has an (admittedly brief and somewhat forced) epiphany about the film's Other. When the two are trying to escape from his former masters, Friday encourages Crusoe to go on alone, but Draper insists: "We're sticking together, buddy." When Friday questions, "Buddy?" Draper answers "Yeah, slang for brother." Thus, *Robinson Crusoe on Mars* momentarily puts in place the standard version of the master–slave dynamic that dominates screen retellings of the Crusoe story down at least to the mid-twentieth century but the film almost immediately backs away from that stance. That *Robinson Crusoe on Mars* is ill at ease about the traditional treatment of the Crusoe–Friday pairing is confirmed by commentary on the Criterion Collection DVD of the film; Mantee reports that he was "uncomfortable" when the script required him to tell Friday: "I'm the boss." He also comments ruefully on the scene with Friday working and Draper at ease by describing it as representing Friday serving the American and the latter sitting on "a throne."[27]

By the 1960s, in short, screen artists in Britain and America clearly saw the need to qualify the racial politics they inherited from earlier versions of the Crusoe story. And after 1964, most screen versions rework the Crusoe–Friday relationship in such a way as to undermine explicitly the racist and colonialist presuppositions of the Crusoe myth. *Man Friday*, released eleven years after *Crusoe on Mars*, not only rejects Crusoe's religion, but also represents him as a pathological racist and imperialist. Caleb Deschanel's *Crusoe*, in which the protagonist is an American slave trader, suggests that Crusoe is corrupted by his view of non-Europeans, and the film turns his encounters with two Friday figures into the occasion for his moral regeneration.[28] In the recent (2009) television *Crusoe* (shown in America on NBC), this tendency has gone so far that when a pirate refers to Friday as a "savage," Crusoe objects, and his description of his companion turns him into a paragon whom the Westerner can only hope to emulate.[29] It seems obvious, in light of these increasingly radical revisions, that works for the screen not only are mindful of crucial elements of the Crusoe myth, but are also aware that they are participating in the continuing elaboration of that myth, both by repeating key inherited elements of it and by at times interrogating or even thoroughly transforming it.

The versions of the Crusoe story that one finds in post-World War II Anglo-American screen appropriations of Defoe's narrative focus, in sum, on a lone individual, isolated in a new and strange environment, who gradually achieves mastery over that environment and acquires an impressive array of technical competencies. These Crusoes generally have at least one encounter with an ethnic, racial, or interspecies Other and in the process assert their natural superiority to the "savage." In the late twentieth century and after, that assertion increasingly comes into question, even by Crusoe himself, and is either qualified or rejected. Most of the retellings of the Crusoe myth, however, retain the encounter with Friday, seemingly acknowledging that this most problematic element in the story is nevertheless crucial to it and that the relationship must be faced and somehow resolved even in popular entertainments. Two new elements in the Crusoe story in the screen age are developments out of Defoe's narrative. The first is that most film and television appropriations of the story insist on the serious psychological distress resulting from prolonged isolation. These late twentieth-century works are at odds with Defoe's narrative, which, although shot through with a sense of "the miseries" arising from the castaway's condition, nevertheless suggests that Crusoe is saved from the worst effects of prolonged isolation by his piety (54). The absence of such religious feeling, however, is the second new element in the Crusoe myth in works for screen after 1950. On television and in the movies, in the twentieth and the twenty-first centuries, the Crusoe myth is insistently secular.

The present account of that myth in recent screen appropriations accords, up to a point, with Ian Watt's discussion of its most basic "meanings," focusing on "the universal appeal of solitude" as well as the sheer, heroic fact of "Crusoe's survival" in the face of immense physical and psychic challenges.[30] Watt sees the myth as largely a matter of Crusoe's mastery: "a model to us all in how he learns to manage his desolated state." We have seen, however, that recent works for the screen abandon this aspect of the book by insisting in varying degrees on the protagonist's psychological debility. Watt, furthermore, has very little to say about race, an issue that looms large in twentieth- and twenty-first-century appropriations of the story. Other scholars, of course, have discussed the treatment of race in Defoe's text. Roxann Wheeler argues that the novel "may be read as using available racial ideology to vindicate the British colonial spirit," a posture that is revealed in "Crusoe's initial, negative assumptions about Africans and Caribbean islanders and in his conviction that Europeans are technological and cultural superiors to all other people." But Wheeler also suggests that there are "fissures" in the novel's racial politics. She points, among other things, to its description of Friday, which she reads as containing "positive connotations" for eighteenth-century readers.[31] Wheeler's work suggests, that is, that even the ambivalence toward matters of race and ethnicity that we find in a number of screen versions made after 1950 can be thought of as rooted in Defoe's original.

Some Defoe scholars may well feel that, despite some salutary revisions of the racial politics of the Crusoe story, more than a fuller representation of the hero's piety is missing from the film and television *Crusoe*s of the last half century or so. Some will decry, that is, the artistic weakness – indeed the vulgarity – of screen versions of Defoe's narrative directed by the likes of Sacha or Haskins or starring the likes of Mantee or Brosnan.[32] It must be said that many of the films or television shows discussed here were low-budget affairs, with not a few of the characteristics of classic B-pictures: far from polished scripts, awkward acting by at best inexperienced actors, and unimpressive technical features rooted in small budgets. Indeed, in the Criterion commentary on *Robinson Crusoe on Mars*, a number of the artists who helped make that film ruefully acknowledge that it includes incongruous elements that undermined its attempt to treat the subject seriously, including the somewhat embarrassing title; the fact that the aliens' spaceships were obviously borrowed from the more famous Haskins' film, *War of the Worlds*; and Friday's "quasi-Egyptian" costume. And aside from the Buñuel film and at least the island segment of *Cast Away*, the television programs and movies treated here cannot claim to be anything other than popular entertainments aimed at a broad and uncritical audience. But Thomas Keymer has recently reminded us of the "lowbrow appeal" of Defoe's novel when it was first published, describing it as a "brazenly commercial production, defiant of traditional literary decorum and accessible to all readers" and, as a result, "one of the most conspicuous successes of the early eighteenth-century market for print" and also "one of the most suspect."[33] An important aspect of the story's seemingly universal appeal – its status as myth – is the fact that is has, throughout its history, first in the novel, then in the Robinsonade, and most recently on screen, been widely accessible. Many of the various appropriations of the myth for the screen may seem vulgar or "lowbrow" but all told, as I have argued, they have likely reached a wider audience in the last hundred years than have the many textual versions of the story, and, as a result, they are an important source for our understanding of the myth as it endures, and changes, in our day. The story may no longer be "the epic of the stiff upper lip" described by Watt, but it continues to embody a powerful image of an isolated human being *in extremis*, surviving and achieving a degree of mastery over nature, Other, and self, albeit a sway much revised from earlier formations of the Crusoe myth.[34]

NOTES

1 IMDB.com lists 101 results for "Robinson Crusoe," eighteen of which are from the silent era. Subsequent historical remarks can be understood to rely upon this resource. I am also indebted to the staff of the Motion Picture, Broadcasting, and Recorded Sound Division of the Library of Congress, especially Rosemary Hanes in the Moving Image Section, for help with research on this topic.

2 I use the word "appropriated" rather than "adapted" because the latter tends to privilege text over image and overlooks the fact that, as Brian McFarlane argues, "There are many kinds of relations which may exist between film and literature, and fidelity is only one – and rarely the most exciting"; McFarlane, *Novel to Film: An Introduction to the Theory of Adaptation* (Oxford: Clarendon Press, 1996), 11.

3 *Robinson Crusoe on Mars*, dir. Byron Haskins, Aubrey Schenck Productions, 1964; *The Adventures of Robinson Crusoe*, dir. Jean Sacha, Franco London Films, 1964. That Haskins' film has attained the status of a cult classic is attested to by its release by the Criterion Collection in 2007, the same year it issued DVDs of Ingmar Bergman's *Sawdust and Tinsel* (1956) and Rainer Werner Fassbinder's *Berlin Alexanderplatz* (1983).

4 Kristin Thompson and David Bordwell, *Film History: An Introduction*, 3rd edn (Boston, MA: McGraw-Hill, 2010), 299, 301.

5 Ian Watt, *Myths of Modern Individualism: Faust, Don Quixote, Don Juan, Robinson Crusoe* (Cambridge: Cambridge University Press, 1996); see also, among others, Anthony Purdy, "From Defoe's 'Crusoe' to Tournier's 'Vendredi': The Metamorphosis of a Myth," *Canadian Review of Comparative Literature* 11 (1984): 217–35; Martin Green, *The Robinson Crusoe Story* (University Park, PA: Pennsylvania State University Press, 1990); and *Robinson Crusoe: Myths and Metamorphoses*, ed. Lieve Spaas and Brian Stimpson (New York, NY: St Martin's, 1996).

6 See "Robinson Crusoe" (1927) on YouTube (accessed October 24, 2013). https://archive.org/details/RobinsonCrus_2.

7 *Mr. Robinson Crusoe*, dir. Edward Sutherland, Elton Productions, 1932. Early sound works include such cartoons as *The Castaway* (1931; Mickey Mouse) and *Robinson Crusoe, Jr.* (1941; Porky Pig), and the fourteen-part serial *Robinson Crusoe on Clipper Island* (1936; Republic Pictures). The latter work is a melodrama far removed from Defoe's original.

8 One can only speculate as to why there is such a change, but it is almost certainly traceable in part to World War II and the long process of decolonization after 1945, historical developments that recast relations between Western countries and the rest of the world.

9 *The Adventures of Robinson Crusoe*, dir. Luis Buñuel, Oscar Dancigers Production, 1954. On this film, see Gillian Parker, "Crusoe Through the Looking-Glass," in *The English Novel and the Movies*, ed. Michael Klein and Gillian Parker (New York, NY: Frederick Ungar, 1981), 14–27; and Robert Mayer, "Three Cinematic Robinsonades," in *Eighteenth-Century Fiction on Screen*, ed. Robert Mayer (Cambridge: Cambridge University Press), 35–51, in which I also discuss *Man Friday* and *Crusoe*.

10 I treat the first seasons of *Gilligan's Island*, *Survivor*, and *Lost* in "Robinson Crusoe on Television," *Quarterly Review of Film and Video* 28 (2011): 53–65. The recent television *Crusoe* actually departs radically from Defoe's narrative.

11 See my essay "Defoe's Cultural Afterlife, Mainly on Screen" in *The Afterlives of Eighteenth-Century Fiction*, ed. Daniel Cook and Nicholas Seager (Cambridge: Cambridge University Press, 2015), 233–4.

12 I discuss the two 1964 works exactly because they are less exalted, more "vulgar" appropriations of Defoe's novel than some other screen versions, and for that reason they give us a better purchase on the appeal of Defoe's narrative in popular culture. (I'll have something to say about "vulgarity" at the conclusion of this chapter.) See "Jean Sacha (1912–1988)," IMDb.com. Both 1964 works are currently available on DVD.

13 I refer here to well-known books published in the 1960s and 1970s by Maximillian E. Novak, J. Paul Hunter, G. A. Starr, John Richetti, and Everett Zimmerman.

14 Filipi is the Director of Film/Video at the Wexner Center for the Arts at Ohio State University; see "Dave Filipi's Top 10" (accessed November 7, 2013). For Haskins' film see www.youtube.com/watch?v=urccNoeKk3Y.

15 See "Comments" at the "Robinson Crusoe (1964), Episode 1, Parts 1 and 2" on YouTube (accessed November 7, 2013). www.youtube.com/watch?v=2FTJ2CZm-xY.

16 Purdy points out that Michel Tournier (in his novel, *Vendredi* [1967]) likewise "follows Rousseau's advice, giving us a novel which begins with the shipwreck and ends with the arrival of the rescue ship"; "The Metamorphosis of a Myth," 222.

17 *Robinson Crusoe*, ed. John Richetti (London: Penguin, 2001). All quotations in the text from the novel are to this edition.

18 *Cast Away*, dir. Robert Zemeckis, ImageMovers/Playtone, 2000.

19 For the comments by Rousseau and Woolf, see Michael Shinagel, ed., *Robinson Crusoe: An Authoritative Text*, 2nd edn (New York, NY: Norton, 1994), 262–3, 287; see also a comment similar to Woolf's by her father, Leslie Stephen, quoted in part at 277–9.

20 *Man Friday*, dir. Jack Gold, ABC Entertainment, 1975; on the Cannes version, see Leonard Maltin, *Movies and Video Guide 1999 Edition* (New York, NY: Signet, 1998), 848.

21 Leslie Stephen observes that Defoe "gives a very inadequate picture of the mental torments to which his hero is exposed"; Shinagel, *Robinson Crusoe*, 278.

22 Watt acknowledges that "scholars rapped my knuckles for suggesting (in *The Rise of the Novel*) that Crusoe's was only 'a Sunday religion'," but after re-examining the issue, he declares himself "not convinced" that Crusoe's religious transformation is "permanent"; *Myths*, 157, 167.

23 In Episode 2, reflecting on his isolation, Crusoe kneels and prays.

24 The first season of *Lost* features a similar scene; Mayer, "Crusoe on Television," 57–8, 61.

25 Mayer, "Cinematic Robinsonades," 41.

26 Michael Lennick observes that the filmmakers began searching for suitable locations "one week to the day after President Kennedy's funeral"; Lennick, "*Robinson Crusoe on Mars*: Life on Mars" on the Criterion Collection website (accessed on October 17, 2013).

27 "Commentary," Criterion DVD.

28 *Crusoe*, dir. Caleb Deschanel, Island Pictures, 1988; Mayer, "Cinematic Robinsonades," 47.

29 "Rum and Gunpowder," *Crusoe*, NBC, 2008; this Friday speaks twelve languages and knows *Paradise Lost* by heart. One more issue needs to be mentioned: sexuality. Although Defoe's book, famously, avoids consideration of its hero's sexual desire, the films by Buñuel, Gold, and Deschanel, in different ways, depart from the original in this respect; see Mayer, "Cinematic Robinsonades," 38, 43, 46. The two 1964 versions, however, leave sex out, as do *Cast Away* and the Brosnan film (although in the latter two, away from his island, Crusoe has a lively, hetero-normative sexual life). The Brosnan film is: *Robinson Crusoe*, dir. George Miller and Rodney K. Hardy, Miramax, 1997.

30 Watt, *Myths*, 167, 171.

31 Wheeler, "*Robinson Crusoe* and Early-Eighteenth-Century Racial Ideology," in *Approaches to Teaching Defoe's* Robinson Crusoe, ed. Maximillian Novak and Carl Fisher (New York, NY: MLA, 2005), 93, 92; see also Wheeler, "'My Savage,' 'My Man': Racial Multiplicity in *Robinson Crusoe*," *ELH* 62 (1995): 844–5. The Friday in Wetherell's 1927 film is also an attractive figure: seemingly cheerful and innocent and boyishly handsome.

32 I draw here upon a discussion of the Brosnan film as an example of "Vulgar Postcolonialism" presented by Andreas Mueller at the 2008 ASECS meeting in Portland, OR.

33 *Robinson Crusoe*, ed. Thomas Keymer (Oxford: Oxford University Press, 2007), ix–x.

34 Watt, *Myths*, 171.

FURTHER READING

Adams, Percy G., *Travelers and Travel Liars* (Berkeley and Los Angeles, CA: University of California Press, 1962).

Alkon, Paul, *Defoe and Fictional Time* (Athens, GA: University of Georgia Press, 1979).

Backscheider, Paula R., *A Being More Intense* (New York, NY: AMS Press, 1984).

    Daniel Defoe: Ambition & Innovation (Lexington, KY: University Press of Kentucky, 1986).

    Daniel Defoe: His Life (Baltimore, MD and London: Johns Hopkins University Press, 1989).

Baine, Rodney M., *Daniel Defoe and the Supernatural* (Athens, GA: University of Georgia Press, 1965).

Bannet, Eve Tavor, *Transatlantic Stories and the History of Reading: 1720–1810* (Cambridge: Cambridge University Press, 2011).

Bastian, Frank, *Defoe's Early Life* (Totowa, NJ: Barnes & Noble, 1981).

Bell, Ian, *Defoe's Fiction* (London: Croom Helm, 1985).

Bender, John, *Imagining the Penitentiary: Fiction and the Architecture of Mind* (Chicago, IL: University of Chicago Press, 1987).

Birdsall, Virginia Ogden, *Defoe's Perpetual Seekers: A Study of the Major Fiction* (Lewisburg, PA: Bucknell University Press, 1985).

Blewett, David, *Defoe's Art of Fiction* (Toronto: University of Toronto Press, 1979).

    The Illustration of Robinson Crusoe 1719–1920 (Gerrards Cross: Colin Symthe, 1995).

Bloom, Harold, ed. *Robinson Crusoe: Modern Critical Interpretations* (New York, NY: Chelsea House, 1988).

Boardman, Michael M., *Defoe and the Uses of Narrative* (New Brunswick, NJ: Rutgers University Press, 1983).

Brown, Homer O., "The Displaced Self in the Novels of Daniel Defoe," *English Literary History* 38 (1971): 562–90.

Byrd, Max, ed. *Daniel Defoe: A Collection of Critical Essays* (Englewood Cliffs, NJ: Prentice-Hall, 1976).

Carey, Daniel, "Reading Contrapuntally: *Robinson Crusoe*, Slavery, and Postcolonial Theory," in *Postcolonial Enlightenment: Eighteenth-Century Colonialisms and Postcolonial Theory*, ed. Daniel Carey and Lynn Festa (Oxford: Oxford University Press, 2009), 105–36.

Cohen, Margaret, *The Novel and the Sea* (Princeton, NJ: Princeton University Press, 2010).

Curtis, Laura, *The Elusive Defoe* (Totowa, NJ: Vision Press and Barnes & Noble, 1984).

Damrosch, Leopold, *God's Plot and Man's Stories* (Chicago, IL: University of Chicago Press, 1983).

Davis, Lennard, *Factual Fictions: The Origins of the English Novel* (New York, NY: Columbia University Press, 1983).

Derrida, Jacques, *The Beast and the Sovereign*, volume II, ed. Michel Lisse, Marie-Louise Mallet, and Ginette Michaud, trans. Geoffrey Bennington (Chicago, IL. and London: University of Chicago Press, 2017).

Downie, J. A., *Robert Harley and the Press: Propaganda and Public Opinion in the Age of Swift and Defoe* (Cambridge: Cambridge University Press, 1979).

Earle, Peter, *The World of Defoe* (New York, NY: Atheneum, 1977).

Edwards, Philip, *The Story of the Voyage: Sea Narratives in Eighteenth-Century England* (Cambridge: Cambridge University Press, 1994).

Ellis, Frank, *Twentieth-Century Interpretations of Robinson Crusoe: A Collection of Critical Essays* (Englewood Cliffs, NJ: Prentice-Hall, 1969).

Flynn, Carol Houlihan, *The Body in Swift and Defoe* (Cambridge: Cambridge University Press, 1990).

Green, Martin, *Dreams of Adventure, Deeds of Empire* (London: Routledge & Kegan Paul, 1980).

The Robinson Crusoe Story (University Park, PA and London: Penn State University Press, 1990).

Hulme, Peter, *Colonial Encounters: Europe and the Native Caribbean 1492–1797* (London and New York, NY: Routledge, 1992; first published 1986).

Hunter, J. Paul, *The Reluctant Pilgrim: Defoe's Emblematical Method and Quest for Form in* Robinson Crusoe (Baltimore, MD: Johns Hopkins University Press, 1966).

Before Novels: The Cultural Contexts of Eighteenth-Century English Fiction (New York, NY: Norton Books, 1992).

Kay, Carol, *Political Constructions: Defoe, Richardson, and Sterne in Relation to Hobbes, Hume, and Burke* (Ithaca, NY: Cornell University Press, 1988).

Lund, Roger, ed., *Critical Essays on Daniel Defoe* (New York, NY: G. K. Hall, 1997).

Mayer, Robert, *History and the Early English Novel: Matters of Fact from Bacon to Defoe* (Cambridge: Cambridge University Press, 1997).

"Three Cinematic Robinsonades," in *Eighteenth-Century Fiction on Screen* (Cambridge: Cambridge University Press, 2002), 35–51.

McKeon, Michael, *The Origins of the English Novel: 1660–1740* (Baltimore, MD and London: Johns Hopkins University Press, 1987).

McKillop, Alan D., *The Early Masters of English Fiction* (Lawrence, KS: University of Kansas Press, 1975).

Meier, Thomas Keith, *Defoe and the Defense of Commerce* (Victoria, British Columbia: English Literary Studies, University of Victoria, 1987).

Napier, Elizabeth, *Defoe's Major Fiction: Accounting for the Self* (Newark, DE: University of Delaware Press, 2016).

Novak, Maximillian E., *Economics and the Fiction of Daniel Defoe* (Berkeley and Los Angeles, CA: University of California Press, 1962).

Defoe and the Nature of Man (Oxford and London: Oxford University Press, 1963).

Realism, Myth, and History in Defoe's Fiction (Lincoln, NE: University of Nebraska Press, 1983).

Daniel Defoe – Master of Fictions: His Life and Works (London: Oxford University Press, 2001).

Owens, W. R., and P. N. Furbank, *The Canonisation of Daniel Defoe* (New Haven, CT and London: Yale University Press, 1988).

Richetti, John J., *Popular Fiction Before Richardson: Narrative Patterns 1700–1739* (Oxford: The Clarendon Press, 1969; rpt 1992).

Defoe's Narratives: Situations and Structures (Oxford: The Clarendon Press, 1975).

Daniel Defoe (Boston: G. K. Hall, 1987).

Richetti, John, *The English Novel in History, 1700–1780* (London and New York, NY: Routledge, 1999).

The Life of Daniel Defoe: A Critical Biography (Oxford: Blackwell, 2005).

The Cambridge Companion to Daniel Defoe (Cambridge: Cambridge University Press, 2008).

Rogers, Pat, ed., *Defoe: The Critical Heritage* (London: Routledge & Kegan Paul, 1972).

Robinson Crusoe (London: Allen & Unwin, 1979).

Schonhorn, Manuel, *Defoe's Politics: Parliament, Power, Kingship, and* Robinson Crusoe (Cambridge: Cambridge University Press, 1991).

Seidel, Michael, *Exile and the Narrative Imagination* (New Haven, CT: Yale University Press, 1986).

Robinson Crusoe: Island Myths and the Novel (Boston, MA: G.K. Hall, 1991).

Sherman, Sandra, *Finance and Fictionality in the Early Eighteenth Century: Accounting for Defoe* (Cambridge: Cambridge University Press, 1996).

Shinagel, Michael, *Defoe and Middle-Class Gentility* (Cambridge, MA: Harvard University Press, 1968).

Sill, Geoffrey, *Defoe and the Idea of Fiction 1713–1719* (Newark, DE and London: University of Delaware Press, 1983).

Starr, G. A., *Defoe and Spiritual Autobiography* (Princeton, NJ: Princeton University Press, 1965).

Defoe and Casuistry (Princeton, NJ: Princeton University Press, 1971).

Sutherland, James R., *Defoe* (London: Methuen, 1937).

Daniel Defoe: A Critical Study (Cambridge, MA: Harvard University Press, 1971).

Todd, Dennis, *Defoe's America* (Cambridge: Cambridge University Press, 2010).

Vickers, Elsa, *Defoe and the New Sciences* (Cambridge: Cambridge University Press, 1996).

Warner, John M., *Joyce's Grandfathers: Myth and History in Defoe, Smollett, Sterne, and Joyce* (Athens, GA: University of Georgia Press, 1993).

Watt, Ian, *The Rise of the Novel: Studies in Defoe, Richardson, and Fielding* (Berkeley and Los Angeles, CA: University of California Press, 1957).

"*Robinson Crusoe* as a Myth," revised from *Essays in Criticism* (1951), reprinted in *Norton Critical Edition of Robinson Crusoe*, ed. Michael Shinagel (New York, NY: Norton, 1994).

West, Richard, *Daniel Defoe: The Life and Strange, Surprising Adventures* (London: HarperCollins, 1998).

Zimmerman, Everett, *Defoe and the Novel* (Berkeley and Los Angeles, CA: University of California Press, 1975).

Zweig, Paul, *The Adventurer* (New York, NY: Basic Books, 1974).

INDEX

Cambridge Companions to Literature

AUTHORS

August Wilson edited by Christopher Bigsby

Mary Wollstonecraft edited by Claudia L. Johnson

Virginia Woolf edited by Susan Sellers (second edition)

Wordsworth edited by Stephen Gill

W. B. Yeats edited by Marjorie Howes and John Kelly

Xenophon edited by Michael A. Flower

Zola edited by Brian Nelson

TOPICS

The Actress edited by Maggie B. Gale and John Stokes

The African American Novel edited by Maryemma Graham

The African American Slave Narrative edited by Audrey A. Fisch

African American Theatre by Harvey Young

Allegory edited by Rita Copeland and Peter Struck

American Crime Fiction edited by Catherine Ross Nickerson

American Gothic edited by Jeffrey Andrew Weinstock

American Modernism edited by Walter Kalaidjian

American Poetry Since 1945 edited by Jennifer Ashton

American Realism and Naturalism edited by Donald Pizer

American Travel Writing edited by Alfred Bendixen and Judith Hamera

American Women Playwrights edited by Brenda Murphy

Ancient Rhetoric edited by Erik Gunderson

Arthurian Legend edited by Elizabeth Archibald and Ad Putter

Australian Literature edited by Elizabeth Webby

The Beats edited by Stephen Belletto

British Black and Asian Literature (1945–2010) edited by Deirdre Osborne

British Literature of the French Revolution edited by Pamela Clemit

British Romanticism edited by Stuart Curran (second edition)

British Romantic Poetry edited by James Chandler and Maureen N. McLane

British Theatre, 1730–1830, edited by Jane Moody and Daniel O'Quinn

Canadian Literature edited by Eva-Marie Kröller (second edition)

Children's Literature edited by M. O. Grenby and Andrea Immel

The Classic Russian Novel edited by Malcolm V. Jones and Robin Feuer Miller

Contemporary Irish Poetry edited by Matthew Campbell

Creative Writing edited by David Morley and Philip Neilsen

Crime Fiction edited by Martin Priestman

Dracula edited by Roger Luckhurst

Early Modern Women's Writing edited by Laura Lunger Knoppers

The Eighteenth-Century Novel edited by John Richetti

Eighteenth-Century Poetry edited by John Sitter

Emma edited by Peter Sabor

English Literature, 1500–1600 edited by Arthur F. Kinney

English Literature, 1650–1740 edited by Steven N. Zwicker

English Literature, 1740–1830 edited by Thomas Keymer and Jon Mee

English Literature, 1830–1914 edited by Joanne Shattock

English Novelists edited by Adrian Poole

English Poetry, Donne to Marvell edited by Thomas N. Corns

English Poets edited by Claude Rawson

English Renaissance Drama, second edition edited by A. R. Braunmuller and Michael Hattaway

English Renaissance Tragedy edited by Emma Smith and Garrett A. Sullivan Jr.

English Restoration Theatre edited by Deborah C. Payne Fisk

The Epic edited by Catherine Bates

Erotic Literature edited by Bradford Mudge

European Modernism edited by Pericles Lewis

European Novelists edited by Michael Bell

Fairy Tales edited by Maria Tatar

Fantasy Literature edited by Edward James and Farah Mendlesohn

Feminist Literary Theory edited by Ellen Rooney

Fiction in the Romantic Period edited by Richard Maxwell and Katie Trumpener

The Fin de Siècle edited by Gail Marshall